TCM TURNER CLASSIC MOVIES

FROM THE MOMENT THEY MET IT WAS MURDER

TCM Turner Classic Movies®

FROM THE MOMENT THEY MET IT WAS MURDER

DOUBLE INDEMNITY AND THE RISE OF FILM NOIR

ALAIN SILVER and JAMES URSINI

RUNNING PRESS
PHILADELPHIA

Hachette Book Group supports the right to free expression and the value of copyright. The purpose of copyright is to encourage writers and artists to produce the creative works that enrich our culture.

The scanning, uploading, and distribution of this book without permission is a theft of the author's intellectual property. If you would like permission to use material from the book (other than for review purposes), please contact permissions@hbgusa.com. Thank you for your support of the author's rights.

Running Press
Hachette Book Group
1290 Avenue of the Americas, New York, NY 10104
www.runningpress.com
@Running_Press

Printed in the United States

First Edition: March 2024

Published by Running Press, an imprint of Hachette Book Group, Inc.
The Running Press name and logo are trademarks of Hachette Book Group, Inc.

The Hachette Speakers Bureau provides a wide range of authors for speaking events. To find out more, go to hachettespeakersbureau.com or email HachetteSpeakers@hbgusa.com.

Running Press books may be purchased in bulk for business, educational, or promotional use. For more information, please contact your local bookseller or the Hachette Book Group Special Markets Department at Special.Markets@hbgusa.com.

The publisher is not responsible for websites (or their content) that are not owned by the publisher.

Print book cover and interior design by Susan Van Horn.

Library of Congress Cataloging-in-Publication Data has been applied for.

ISBNs: 978-0-7624-8493-5 (hardcover), 978-0-7624-8495-9 (ebook)

LSC-C

Printing 1, 2024

In memory of

Richard Schickel

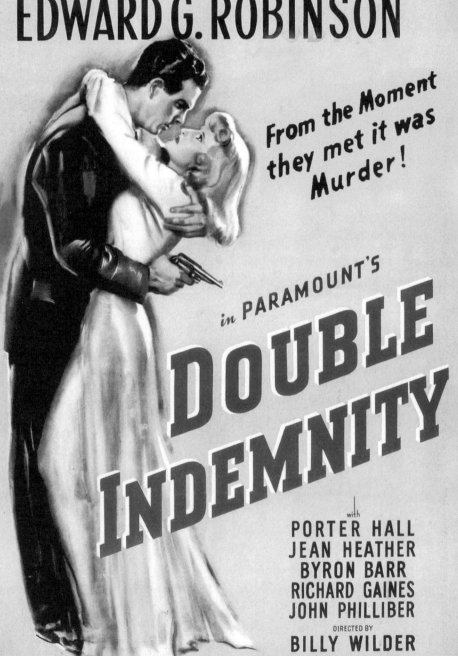

CONTENTS

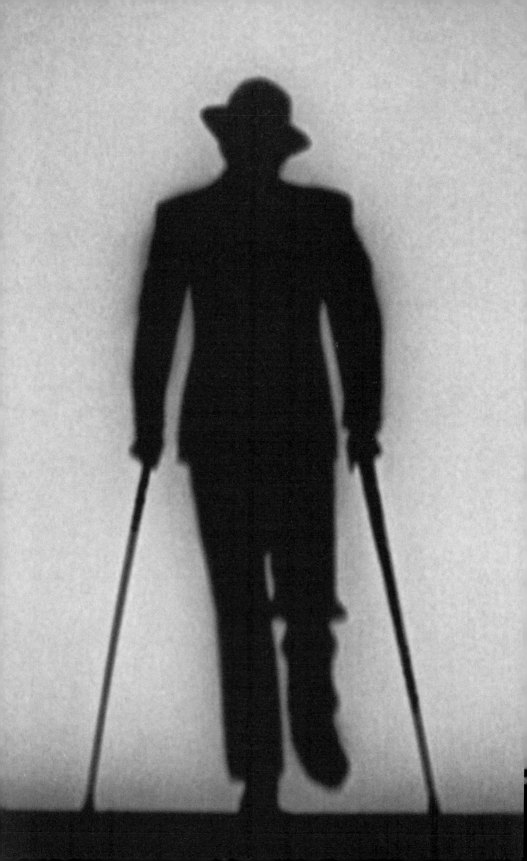

PROLOGUE:
MOONLIGHT AND ROSES

It had rained heavily in Ossining, New York, that afternoon. The air was still heavy with moisture, as three men braved the chill to stand behind a stone railing on a second-floor balcony and smoke. They were outside one of the two newest cell blocks of the up-state village's celebrated correctional facility, those that were reserved for the condemned. Being on the prison's east side, it was away from the brisk wind off the Hudson. But it was an hour before midnight on January 12, 1928. Had there been a mercury thermometer hanging on the cinderblock wall, it would have read exactly 42 degrees Fahrenheit.

There was a full moon. The sky was cloudless. Visible in the yard below was a most incongruous rose garden.

Puffing on his worn briar pipe, the oldest person on the balcony was Robert Greene Elliott.[1] He was an affable man two weeks from his 54th birthday and called "Bob" by his friends. Of course, none of them knew that he reported to work with a face mask in his back pocket that matched his black suit. Other than his wife and his eldest son only a handful of prison wardens in the tri-state area were aware of what Mr. Elliott did for a living. None of those officials ever addressed him by name in public. Lewis Lawes, the overseer of Sing Sing, disapproved of capital punishment but appreciated Elliott's professional demeanor and discretion, how he waited exactly four seconds after Lawes signaled a go-ahead before he pulled a lever that sent whoever was seated in the electric chair to meet their maker.

The youngest smoker on the balcony still looked like a kid. Thomas James Howard Jr. was 32 years old but had a baby face. Normally he worked for the *Chicago Tribune*; but its sister paper and New York City's preeminent tabloid, *The Daily News*, had brought him east on the 20th Century Limited in mid-December. The paper put him up at the Roosevelt Hotel and paid him the significant sum of $100 per week to spend the holidays preparing for tonight. He had dutifully practiced for his unusual assignment every day except Christmas. There was a small Leica with a single-plate negative strapped to his leg, and a cheap stogie between his lips. He puffed on it heavily and nervously, so unable to conceal his anxiety that Bob Elliott wondered what was the matter with this fellow.

The last man was the human-interest writer for the *New York World*. James Mallahan Cain knew of but had never met Sing Sing's "Rose Man":

Thomas Howard's secretly taken photograph of Ruth Snyder being electrocuted. Four hours after the event, sidewalk news hawks were waving the front page of the *Daily News*, "New York's Picture Newspaper," for Friday, January 13, 1928, with a one-word headline. For a measly two pennies anyone could buy the tabloid and read the "story on page 3." The same image appeared on the front of the Saturday special edition with a new boldface caption: "CROWDS follow Ruth and Judd to GRAVE."

Charles E. Chapin, the convict who had planted and tended the garden and had been the editor of the *New York Evening World* until he shot his invalid wife in the head and was sent up the river for a 20-year stretch. Cain was less than three years older than Tom Howard but had the weathered face of a peripatetic journalist who wanted to write fiction. He held his cigarette effetely between his index and middle fingers, exhaled, and wished he were home with his new wife and two stepchildren. With a nod to the others, he crushed his coffin nail underfoot and went back inside through a gray-metal door. Within a few minutes he would see what he came for. It certainly had human interest...of the most morbid variety.

More than 15 years later, in a prison on the other side of the country, a group of men from Hollywood toured the gas chamber at San Quentin. Paramount Pictures has sent director Billy Wilder, producer Joe Sistrom, and other filmmakers 400 miles north to see for themselves what California's death row looked like. They were all there because of what had happened on January 12, 1928: the execution of the "double indemnity" killers Ruth Brown Snyder and Henry Judd Gray.

The cost of the research, set construction, and shooting of "Sequence E" from the movie script for *Double Indemnity* would exceed by slightly more than forty-five times what the State of New York spent on January 12, 1928. The largest line item in the prison's cost report would have been $150 paid to Mr. Elliott to fry Ruth Snyder in "Old Sparky" at 11:06 pm. As part of a special two-fer arrangement the execution of Judd Gray 29 minutes later—in the same chamber where the acrid smell of Ruth Snyder's singed hair lingered long after her howls had stopped echoing—would earn affable Bob a mere $50 extra.

Tom Howard's photograph, which cost *The Daily News* around $800 to obtain, was widely circulated in the next morning's extended press run, the paper printed 500,000 more copies than its 1.2 million daily average. Those copies all sold out before noon. The photograph itself was reprinted in next day's paper and many thousands of times since.

"Sequence E" was cut before the first preview and no longer exists.

A production still of the discarded "Sequence E" from *Double Indemnity:*
Barton Keyes (Edward G. Robinson, right) is at San Quentin to witness the
execution of Walter Neff (Fred MacMurray).

A fur-coated Ruth Snyder flanked by sympathetic Matrons

1.

TRUE CRIME

The dark-haired, young woman stared at the dressing-room mirror backstage at the Plymouth Theatre. Her breathing was nervous, shallow. She had worked hard on her lines. She had them cold. But there were so many of them. And not all of them made sense. She had learned English as a second language when still a child. Now navigating through a jumble of complex phrases sometimes revealed a trace of German accent. That worried her, too.

It didn't help that it was standing room only on opening night, September 7, 1928. She knew why almost all the people in the audience had bought tickets to a play in nine episodes called *Machinal*. It wasn't because they admired the work of expressionist, female playwright and former war correspondent Sophie Treadwell. Even though it was her third lead role on Broadway, she understood that few if any had come to see her, 23-year-old Zita Johann, born in Deutschbentschek in the Austro-Hungarian empire. No, it was because of her role: based on a real person, a secretary, a wife, a mother…then a killer, who, after a sensational arrest and trial, had met a grisly fate earlier that very year. Zita had seen the picture of Ruth Snyder in the death chair on the front page of *The Daily News*. What she did not, could not, know was how many people in the full house had seen it also, or how their underlying salacious interest might color the reaction to her character.

What Zita Johann did not, could not, know, as she finally stood in the wings, was this play would have a decent run, would break the 60-performance mark. She breathed out. Curtain up. On stage the four other characters already in the office set began a staccato chorus of ostensibly detached, ironically connected words and phrases. The first of what would be only 91 performances had begun.

What Zita Johann did not, could not, know was that the only nascent star in this show was not her, but the man dressed as her character's lover: He was also standing backstage with a cigarette and flashed her a broad, encouraging smile. Clark Gable only appeared in episodes five and six and would soon leave Broadway for Metro-Goldwyn-Mayer.

What Zita did not, could not, know was that her engagement to Romanian born John Houseman would lead to a short marriage, that Houseman would become partner of *wunderkind* Orson Welles, would move from Broadway to Hollywood, and almost twenty years later produce mystery writer Raymond Chandler's first original screenplay for Paramount Pictures *The Blue Dahlia*.

"In the pan!" said a voice on stage. "Hot dog," said another. The next line was her cue. Zita Johann exhaled and strode out.

Zita Johann as "A Young Woman" in a tryst with "A Man" (Clark Gable) in the 1928 production of *Machinal*.

*"It was drizzling rain.... When I walked I listened for
my step—no sound seemed to follow.'*
Corset Salesman Henry Judd Gray, in his memoir *Doomed Ship*[1]

*"It sounds crazy, Keyes, but it's true, so help me.
I couldn't hear my own footsteps. It was the walk of a dead man."*
Insurance Agent Walter Neff, Dictaphone memo to Barton Keyes

Where to begin the story of the true crime that underlies *Machinal*? "It was unfortunate," contemporary critic Perriton Maxwell wrote of the play, "that its theme and characters grew out of the notorious Snyder-Gray murder case.... The play bears no likeness to the sordid facts of that cheap tragedy."[2] Given that Treadwell's heroine, "A Young Woman" aka Helen Jones, is executed for the murder of her abusive husband, Maxwell's comment is more than a trifle ingenuous. In his *New York Times* review the morning after the premiere, J. Brooks Atkinson had a better grasp of the playwright's process: "to retrieve a frail and somber beauty of character. In superficial details, the play resembles the Snyder and Gray murder case. But Sophie Treadwell has in no sense capitalized on a sensational trial in her strangely moving, shadowy tragedy of one who lacks strength."[3] Of course, this assertion that *Machinal* in no sense capitalized on recent events is even more ingenuous. "Whatever her faults Ruth Snyder had fire, and vigor, and a great lust of life," wrote Charles Brackett years before his first screenplay with Billy Wilder, "this heroine is a whining, neurotic girl full of self-pity and repressions...and Zita Johann is touching, though possibly some responsibility for the monotony of the character lies with her."[4]

Questions of fire and vigor aside, the true crime was certainly both glamorous and sordid. But were either of its proletarian lovers tragic figures? Was the murderous wife a cold-blooded killer or the victim of an abusive husband? Did "one who lacks strength" commit self-serving violence or rise up in early feminist revolt against a cruel patriarchy? Was the lover a true co-conspirator or just haplessly enmeshed by a scheming fatal woman?

9

Henry Judd Gray

The facts: in 1925 a disaffected 30-year old housewife named Ruth May Snyder (née Brown) was unhappily ensconced in Queen's Village, Long Island, with her stuffy, 42-year-old husband Albert, who was an art and design editor for *Motor Boating* magazine. Her young daughter, a grade-schooler named Lorraine, and her mother Josephine "Granny" Brown were also part of the household. That June, on one of her many shopping outings to Manhattan, the tall, blonde-haired Ruth was introduced to a traveling salesman named Henry Judd Gray. She didn't care that he wore thick eyeglasses, was shorter than her, or that he had a wife and child living on the Jersey shore. Maybe it was his cleft chin, maybe she was just that bored, but, on the promise of a free corset, they went to his workplace, quickly fell into each other's arms and began a liaison full of cringe-worthy cuteness.

"My own loverboy," Ruth wrote less than a month before the crime to the man who brought newfound joy into her dreary existence, "Gee, but I'm so very happy, dear, I can't sit still to write. I'm thinking of: you, you darn lovable little cuss. I could eat you up, could get lit and put out this blaze what is so much bother to me. Ah, yes, hon, let us get good and plastered."[5]

When cross-examined about said missive at the murder trial, Ruth maintained she was not much of a drinker. But she could not deny that, as the affair progressed, she was soon no longer content with the occasional rendezvous in speakeasies that served throat-searing Prohibition-era cocktails, to be followed by mid-day dalliances at the Waldorf-Astoria. Their meetings became frequent enough that the couple kept a checked bag with the clerk in the hotel coatroom. She had an unofficial sort of domesticity with her "lover boy" Gray, as evidenced by the bag's contents that included his-and-her PJs, toothbrushes, a deck of playing cards, and a copy of the quasi-feminist novel by Anita Loos, *Gentlemen Prefer Blondes*. Often sweet Lorraine accompanied Mommy and "Uncle Judd" to lunch before she was left alone in the lobby to entertain herself riding the elevators up and down.

Ruth needed more. She nursed her resentment about Albert, who earned a good living (but it wasn't a fortune), who still doted on a dead girlfriend from ten years past, and who enjoyed bootleg whisky that turned him into an angry drunk. She had been thinking for a while about removing the punctilious editor from her life, and purportedly tried it once or twice with poison or gas. But all that did was give the unsuspecting Albert a stomach ache or headache. Now she wanted him gone more than ever, and divorce was still not her chosen method to accomplish that.

Unlike *Double Indemnity*'s Walter Neff and Phyllis Dietrichson (née Nirdlinger), "Momsie" and "Bud," as the real-life conspirators called each other, were not the careful planners they thought themselves to be. "She told me that she would like to have her husband buy a large insurance policy. She stated that he would be home on a certain night and requested that I call…that I should try my best to sell him a policy, in the event that he was not interested to at least get his signature and that she would probably be able to persuade him later."[5] Sound familiar? That's not a line from the movie or the novel that came before it. In November of 1925, Ruth Snyder met in her parlor with Leroy Ashfield, an insurance agent for Prudential, to discuss putting a price on the life of her dear Albert. Ashfield's recollection of what Ruth wanted is taken from the trial transcript of his testimony.

After the inept lovers were charged, their prosecution became a sensational event covered not merely by all the papers in the New York area, but also by reporters from every major city in the country and around the world. Even the staid *New York Times* kept it on the front page for weeks and reproduced the entire transcripts of the testimony of the defendants. In the tabloids they became known as Ruthless Ruth, the Granite Lady, the Bloody Blonde, or the Tiger Woman, who had misled Poor Judd or the Putty Man.

It's not clear from the trial testimony of insurance agent Leroy Ashfield, if Ruth served him any iced tea; but she ended up with a double indemnity policy that would pay out $90,000—that's over $1.5 million in today's money— and $5,000 more in straight life. After sloppily acquiring this small fortune in insurance coverage, the lovers just got clumsier. Ultimately, in the wee hours of March 20, 1927, Judd Gray brought chloroform, a sash weight, and some picture wire (see page 23) to the Snyder house in Queens Village. After using those items to do the deed, drawers were opened, contents strewn everywhere, and Albert's top-break revolver was displayed on the bed, as if it had failed to thwart a burglary. Left behind was the wire tightened around the victim's neck, and on the floor a stickpin with the initials "J.G." For a while, the detectives smirked about how Judd Gray had carelessly implicated himself by leaving his monogram behind. In fact, the stickpin was Albert's keepsake of his dead fiancée, Jessie Guishard.

Ultimately that detail hardly mattered, because less than an hour after being summoned to the crime scene, the police had Ruth in handcuffs and were looking to slap another pair of nippers on Judd. Writing in his column for the Hearst syndicate a mere four weeks after the killing, Damon Runyon would describe the start of the trial:

> *A chilly-looking blonde with frosty eyes and one of those marble, you-bet-you-will chins, and an inert, scared-drunk fellow that you couldn't miss among any hundred men as a dead set-up for a blonde, or the shell game. Mrs. Ruth Snyder and Henry Judd Gray are on trial in the huge weather-beaten old courthouse of Queens County in Long Island City…for what might be called the Dumb-bell Murder, it was so dumb.*[7]

Never at a loss for words or prone to understatement, Runyon wasn't referring to the sash weight, but the fact that he believed that the details of their plan "for sheer stupidity and brutality have seldom been equaled in the history of crime. It was stupid beyond imagination, and so brutal that the thought of it probably makes many a peaceful, home-loving Long Islander of the Albert-Snyder type shiver in his pajamas as he prepares for bed."[8]

The crowd outside the courthouse on Day 1 of the trial.

Shortly after testifying about bending the rules to earn a hefty commission, insurance salesman Leroy Ashfield was given the boot. Bud and Momsie were found guilty and sent to Sing Sing to meet their maker. In November of 1928, Prudential won a lawsuit that declared little orphan Lorraine Snyder was not entitled to a penny.[9]

As one of the best-known of over 180 certified journalists covering the trial, Damon Runyon was first in line every day to enter the packed courtroom with 1500 people crammed inside, where "all standing room was occupied [and] some of those in the last rows had thoughtfully provided themselves with field glasses…" Runyon didn't need binoculars in his front-row seat, from which he could see and hear quite well without "…the electronically operated loudspeakers [that] carried voices to all parts of the courtroom."[10]

13

A phalanx of press photogs line up with press passes in hatbands.

Surrounded by scores of journalists and writers (including Sophie Treadwell, James Cain, Fannie Hurst, David Belasco, and Ben Hecht), celebrities (from evangelist Aimee Semple McPherson and comedian Jimmy Durante to director/producer David Wark Griffith and tunesmith Irving Berlin), and a few ordinary folks who somehow managed to buy a pricey ticket (that could cost fifty to one hundred 1927 dollars) from the scalpers outside, what Runyon must have realized was, however stupid the particulars, the trial had an extraordinarily high potential for dramatization. Even the anonymous reporters assigned by the *New York Times* wrote about "performances" by the witnesses that at times elicited "suppressed laughter [from] a typical Broadway crowd" but could also be riveting enough for "no general sarcastic whispering and no atmosphere of frank skepticism."[11]

When he entered the courtroom on day one, D.W. Griffith told the press he might make a movie about the case (he never did). "Poor unfortunate woman," opined dramaturge Belasco, "drawn into this mess as she embarked on what she thought was the great romance of her life. I have looked at her with much sympathy."[12] While not yet Hollywood's preeminent

14

polisher of cynical screen dialogue, as Reporter at Large for *The New Yorker*, Ben Hecht openly disparaged the allure of "the Snyder-Gray trial, preoccupying the attention of the town, turned over to a whole raft of Noted Authors, Gland Experts, Philosophers, Analysts and Dramatists." Per Hecht the paid observers were charged "not to turn in a mere journalistic account.... They didn't like the plot. It was very poorly invented, and any one

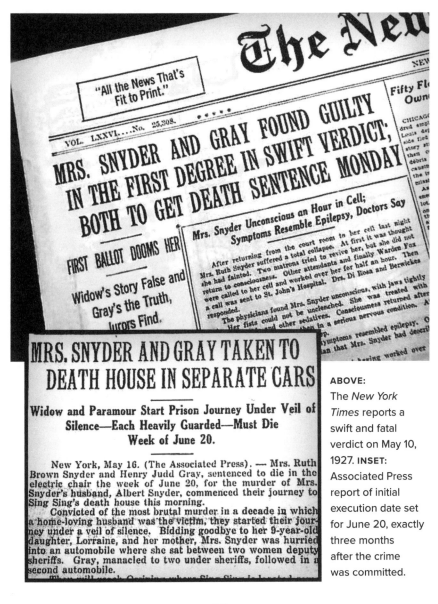

ABOVE: The *New York Times* reports a swift and fatal verdict on May 10, 1927. INSET: Associated Press report of initial execution date set for June 20, exactly three months after the crime was committed.

15

of them could have written a much better murder."[13] While not all who were aboard this whole raft saw literary potential in the trial's daily chronicle of tawdry events, many bought into the bathos with which defendants Snyder and Gray cloaked themselves. No less a curmudgeon than James Cain's mentor H.L. Mencken had more pity for Gray: "A more wicked man, caught in the net of La Snyder, would have wiggled out....But once poor Judd had yielded to her brummagem seductions, he was done for and...he shriveled like a worm on a hot stove."[14]

Her eyes were closed and her breathing shallow. Was it time yet? How long had she been lying there waiting. The hard part was done. She chewed on the cheesecloth stuffed in her mouth. Why was it called that? It had no taste.

It was dark in this upstairs hallway and cold on its hardwood floor. Glistening off of it, when she blinked, she could see sunlight. "Lorraine," she croaked, "Help me, Lorraine." She listened for small footsteps, for a bedroom door. Nothing. She called again, louder, and added a moan of pain, as might befit someone brutally struck in the head. Finally a rustle, a child's shriek, a whimper. Then the funny sound of tiny feet running to get help.

Ruth Snyder did not laugh. She was ready. She had rehearsed endlessly in her head over the past few hours. What she did not, could not, know was how phony her tale of a botched burglary would sound. What she did not, could not, know was how quickly the doctors and police would scoff at her recitation. What head wound? None was apparent. You fainted and stayed unconscious for hours? What Ruth did not, could not, know was how quickly she would confess, how quickly they would try and convict her, how not even sixty days from that moment lying on the hardwood floor she had painstakingly polished, she would be in a black town car transporting her north to Ossining, where they kept the electric chair.[15]

Damon Runyon notwithstanding, in the annals of true crime Ruthless Ruth and Poor Judd were hardly the dumbest ever. Less than three years earlier teenage thrill killers, Nathan Freudenthal Leopold Jr. and Richard Albert Loeb, self-annointed *übermenschen*, planned their own perfect crime, which unraveled almost as quickly as the Snyder-Gray scheme. It took all of ten days for Chicago police to figure it out, dismiss an alibi even phonier than Gray's, and extract confessions from the young men in which each blamed the other. Did Ruth and Judd know any of these details from the earlier case when they enacted their own homicide plan? They must have followed the case as it splashed all over New York's three muckraking tabloids the *Daily News, Daily Mirror*, and *Evening Graphic*. Of course, Leopold and Loeb had Clarence Darrow to save them from a walk to the gallows for what—until Snyder-Gray displaced it—headlines worldwide had universally chronicled as the "crime of the century."

It is hard to reckon what number "crime of the century" the Snyder-Gray actually was. Besides Leopold-Loeb earlier candidates for this illustrious title include: Roscoe "Fatty" Arbuckle, tried three times (in 1921-22, two hung juries then an acquittal) for the death by misadventure of Virginia Rappe. Chester Gillette went to the chair in 1908 for drowning his pregnant girlfriend Grace Brown in New York's Big Moose Lake. Gillette tried to claim the woman he clubbed with a tennis racket had committed suicide. If those details are vaguely familiar, so might be the sad tale of Leo Frank, who was lynched in 1915 by Georgia vigilantes that disagreed with the commutation of his death sentence for the rape and murder of "Little Mary Phagan."

Bomber and labor activist Albert Horsley (better known as "Harry Orchard") made a deal to escape the noose by implicating Industrial Workers of the World leader "Big Bill" Haywood; but in 1907 Clarence Darrow got Big Bill off. In the consensus first "trial of the century" wealthy playboy and cocaine addict Harry Kendall Thaw—in a prime example of gilded age grievance—managed to blow off noted architect Stanford White's face with three shots from a .22-caliber pistol. This happened during a 1906 performance on the roof of Madison Square Garden. Thaw's issue: as a teenager his showgirl wife, Evelyn Nesbit, had been seduced and abandoned by White. The press coverage was so intense that for the first time ever in a murder trial the jurors were sequestered. After the first jury hung 7-5 in favor of conviction, a second deemed Thaw not guilty by reason of insanity. He was freed in 1915.[16]

Before any of these deadly, male endeavors, tales of true crime had no shortage of women who killed for love or money. In the 1868 Cold Springs Murders, and despite leaving the weapon behind, Nancy Clem and her crew ultimately got away with shooting a couple in the head over a business debt. For a while in 1895 Maria Barbella sat in the Ossining death house for slashing her ex-lover's throat with a straight razor. She got a second trial because there were no Italians on the jury, she could barely understand English, and her victim had physically abused her.[17] Was it possible Ruth was thinking about Maria when she filed her unsuccessful appeal?

It is hard to imagine what the nascent crime of the 21st century might be, given that murders have been committed over ill-timed texting and interrupted video games, over a roll of toilet paper and a bag of Cheetos. A TV docu-series dedicated to finding even dumber reasons for homicide aired for two seasons. One episode of *Killer Motive* highlighted a deadly dispute over concert tickets, another over wi-fi passwords. One young woman "just didn't like Mondays." In this context, the simpler motives of the Snyder-Gray case might not have enough weirdness to go viral, to be as truly sensational—as much a crime of the century—as it was almost a hundred years ago.[18] What remains easy to imagine is that true crime stories continue to become fodder for fiction. In their 2005 essay "Multiple Indemnity: Film Noir, James M. Cain, and Adaptations of a Tabloid Case," Penelope Pelizzon and Nancy West note that:

> *Tabloids were constantly adapting material themselves, employing a remarkable range of discursive strategies for recasting, remaking, and revising current events into popular amusement. To emphasize their status as adaptation-ready sites, tabloids borrowed from the stage, cinema, and fiction while simultaneously suggesting that their stories—gripping tales plucked right from the street—were simply waiting to be recycled in turn by these other forms.*[19]

Is that not just as true today?

As the jacket copy for the anthology by early crime collector William Roughead asserted, no less an intellectual than Henry James savored

18

walking "along the gallery that I can't tread alone...the gallery of sinister perspective."[20] Certainly dramas based on true crimes have been staged for centuries. Perhaps Oedipus' murder of his father was more mythical than actual, but the marketing of many Shakespearean efforts (think of *Julius Caesar*'s eponymous character cut down by diverse daggers) could feature grisly, historical assassinations.

A true crime inspired Edgar Allan Poe's incomplete play *Politian*, which, though transposed to Renaissance Rome and written in faux Elizabethan blank verse, is based on the notorious 1825 fatal stabbing of Solomon Sharp by Jereboam Beauchamp (Poe's Politian) with a poison-dipped blade. In a killing that remarkably foreshadows both Thaw/Nesbit/White and Snyder-Gray, after revenging his wife, whom Sharp had impregnated and abandoned, Beauchamp obtained a delay on his meeting with the hangman in order to complete his jailhouse memoir. This early sensational crime inspired sundry other plays and novels.[21] Poe also changed the actual setting in his much-better-known crime fiction, "The Mystery of Marie Rogêt," by moving the locus of the 1841 murder of Mary Cecelia Rogers from New York City to Paris.[22]

Examples from Poe aside, starting at the same time as the Civil War in America, the *Beadle's Dime Novels* series and its hundreds of imitators mined society's desire for based-on-a-true-story narratives. While most often glorifying heroic characters from Buffalo Bill to Wyatt Earp, there was also a profusion of lurid tales of real criminality from the celebrated outlaw Jesse James to the last stagecoach robber in America, a woman named Pearl Hart, aka The Bandit Queen. Hart was a proto-femme fatale in that she sweet-talked a local miner into lending her a hand with a robbery. While she was certainly not a killer (she let her victims keep enough money to buy lunch at the next relay station), the saga of Pearl Hart's desperate acts—the robbery, flight, capture by a pursuing posse, escape, recapture, trial, acquittal, retrial, sentence to three years in Yuma penitentiary—was covered by *The Times* of both New York and London and spun-off into a "first-person" (purportedly) life story, published in a national literary magazine—the very magazine where 20 years later Ruth Snyder first worked as a secretary—and introduced with the comment: "The evolution of the new woman has many strange phases."[23]

When the dime novels were dying off at the turn of the 20th century, American naturalist writers began the transformation of true crime into literature. War correspondent turned novelist Frank Norris based his physical description of the titular character in his 1899 first novel *McTeague: A Story of San Francisco* on a spousal abuser, who stabbed his wife thirty-five times. That event got scant coverage outside of the Bay Area but happened while Norris studied at UC Berkeley.[24] Even without knowing that author Theodore Dreiser had a folder full of old newspaper clippings in his desk drawer, it was easy for almost any reader to recognize that the inspiration for the fictional Clyde Griffiths was the similarly initialed Chester Gillette in Dreiser's 1925 novel, *An American Tragedy*.

The naturalists, of course, followed the literary trail blazed by French realists. Norris especially admired Émile Zola, whose *La Bête Humaine* and *Thérèse Raquin* were inspired by real crimes. In particular, the guilt-haunted, adulterous killers in *Thérèse Raquin*, who end their anguish in suicide, somewhat closely anticipate the story-arc of Cain's *Double Indemnity*. Equally if not more on point is the metamorphosis of the licentious and sad Veronique Delphine Delamare into the profligate Emma Bovary by Gustave Flaubert. While Emma never tries to do in Monsieur Bovary, the Madame Bovary Syndrome or "chronic affective dissatisfaction" based on the character was clearly a factor in how Ruth perceived hubby Alfred and tinged the perceptions of both the *Double Indemnity* novel's Phyllis Nirdlinger and the movie's Phyllis Dietrichson.

Surprisingly not all the pre-Snyder-Gray crimes of the century have been extensively fictionalized in prose or film. The 1955 movie *The Girl on the Red Velvet Swing*, produced and co-written by Charles Brackett, does not even credit the nonfiction book of the same name by Charles Samuels.[25] Only Jerry Stahl's *I Fatty* fictionalizes comedian Arbuckle's prosecution, as part of a complete "autobiography."

Dreiser's novel was adapted as both a Broadway play (Patrick Kearney, 1926) and a movie directed by Josef von Sternberg for Paramount in 1931.

George Stevens' post-*Double Indemnity*, noirish 1951 remake, *A Place in the Sun* (co-written by Michael Wilson from the play), is better known. More recently there have been an opera (Tobias Picker, 2005) and even a musical (developed for Broadway but never staged in 1995) based on the Dreiser work.

Also surprising is that Leo Frank and Leopold and Loeb are running neck-and-neck as the second most frequently portrayed criminals of the century. The Frank case got out of the gate first with Oscar Micheaux's 1921 race film (now lost), *The Gunsaulus Mystery*, in which ethnically Irish "Mary Phagan" becomes a Black girl named Myrtle Gunsaulus. Micheaux remade this as a talkie, *Murder in Harlem* (1935), and both movies portray the accused man as white (but not Jewish) and guilty. Shortly thereafter in the novel *Death in the Deep South* (1936) and the film based on it, *They Won't Forget* (directed by Mervyn LeRoy for Warner Bros., 1937), the protagonist, now an outsider from New York but still not portrayed as Jewish, is lynched; and his guilt or innocence remain uncertain. Most recently endemic antisemitism is in the forefront of the Broadway musical *Parade* (Jason Robert Brown, 1998), which won Tonys for both its original staging in 1998 and as 2023's best revival.

While better-known for *Gas Light*, British playwright Patrick Hamilton's dramatic version of the Leopold-and-Loeb case (which focused on the crime and its philosophy only, not the trial), *Rope*, successfully debuted in London and on Broadway in 1929. It is better known as Alfred Hitchcock's 1948 film version (comprised of stitched together, ten-minute long takes). The trial is the climax of *Compulsion*, a 1956 novel by Meyer Levin, which he adapted for Broadway in 1957. The movie version was released in 1959 (directed by Richard Fleischer). The homosexual nature of the relationship between Leopold and Loeb was implied but not explicit in either movie. More recently variations of the thrill-killing/perfect crime/*übermench* aspects underlie both Barbet Schroeder's 2002 *Murder by Numbers* and the 2020 third season of the TV series *The Sinner*. And, yes, there is a musical version, albeit off-Broadway: *Thrill Me*. While Albert Horsley/"Harry Orchard" also contributed to the "confessions and autobiography" genre, no one has yet seen fit to tell his story in music and lyrics.

Are there more versions of Snyder-Gray in fiction than any of its predecessors? Given that through Cain their crime inspired both *Double Indemnity* and *The Postman Always Rings Twice* and that the film *Double Indemnity* in turn spawned numerous imitators, the answer is, "Of course." As recently as 2022, in *Out of the Blue* a fatal woman descended from Ruth Snyder—although more closely aligned to writer/director Lawrence Kasdan's iteration of her as Matty Walker in his 1981 *Body Heat*—seduces and discards a chump and gets away with matricide.[26]

What is less clearly delineated is the future of Snyder or Gray as true-crime characters. Despite Sophie Treadwell's sympathetic depiction of Ruth in *Machinal* mere months after her death, the preponderant perception of her is still mostly colored by the characterizations of scoffing, sexist pundits such as Runyon or Mencken. Pearl Hart's feminist position was defiantly opined in court as "I shall not consent to be tried under a law in which my sex had no voice in making," and possibly her trim figure ultimately swayed the all male jurors, who originally acquitted her, and enraged the judge. Deciding Pearl had "flirted and bent the men to her will," he put a lesser charge on her and got a conviction.

As four weeks of countless newspaper columns confirm, this was a tactic that Ruth Snyder could not pull off. Both Pearl and Ruth on more than one occasion expressed the belief that they would never have been found guilty had there been a single woman on the jury. In Ruth's case, the State of New York at that time prohibited women from serving on capital-case juries. If the comments of the wife of juror Charles Meissner are indication, that may have been a misguided belief on Ruth's part: "If there were any women on that jury I know what Mrs. Snyder would get. From all I've heard Albert Snyder was one of the few good husbands left in the world. The fact that Mrs. Snyder is a woman should not be considered."[27] Given the intensity of the coverage preceding the trial, was there anyone, male or female, not predisposed to convict? It took five days and the questioning of almost 400 candidates to find twelve "open-minded" men.[28] On the next court day, the start of the actual trial was again delayed while reports of possible prejudice

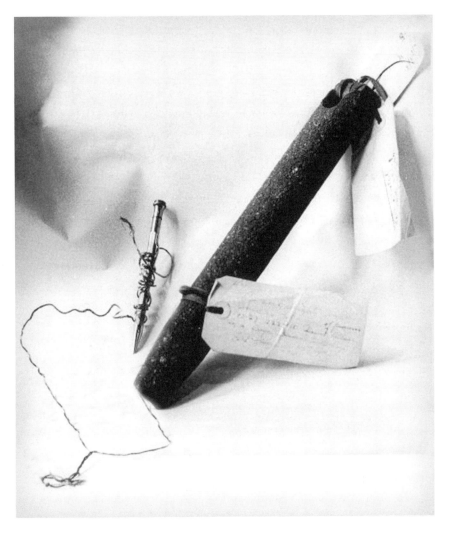

The sash weight, wire, and nail used to bludgeon and choke Albert Snyder to death.

of two of the twelve jurors were reviewed, including the comment of Mrs. Meissner and a *Daily News* report that the foreman, William Young, and his wife attended a play where the case was mentioned.[29] Shortly after the trial, no less than Clarence Darrow himself, who had no involvement with the defense, "deplored the 'feeling of hate that had been worked up' against Mrs. Snyder and Gray."[30]

Whatever the gender of any juror, portraying herself as the victim was a limited option for Ruth, precluded by both the irrefutable premeditation of the double indemnity insurance policy and Judd Gray's assertions of being her pawn. Pearl Hart opens her life story this way: "We were married. I was happy for a time but not for long. My husband began to abuse me."[31] Ruth Snyder could have used exactly the same words in her confession, where she actually said: "I began having difficulty with my husband almost immediately after our marriage....I certainly thought he would do anything in a fit of awful temper."[32] "For a time" for Pearl, "immediately" for Ruth, in Sophie Treadwell's dramatization unhappiness is entirely foreseen: "I don't care whether he's decent or not...when he puts a hand on me, my blood runs cold."[33]

Sometimes in the subway, I think I'm going to die. Maybe I am crazy—I don't know.

I don't know what. Maybe I'm crazy. But there's something in me that loves Death.

All the same, life can be horrible. There's cruelty and emptiness and death.

Sometimes we sit all evening without saying a word to each other.

I had another argument with my husband when he said he was going to blow my brains out.[34]

Those are five sentences from a real and imaginary Ruth Snyder and her alter egos, Phyllis Nirdlinger, Helen Jones, and Phyllis Dietrichson. Madame Bovary Syndrome? Who said what? Does it matter?

While Harry Thaw's pre-crime behavior indicated some validity to his defense, like their other fellow criminals of the century, neither Ruth Snyder nor Judd could play the insanity card. What held more promise for Ruth,

given that being the victim of abuse got Maria Barbella a retrial and acquittal, was to pose as the meek and menaced wife. But to this day, desperate women who kill their abusers are far from certain to be exonerated. "If
my husband had not said that he would take my life," said Ruth, gingerly
dipping a toe into the murky waters of self-defense during her confession,
"we would not have…decided that the only way out of difficulties was to
take his."[35] In the end her melodramatic testimony revealed an even simpler
strategy: point the finger at the other guy. "I said to him, 'Good God, what
are you going to do, Judd?' I tried to plead with him, reason with him."[36] As
the sub-headlines of the *Times* pointedly recapped the high drama: "Gray
alone killed Snyder, as she tried to save him"; "Life menaced, she says"; and
"Tries to show duress—weeps twice in 2-hour story of line."[37]

After listening to Ruth and his lawyer's cross-examination—"Gray is
alert for the first time," said another sub-head, "his lawyer lays basis for
an insanity plea"[38]—Judd Gray flipped the script: "It was after I had four or
five highballs, she asked me if I wouldn't please help her by shooting her
husband. I said 'Absolutely no,' that she must see the thing through alone."[39]
While writing *Doomed Ship* in the death house, Gray quotes no less than
feminist revolutionary and champion of the misunderstood woman Ger-
maine de Staël to explain how he was fooled, "a mad mirage born in infat-
uation…would that I could have sanely viewed it."[40] It being unlikely there
was a copy of de Staël's *Corinne* in the Sing-Sing library, Judd presumably
saw her "Love is an emblem of" motto on a greeting card from a fan. Had
he explained Harry Thaw-like on the stand how La Snyder not only plied
him with liquor but outright bewitched him, might poor Judd have beaten
the rap?

What must David Belasco or D.W. Griffith, Sophie Treadwell or James
Cain, or any of the other observers packed into that standing-room-only
space have thought of their performances? In the end, the only audience that
mattered went into the jury room "at 5.20 P.M.…and returned to the courtroom at seven o'clock P.M."[41] with a unanimous verdict of first-degree murder. On Friday the 13th of May, 1927, a major bad luck day for Momsie and
Bud, Judge Townsend Scudder issued their death warrants.

The opinion of Mrs. Meissner notwithstanding, Sophie Treadwell and many women since have seen Ruth as a victim. "This is a play written in anger," says a 1993 back-page blurb by dramatist Nicholas Wright regarding a new edition of *Machinal*. "In the dead wasteland of male society—it seems to ask—isn't it necessary for certain women, at least, to resort to murder?"[42] Yet for more than a decade following that new edition of *Machinal*, true-crime anthologies written by both women and men continued to portray "iron-widow" Ruth and "simpleton" Judd in the tabloid tradition: like Pearl Hart in Yuma prison, with Ruth inviting reporters to her cell in Ossining, still calling her dead husband "the stingy old crab" and opening envelopes with over 150 marriage proposals "mainly from men desperate to take Judd Gray's place as her slave" or "the plastic to be moulded to her will."[43]

The ethics of how Snyder and Gray were and have been portrayed from arrest, to trial, to grisly end are easy to question from a later perspective. In *Moral Reasoning for Journalists* ethicist Steven Knowlton quotes a pre-execution tabloid edition: "Think of it? A woman's final thoughts just before she is clutched in the deadly snare that sears and burns and FRIES AND KILLS! Her very last words! Exclusively in tomorrow's *Graphic*." In the no-holds-barred fight for market share, "the counterpunch from *The Daily News*" was, Knowlton notes (in his 1997 first edition), Thomas Howard's "blurry photograph of a blindfolded woman strapped to the electric chair that has long served as the symbol of the wretched excess of tabloid journalism." Knowlton rhetorically questions why "more than sixty years later, the staid *New York Times*, the world's very definition of responsible journalism...[publishes] that photograph again."[44] While the *Times* used details rather than punctuation to create melodrama, its own front page chronicle of the execution was hardly staid:

> *The thin deep-lined gray haired man, Robert Elliott, the official executioner, worked slowly and carefully leaned over, his gray hair falling into his eyes, and adjusted the electric plate. All the while Mrs. Snyder was sobbing and crying "Father, forgive them, for they know not what they do." The strap across the chest, which covered*

the khaki-colored smock, was tightened. The two matrons, both in tears, retired from the room, as twenty-four witnesses, packed in four church benches borrowed from the prison chapel, looked on.[45]

Pelizzon and West assert that "although straight newspapers like *The New York Times* reported on the case as well, their coverage was less extensive."[46] Given that "all the news that's fit to print" included the full text of the defendant's testimonies, "less extensive" is a relative concept.

Still as early as 1980, women writers began a serious reconsideration of Snyder-Gray. "It was to the tabloid *Mirror* that readers turned for murder news," noted Ann Jones, "and in its pages Ruth Snyder was compared to Lucretia Borgia, Messalina, and Lady Macbeth. Snyder became the 'fiend wife,' the 'blonde fiend,' and 'Ruthless Ruth the Viking Ice Matron of Queens Village.' "[47] Jones also details the spurious science of the phrenologist hired by the newspaper, who found indications of cruelty in the slope of Ruth's chin and an inclination to infidelity in her eyelids. More recently, Jessie Ramey exhaustively reviewed myriad contemporary opinions that portrayed Snyder as "a sexual aggressor who overstepped gender boundaries.... In other words, the patriarchal institution of the traditional family—a crucial locus of power—was directly threatened by a woman, whether she was a young, attractive, modern woman, an industrious housewife and mother, or an evil serpent and passionate vampire."[48]

On the Monday after the sentencing, the *Times* reported that a woman named "Alice Johnson shot down her husband last night in a quarrel over the result of the Snyder trial. The police say both had been drinking."[49] What was not reported is whether Alice "emptied the pistol at the breast of her husband" because he was for or against the verdict.

According to Pelizzon and West, a decade before Cain, in thirteen weekly *Daily Mirror* installments of "Ruth Snyder's Tragedy: The Greatest True Story Ever Written," Russell Birdwell wrote the first "novella [that] crystallized all the melodramatic elements."[50] Who could dispute that from the quote they chose: "After meeting Gray in a hotel room, Snyder passed a movie theatre and paused before a flaming placard which announced

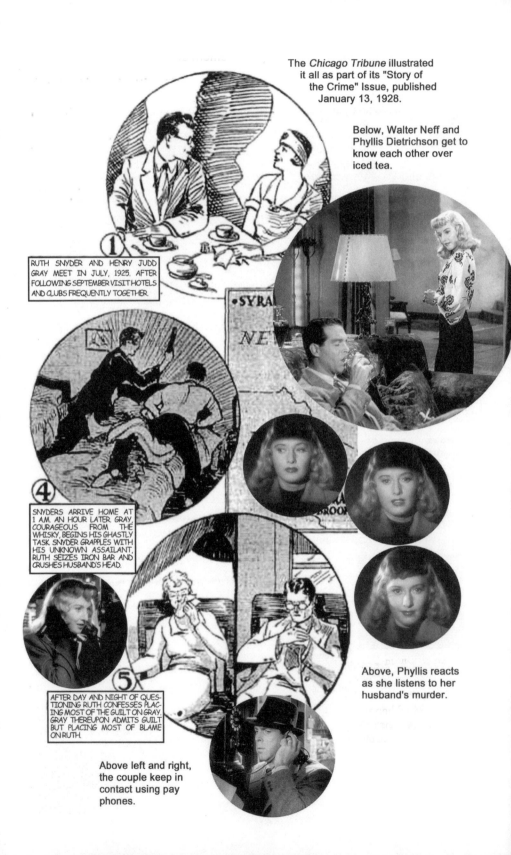

The *Chicago Tribune* illustrated it all as part of its "Story of the Crime" Issue, published January 13, 1928.

Below, Walter Neff and Phyllis Dietrichson get to know each other over iced tea.

① RUTH SNYDER AND HENRY JUDD GRAY MEET IN JULY, 1925. AFTER FOLLOWING SEPTEMBER VISIT HOTELS AND CLUBS FREQUENTLY TOGETHER

④ SNYDERS ARRIVE HOME AT 1 AM. AN HOUR LATER GRAY, COURAGEOUS FROM THE WHISKY, BEGINS HIS GHASTLY TASK SNYDER GRAPPLES WITH HIS UNKNOWN ASSAILANT, RUTH SEIZES IRON BAR AND CRUSHES HUSBAND'S HEAD.

⑤ AFTER DAY AND NIGHT OF QUESTIONING RUTH CONFESSES PLACING MOST OF THE GUILT ON GRAY. GRAY THEREUPON ADMITS GUILT BUT PLACING MOST OF BLAME ON RUTH.

Above, Phyllis reacts as she listens to her husband's murder.

Above left and right, the couple keep in contact using pay phones.

RUTH AND GRAY CONCOCT PLOT TO GET RID OF ALBERT SNYDER, RUTH'S HUSBAND. SHE OBTAINS $97,000 INSURANCE ON HIS LIFE AND TRIES WITHOUT SUCCESS TO KILL HIM BY POISON AND GAS.

Above, Neff tells the weary Mr. Dietrichson to "Just sign here."

SATURDAY NIGHT, MARCH 19, 1927 GRAY CREEPS INTO SNYDER HOME THROUGH KITCHEN DOOR LEFT OPEN BY RUTH. HE DRINKS WHISKY LEFT FOR HIM BY WOMAN.

Below, there are no friendly matrons for Neff in the gas chamber.

JAN 12, 1928. RUTH GOES TO DEATH CHAIR AFTER VAIN EFFORTS TO POSTPONE DEATH PENALTY. GRAY FOLLOWS SOON AFTER.

the latest picture of the screen's most celebrated vampire. A cynical smile twisted the lips of this crowned conqueror of men"[51] The overheated prose of tabloid-essayist Birdwell aside, the key point of "James Cain and the Tabloids," is that

> *In his depiction of femme fatale Phyllis, Cain used imagery nearly identical to that portraying Ruth in the tabloids... The "one big square of red silk" Phyllis wrapped around herself before her symbolic "marriage" with Death [is] an image right out of the Daily Mirror's coverage, which described Ruth as donning a "flaming red" kimono while waiting for her lover to appear.[52]*

Pelizzon and West open their essay with the excision of the gas chamber from the final cut of *Double Indemnity* and the claim that "the significance of the Snyder-Gray case for Wilder's *Double Indemnity* has been completely obscured in cinema scholarship."[53] While that may be something of an overstatement, given all the mediating influences that affect any Hollywood movie, the direct line from Ruth Snyder to Phyllis Dietrichson (and by extension, to *Body Heat*'s Matty Walker, and who knows how many future fatal women in cinema) cannot be disputed. Nor can the parallel line linking true crime to hard-boiled fiction, to the movie *Double Indemnity* and the rise of film noir.

Of course those who dramatize true crime will always get to pick their protagonist. In the unproduced original screenplay, *Dead!*, Pulitzer-prize-winning novelist William Styron chose Judd Gray.[54] That concept, the invocation of a fatal woman, might sound a bit retro, given contemporary film's focus on empowered women. But even fifty years ago, almost a decade before *Body Heat*, Styron and his co-screenwriter dramatize the actual events of Snyder-Gray, from first meeting to execution, without making Ruth a serpent or vampire or even a brummagem seductress. Like a character out of Dos Passos (or Frank Norris), Judd Gray is affected by a forlorn ennui: "A man can have all those things you talk about and there still can be something wrong." When Ruth talks of "emptiness and death," Judd wants her

30

to perk her up: "You shouldn't chide yourself. What I see you as is sensitive." If anything, this Ruth is too clear-eyed, not the opposite of Treadwell's disappointed Helen but more keenly self-aware: "My home life is *not* one of perfect bliss." In the death house, Ruth discusses the tabloid comments about her with a Matron: "If I wanted to put on an act, I could have cried all through the trial. That would have charmed them." But even this Ruth can detach from reality when she imagines life with the rancher who sent her a marriage proposal (another echo of Pearl Hart). It's a moment of disaffection not unlike Helen Jones' rant against her head being shaved ("I will not be submitted—this indignity!"). But the end is the same.

Next in the line from Bloody Blonde Ruth May Brown Snyder to Phyllis Dietrichson is Mrs. Nirdlinger, the creation of James Cain. Was it "chronic affective dissatisfaction" that permitted her cool rationalization of her husband's eminent demise?

He's not happy. He'll be better off—dead . . . it doesn't seem terrible. It seems as though I'm doing something—that's really best for him.[55]

DOUBLE INDEMNITY
BY JAMES M. CAIN
THE
General Fidelity
Insurance Company
HEREBY AGREES TO PAY
DOUBLE INDEMNITY
$50000.00
AN AVON BOOK

2.

HUMAN INTEREST

As soon as he walked into the courtroom—packed beyond all reason, acrid with stale tobacco smoke from hundreds who were nervously indulging the same filthy habit—he realized that he should not have worn the heavier suit. An overcoat for the cold outside over some lightweight suit. Tomorrow. If he needed a cigarette, which was likely, he had planned to step outside. What he did not, could not, know is that more than 3,000 cigarettes would be smoked in there today.

His ticket entitled him to the third row, and he clambered over colleagues to get to his seat. He recognized a few: Runyon, of course, how could he miss something like this; and Ben Hecht, ever the sour look on his puss. Fannie Hurst, that was a surprise, but not Mary Roberts Rinehart, the clumsy mystery hack. What an odd crew, even Jimmy Durante—why the hell was he here? Cain had his own ambitions, but what the 34-year-old in wire-rim glasses and three-piece suit did not, could not, know is that in less than a decade, he might be more famous that any of these people.

Everybody stood when the judge came in. When all sat back down, he spotted the Granite Woman Blonde herself flanked by two attorneys, as she glanced back at the crowd. Were her eyes red? From crying? He scoffed at the melodramatics. That sap who helped her kill her husband had his face in his hands. Oh, brother. Thank God, he had missed the first week. Five days to pick a jury? Everyone here had read the confessions, so all he and most everyone squirming in these cramped seats expected, all they wanted to hear was the testimony. How would these inept killers get around what they had told the police? What he did not, could not, know was that the jury process was not yet done.

33

So, he stayed in his seat and unfolded his handkerchief once or twice to mop his forehead, while the judge peppered two of the "rubes" selected for the jury with more questions: what had they done, how had they managed to get their names in the papers over the weekend? Why had one of the wives opened her yap? What he did not, could not, know but was starting to feel was that there was nothing new to be learned in this courtroom that day. He, like just about all of New York City, had already passed judgment. The prosecution had a dozen boring witnesses swearing to facts he had already read four times. The defendants would not make it to the stand today. A stringer next to him got up to leave. He followed in his wake.

Stepping outside the courtroom, scalpers were still hawking SRO tickets. What he did not, could not, know was that in less than 10 months his human-interest assignment would carry him to Ossining, to the death house. What James Cain did not, could not, know was what else he might make of all this.

A woman was standing there. She was maybe thirty-one or two with a sweet face, light blues eyes, and dusty blonde hair. She was small and had on a suit of blue house pajamas. She had a washed-out look...But all of a sudden she looked at me and I felt a chill creep straight up my back and into the roots of my hair.

Walter Huff

Insurance Salesman for General Fidelity[1]

From March 1927 through January 1928, for almost an entire year while the Snyder-Gray murder case was the talk of the town, journalist for the *New York World* Jim Cain must have thought a bit about his mother, Rose Mallahan Cain. Like Ruth Snyder, Rose married an older, successful man for a sense of security. Rose loved opera and pursued training as an opera singer for seven years (a motif that would run through many of her son's novels). She even gave public concerts. But ultimately, like Ruth, she "sold out." She settled down to give birth and to raise five children (James being the first) in Annapolis, Maryland, where her husband Dr. James Cain was a respected

James M. Cain in the 1930s.

professor and intellectual, a "Yale man." Rose may have never yearned for more; but her oldest son did, over and over again.

"It is true that I write about singers, but not, you will notice, swooning over their voices. Real dramatization is focused on their minds, their skill at reading music, and improvising to cover emergencies at comprehension... This, I suspect, is all a bouquet on the grave of my mother. She had a beautiful voice, a big hot lyric endlessly trained and equal to any music written for

35

soprano…"[2] Not only in *Career in C Major* but in *Mildred Pierce, Serenade*, and others did singers and/or opera rear their mytho-poetic heads. Rose, unlike Ruth Snyder, did not pursue the freedom she was denied by a repressive, puritanical America. Even though the U.S. was reveling in the "Jazz Age," when flappers reigned supreme—at least in books and movies—the reality was grimmer: most middle-class women were trapped in loveless marriages or, if they were working class, compelled to take on menial jobs to support their children and often drunken husbands.

Plainly put Rose did not have the Bloody Blonde's audacity. Did she ever contemplate doing away with her boring bourgeois husband and collecting on a double indemnity insurance policy (yes, Cain's Dad had double indemnity coverage)? Perhaps. Just like Ruth and corset-salesman Judd, money would have given Rose the freedom to live whatever life was desired. After Ruth's unrest (so brilliantly evoked in groundbreaking playwright Sophie Treadwell's 1928 modernist play *Machinal*) erupted in an orgy of violence that left hubby Albert garrotted and dead, her immediate vilification by the press (including Cain's own *New York World*), tabloid and mainstream alike, was pretty much as might be expected.

As a youth Cain doted on his mother. He called himself a "mama's boy" in many interviews. He idolized her so much that he even tried to become an opera singer himself. But Rose refused to live her dreams through her son. Instead, according to biographer David Madden, upon hearing of his plans, she was "aghast" and "forcefully informed him that he had little talent."[3] Like many of his characters, that made young Cain pursue this dream with even more determination. So, he took on "menial jobs," among them an insurance salesman—yes, a little like Walter in *Double Indemnity*—to support his singing lessons. Then, as happens so often in Cain's fatalistic novels, the dream died. Mother knew best.

Of course, this Mom-worship did not exclude resentment of her power over him. At its worst, it never came close to the opprobrium reserved for his imperious father, who endlessly expressed disappointment in a son he saw as underachieving. Cain told the childhood story of a foot race with his athletic father. The elder Cain humiliated his son by leaving him in the dust and then greeting him with disapproving looks.[4] Although the young James was a remarkably agile scholar and accepted to Washington College—where his father was president—when he was just fifteen, none of this was ever enough for the self-absorbed Dr. Cain.

A version of this oedipal, familial tangle would become a recurring theme in Cain's fiction including *Double Indemnity*. Often it was the father/father figure or sometimes mother/mother figure who had to be subdued, seduced, or both as in: *The Butterfly* (the young protagonist and her "father" Jess); *The Postman Always Rings Twice* (the cheating couple and the domineering older husband); *Mildred Pierce* (spoiled daughter vs. permissive mother); *Double Indemnity* (salesman and mentor). On occasion, there were even extreme versions of these oedipal characters such as the manipulative mother in *A Modern Cinderella* (later published as *The Root of His Evil*) or the rapacious father in *The Enchanted Isle*.

What added to Dr. Cain's growing dissatisfaction with his firstborn was his son's inability to settle on a career. Initially he became and remained a drifter. After moving to Baltimore to live on his own, Cain went from job-to-job—clerk for a public utility, road inspector for the state of Maryland, terrible insurance salesman—all for brief periods. There were of course side effects from this peripatetic phase in his youth of which Cain was then unaware. Raised by his mother to always speak in upper-class English with precise grammar, once out amongst the working class, he acquired a sense of prole-speak, "that hard-bitten Cain dialogue" that got him hired to write screenplays. In fact, studios paid a premium in the 1930s and 1940s to have him punch up scripts with the patois of the working class. Cain himself was never comfortable with the hard-boiled label. In Cain's preface to *Three of a Kind* he pointedly says:

> *I make no conscious effort to be tough, or hard-boiled, or grim, or any of the things I am usually called. I merely try to write as the character would write, and I never forget that the average man, from the fields, the streets, the bars, the offices, and even the gutters of his country, has acquired a vividness of speech that goes*

beyond anything I could invent, and that if I stick to this heritage, this logos of the American countryside, I shall attain a maximum of effectiveness with very little effort. In general my style is rural rather than urban; my ear seems to like fields better than streets. I am glad of this, for I think language loses a bit of its bounce the moment its heels touch concrete.[5]

He saw himself more in the potboiler mode of naturalistic writers from Émile Zola to Ernest Hemingway or Theodore Dreiser. He felt more akin to the smart-talking journalists he would soon befriend (and in some instances work with), such as H.L. Mencken, than to contemporary writers of noir-style fiction writers such as Dashiell Hammett or later Raymond Chandler. In fact, Cain always bristled at being compared to detective or murder-mystery novelists. His novels were not mysteries, and his investigators were not private detectives, not in the mold of either Hammett's hard-bitten Sam Spade or Chandler's sardonic idealist Philip Marlowe. There is no perpetrator to be unmasked in a grand finale by a version of Agatha Christie's Poirot in *Double Indemnity*—its third sentence invokes the "House of Death"—or any of Cain's crime stories. Who murdered Albert Snyder—that is Mr. Nirdlinger in the novella—is never in question.

The second lesson for young Cain was a bit more erotic and exotic. His "teachers" (much like his mother) were beautiful femmes fatales. All his biographers report that Cain frequented bordellos in Baltimore and later Nevada. He actually claimed that he often just talked to the women there (research?). Whether that was true or not, his four marriages—the last to Florence Macbeth, an opera singer with whom he had been obsessed as a young man—and his numerous affairs suggest a strong interest in sex, which would become a hallmark of his steamy novels. Like their author, Cain's characters often explored the outer dimensions of sexuality. His "perverse" heroes could be in sadomasochistic relationships (*The Postman Always Rings Twice* or *Serenade*), manipulated by strong and ambitious women (*Double Indemnity, Postman, Mildred Pierce,* or *The Root of His Evil*), or obsessed with sexually precocious teenagers (*The Butterfly, The*

Renowned opera singer of the early 20th century, Florence Macbeth (left), whom Cain idolized in his youth and finally married late in life, when she no longer resembled the young and fresh Ruth Snyder (right) before her own disappointing marriage.

Enchanted Isle, Mildred Pierce, or Phyllis' nubile stepdaughter Lola in *Double Indemnity*).

"But then one day, just for no reason, I was sitting in Lafayette Park, and I heard my own voice telling me, 'You're going to be a writer.' For no reason at all. Just like that."[6] This is the story Cain frequently repeated: his epiphany on a park bench. It's a good story and in line with the sometimes surreal moments in Cain's otherwise naturalistic stories.

Witness the feverish final scene on the boat in the novel (not in the movie of course, it being much too arcane for 1940s Hollywood).

Walter, still weak from the bullet Phyllis put in him earlier, writes his confession to save Lola and her boyfriend. Wearing a red shroud-like dress, Phyllis beckons to him to join her beneath the moon and then out into the shark-infested sea. It is a gothic scene worthy of a fantasist director—something that might be expected in Luis Buñuel's *Belle de Jour* or

That Obscure Object of Desire or a neo-noir from Guillermo del Toro. This ending was one of Cain's own excursions into "amour fou" as well as an allusion to the suicidal murderous couple in Zola's *Therese Raquin*. Phyllis starts the ball rolling on this litany of expiation with a soupçon of cos-play:

"For me to meet my bridegroom. The only one I ever loved. One night I'll drop off the stern of the ship. Then, little by little I'll feel his icy fingers creeping into my heart."

"...I'll give you away."

"What?"

"I mean: I'll go with you."

Keyes was right. I had nothing to thank him for. He just saved the state the expense of getting me. We walked around the ship. A sailor was swabbing out the gutter outside the rail. He was nervous, and caught me looking at him.

"There's a shark. Following the ship."

I tried not to look, but couldn't help it. I saw a flash of dirty white down in the green. We walked back to the deck chairs.

"Walter, we'll have to wait. Till the moon comes up..."

I'm writing this in the stateroom. It's about half past nine. She's in her stateroom getting ready. She's made her face chalk white, with black circles under her eyes and red on her lips and cheeks...She looks like what came aboard the ship to shoot dice for souls in the Rime of the Ancient Mariner.

◆

Cain's career as a journalist began with one of his hometown newspapers. *The Baltimore American* hired him in 1917 and assigned him to the police beat. Very rapidly he picked up the skills of a reporter and segued into a better job as a "human interest" columnist with the more prestigious *Baltimore Sun.* But before he could make a name for himself, he was drafted into World War I, a conflict that Cain decried.

Cain volunteered for the signal corps in the hopes he could refine his reporting skills. Dispatched in 1918 to the meat grinder that was the front lines in Europe, Cain became editor-in-chief of the 157th's newsletter *The Lorraine Cross.* He covered what he saw as an example of purposeless violence, a clash of colonial powers for control of the third world. Ultimately, he was seriously debilitated in a mustard gas barrage. (In one of those ironies with which the noir universe is rife, at the very same time and not so far away, the man who would eventually adapt the as yet unconceived *Double Indemnity* into a screenplay was also hospitalized.)

Discharged and back home, Cain was now a seasoned reporter. So, *The Sun* sent him on a dangerous mission into a miner's strike in West Virginia. Cain covered the labor struggle by going into the collieries to interview the miners. Many of Cain's proletarian sympathies were born from his military service and this experience. Cain always favored underdogs and proletarians, whether drifters/handymen like Frank in *The Postman Always Rings Twice,* the waitresses in *Mildred Pierce, The Root of His Evil,* or *The Cocktail Waitress,* and of course the incautious peddler of policies Walter Huff in *Double Indemnity.* Hard-hitting articles like the one on the coal strike, brought Cain to the attention of such journalistic legends as H.L. Mencken and Walter Lippmann. Mencken hired Cain to write regularly for his new magazine called *The American Mercury.* In 1924, with Mencken's recommendation in hand, he was hired by Lippmann at *The New York World* to write, once again, human interest stories. His output there was prolific. And in 1928, while at the *World,* Cain crossed paths with defendants Tiger Woman Ruth Snyder and Putty Man Judd Gray.[7]

Cain's reputation in the world of New York journalism grew to such an extent that in 1931 Harold Ross, the founder of the legendary *New Yorker,* asked Cain to become its editor. For a tempestuous year, Cain oversaw the magazine, where he had to deal not only with the egos of writers like James Thurber and E.B. White, but also with the interference of Ross. He soon resigned in exasperation.

As he began to dabble with fiction, Cain struggled with the format. He explained it this way: "I have no capacity to be Cain. I can't be Cain. I can be anybody except Cain."[8] So writing in the third-person, objective voice was abandoned; and he found his voice in becoming someone else, the fictive first-person narrator, which Cain refined over and over again in his novels with just three exceptions (*Mildred Pierce*, being one).

A successful early story that caught Hollywood's attention was "The Baby in the Icebox," published in 1932 by Mencken's *American Mercury*. All the basic Cain elements were there, the violence and sex, a frustrated wife dominated by an overbearing man, some variation of which (including role/gender reversals) would characterize Cain's future novels, most notably *Double Indemnity* and *The Postman Always Rings Twice*. A version of Cain himself acts as the unnamed narrator, who is more of an observer than a participant in the twisted triangle of Lura, Duke, and Wild Bill. It was also his first fiction set in Southern California. The story rights were purchased by Paramount, which produced a bowdlerized version called *She Made Her Bed* in 1934, with ingenue Sally Eilers (who worked as a Mack Sennett bathing beauty and first starred for producer/director Frank Borzage in *Bad Girl* [1931]) somewhat miscast as the formidable Lura.

Despite its "happy" ending, "The Baby in the Icebox" became the basis for *The Postman Always Rings Twice*. Arguably its narrative voice and setting are a blueprint for both Cain's later adaptations of the Snyder-Gray case and many later novels. For its different dramatic structure Cain credits his friend and mentor, playwright and screenwriter Vincent Lawrence. Cain recalled how Lawrence initially changed his perspective:

> *Until then, my ideal of writing was that the story correspond with life, mirror it, give a picture whose main element was truth. Lawrence had no objection to this, but insisted that truth was not all.*

42

He said if truth were the main object of writing, I would have a hard time competing with a $3 camera... He then recalled to me Dreiser's play The Hand of the Potter. *He recalled that this play was truthful enough, but utterly pointless, since it made a plea for a degenerate, without once ever attempting to get you interested in that degenerate.*[9]

As the lightbulb above Cain's head started to glow, Lawrence "then expounded to me the principle of the love-rack, as he calls it;—I haven't the faintest idea whether this is a rack on which the lovers are tortured, or something with pegs to hold the shining cloak of romance, or how the word figures in it;—and it was this which has such an effect on Hollywood picture writing."[10] As cryptic as Cain makes it sound, it is really an obsessive love story in which the lovers torture each other as well as themselves to reach their twisted ends, hence the noir crime thriller genre Cain almost single-handedly created and of which *Double Indemnity* is a prime example.

In 1932 Cain's agent, James Geller, convinced him to move out to Hollywood to pursue a potentially lucrative shift to screenwriting. Hollywood would lure many novelists into its arms in the 1920s and 30s, from "serious" literary luminaries such as William Faulkner and F. Scott Fitzgerald, to hard-boiled school members Horace McCoy and Frank Gruber and proletarian authors, guys with initials like W.R. Burnett and A.I. Bezzerides—all came in search of the "golden calf." The results were often disastrous. Their talents were either ill-assigned or underutilized, their unhappiness at being trapped after selling out was often drowned in the bottle. Cain, too, fell into alcoholism; but he never experienced the profound despair of many of his literary comrades in the studio system. For all his darkness Cain had an inherent optimism, which would shine more brightly in some of his later novels.

While traveling in his car around Southern California, Cain gained an appreciation of the rural areas around Los Angeles, the people, the dialect (what his mentor Mencken called pretentiously the "Vulgate"), as well as their struggles to attain the American dream. He was particularly fond of a wild animal preserve which figured into the plot of his first novel. In that milieu he hatched an idea for a first novel that would come to cement his reputation as the father (long before the term came into prominence) of the "noir" novel: *The Postman Always Rings Twice*. Thinking back to Ruth Snyder and her submissive lover Judd Gray, he concocted a plot set in the rural countryside around L.A., a story that epitomized Lawrence's "love-rack" concept and somewhat reworked the Snyder-Gray dynamic.

Drifter Frank Chambers, the narrator, stumbles upon a diner off the highway. He falls for Cora, the young wife of Nick, "the Greek," the owner of the business, who needs to go. As with Ruth and Judd the execution of the murder is sloppy. The couple is arrested and under pressure they turn on each other. Unlike ruthless Ruth and hapless Judd, a clever attorney gets them off. Like Lura and Wild Bill, Cora actualizes her dream by turning the diner into a success and turns her wayward lover into a handyman then husband. Unlike Ruth, a pregnant Cora dies in a car accident. In a final irony, like the Postman of the title, death comes around the bend a second time. Frank is arrested for murder and convicted. He finishes his confession from death row, a scene which greatly influenced a young French writer named Albert Camus when writing his novel, *The Stranger*.

On the advice of friend Walter Lippmann, Alfred Knopf picked up Cain's novel. When it was published in 1934 it garnered rave reviews and best-selling status. As a Cain biographer put it, "By mid-1934, the whole country was talking about the book, which was well on its way to becoming one of the most phenomenal successes in publishing history."[11] The cherry on top was a bidding war by the Hollywood studios that had previously used Cain's talents in a desultory manner. MGM won out but their adaptation of the novel was stopped dead in its tracks by the Production Code Administration and its czar Joseph Breen.

The PCA dated back to 1922, when Postmaster General Will Hays—who had just survived the Teapot Dome Scandal in the corrupt administration of Warren G. Harding—found a cushier and safer job with the Motion Picture Producers and Distributors Association. Hollywood was experiencing a series of scandals including the crime-of-the-century candidate manslaughter trial of Roscoe "Fatty" Arbuckle. To quell the wrath of religious

A slightly more distended Cain after he discovered alcohol, here posed with the star of *The Postman Always Rings Twice*, Lana Turner.

organizations, particularly the Catholic bishops, the MPPDA decided to appoint a morality supervisor for its content.

Although Hays came up with a list of dos and don'ts for filmmakers, there was little in the way of enforcement. It was not until the 1930s when Hollywood produced a series of violent and sexually liberated films like *Scarface* (1932) and *Baby Face* (1933, which featured Barbara Stanwyck in a warm-up for her role in *Double Indemnity*: "She had *it* and made *it* pay") that a phalanx of Catholic celebrities like Martin Quigley of the *Exhibitors Herald-World*, Bank of America founder A.P. Giannini (as always, follow the money), and a high-minded mouthpiece Joseph Breen put the pressure on

Hays and the studios. They finally agreed by 1934 to follow a new list of rules and regulations even more restrictive than the original.

So, Breen informed MGM that Cain's book, in which the adulterous murderers did pay for their crime, albeit indirectly, was just not morally acceptable, as it violated several provisions of the code. In response, despite the novel's acclaim and commercial success, MGM shelved their plans to make a movie out of *The Postman Always Rings Twice*. Where, of course, it stayed until *Double Indemnity*'s explosive box office made Cain's earlier work too valuable a property to lie fallow.

Undaunted, as per his optimistic modus operandi, Cain started writing another "love-rack" piece, again based on the seminal Snyder-Gray trial, its title this time promised a big score: *Double Indemnity*. His agent encouraged him to assemble this new vessel with all possible alacrity and to launch it in the wake of his first bestseller. Standing by to break a bottle of champagne over its bow and publish a serial version was *Liberty* magazine.

Illustration of the disposal of the body from the original publication in *Liberty* magazine. Compare with the movie on page 107.

Cain's *Double Indemnity* is not the Chandler/Wilder *Double Indemnity*. It is up front in its sexual steam and in its daring combination of detailed naturalism with surreal imagery. Its narrator, Walter Huff, does find himself under the spell of a "sweet-faced" but psychotic sex kitten named Phyllis Nirdlinger, who does not immediately reveal her nerves of steel or vision of herself as Death's bride. Equally important for Huff is the prospect of a payday by cheating his own insurance company and flummoxing his own father figure—named Keyes, and in the same position as a fraud investigator in both the novel and film. For Chandler and Wilder, this became the simple invocation "I killed him for money...and for a woman."

In her book *The Street Was Mine: White Masculinity in Hardboiled Fiction and Film Noir* notable noir critic and novelist Megan Abbott presents a fresh perspective on writers like James Cain and Raymond Chandler. In Cain's work and more specifically in *Double Indemnity* she zeroes in on the fear and anxiety that grips the methodical Walter in the novel. These elements were either absent or underplayed in Chandler-Wilder's more traditionally masculine Walter. Abbott identifies several scenes that epitomize this male anxiety which marks much of Cain's work:

> *From his first meetings with Phyllis, Walter experiences inexplicable physical reactions to her, up his spine, on his neck. Although he also experiences a comparatively uncomplicated sexual desire for her, Walter's primary bodily reaction to Phyllis is one of ghastly horror. Walter's hysterical symptoms cluster in two places, the spine and the throat. After the murder, Walter describes feeling "something like a drawstring pull in my throat, and a sob popped out of me." His voice has become independent from his consciousness; his sob has the agency here, not Walter, suggesting a cognitive dissonance of sorts. His voice's subjectivity signals Walter's lack of mastery over his own body; he notes, "It was getting to me. I knew I had to get myself under some kind of control." To regain control over his voice he decides to sing, hoping it will "make me snap out of it." The effect is chilling as he attempts to croon "The Isle of Capri," and*

47

after two notes "it swallowed into a kind of wail." He ends up mum-
bling the Lord's Prayer as a seemingly more solid, stabilizing choice,
but gets through it shakily twice before he suddenly forgets "how it
went." Walter proceeds to dig his fingernails into his hands "trying
to hold onto [him]self" and ends up vomiting and experiencing a vi-
olent shaking fit. His body is a rash of vibrating, convulsing entities,
all operating independently. There is no center.[12]

On the other hand, both Mrs. Nirdlinger and Mrs. Dietrichson exhibit considerable strength and willpower. It is she who carries the novel's dead body of
her husband to the tracks with little effort, while Walter watches in amaze-
ment. It is she who can murder her husband's wife and possibly even children, who can be a serial killer, in order to get the money (who needs the man,
really). It's the patriarchy's American glittering dream that many Cain women
want and which, as with Cora and many subsequent Cain female protagonists,
quickly tarnishes and turns to ash. It is Phyllis Nirdlinger who can shoot her
lover yet still convince the wounded and emasculated Walter to follow her
into the arms of death in the waters around their cruise ship.

Even after *Double Indemnity* was serialized to great success, Knopf
held up publication in book form until 1943 as part of a Cain trilogy called
Three of a Kind. Nevertheless and despite the PCA putting the kibosh on
Postman, Hollywood execs flocked to another rights auction. Cain expected
he could earn $25,000 for this sale (which may not sound like much, but
those 1936 dollars would easily exceed half a million today). However, neither Cain nor agent Geller had factored in the obstruction of Joseph Breen
a second time.

When various studios and producers like the newly independent David
O. Selznick queried the PCA pontiff about the viability of *Double Indemnity*,
his responses to all were identical: "The general low tone and sordid flavor
of this story makes it, in our judgment, thoroughly unacceptable."[13] Despite
its auspicious launch *Double Indemnity* was just like *Postman* ... dead in the
water; and by the time it was finally sold to Paramount in 1943 the price had
dropped considerably.

Cain's next published novel was the even more controversial, *Serenade* (1938). Knopf was particularly enthusiastic about Cain's latest product and with good reason. Once again Cain explored a taboo subject, this time homosexuality. The narrator of the piece was an anxiety-ridden opera singer named Sharp struggling with his sexual identity who believes that his queerness causes him to lose the power of his voice. Like the good journalist he was, Cain consulted several psychologists about this premise (just as he had talked to insurance investigators as research for *Double Indemnity*). Drawing on their feedback, he went ahead with his daring premise.

Sharp tries to find respite from his conflicts through a Mexican getaway. There he meets Juana—who was based on a prostitute Cain "hung out" with during a trip to Guatemala—who seems psychically to sense his torment. While seeking shelter from a storm, Juana performs ancient rituals that Sharp dubs "how an Aztec treats a God." Then they have sex, which acts as a form of magic, after which Sharp regains both his heterosexual sex drive and his powerful operatic voice. With Juana as his protector, back in the United States, Sharp comes under the influence of Hawes, a wealthy gay "angel," who wants him as lover in return for aiding Sharp's career. Again seeing this man struggling with his sexual identity and his voice, Juana steps in and kills Hawes (it's a mock bullfight with Juana taking on the role of matador). After escaping back to Mexico, as with most of Cain's couples, the relationship all but disintegrates. When Juana is killed by a jealous policeman, Sharp sinks into depression and vows never to sing again.

Knopf was right to be keen. The book was another critical and financial success, making Cain among the most famous crime/thriller/noir novelists worldwide. The renowned critic Edmund Wilson published an essay in 1941 called "The Boys in the Back Room." In surveying the hard-boiled novelists of the period, Wilson anointed Cain "the best of these novelists," hierarchically situated ahead of such *Black Mask* writers as Dashiell Hammett and Horace McCoy. He praised Cain for being "ingenious in tracing from their first beginnings the tangles that gradually tighten around the necks of the people involved in those bizarre and brutal crimes that figure in the

American papers; and is capable even of tackling—in *Serenade*, at any rate—the larger tangles of social interest from which these deadly knots derive."[14]

In 1941 Knopf published Cain's first third-person narrative novel—*Mildred Pierce*. It, too, was a hit. *Mildred Pierce* delineates the social and economic inequalities of Depression-era America through another one of Cain's long line of ambitious women. Mildred overcomes her husband's inertia and even the personal avarice of her opera-singing daughter (Velda) to become a small-time business owner, who utilizes ingenuity to capture the American dream. It then spirals into a nightmare under unrelenting pressure from Velda.

Then World War II changed everything, even Hollywood. Studios began to produce films with anti-fascist and pro-War propaganda. Reflecting the worldwide psychic trauma, as might be expected, these films often had to be dark and violent. As these darker visions became more acceptable, even desirable, to audiences, the studios took greater risks with their range of subject matter. Many historians have noted that what became film noir took root with the war's inception and then "blossomed." In this context, when *Three of a Kind* was published, there was renewed interest in the film rights to *Double Indemnity*.

There are several apocryphal stories of how *Double Indemnity* came into the hands of émigré director-writer Billy Wilder in 1943. They began with an article in the *New York Times* by Lloyd Shearer in 1945, one of the earliest to recognize the film noir movement, in fact if not in name. In "Crime Certainly Pays on the Screen," Shearer moralistically laments the growth of "homicidal" films,[15] in many ways parroting the position of the PCA and Joe Breen. He also relates a colorful, if imaginary, story of how a secretary (to producer Joseph Sistrom and, in later versions, to Wilder) could not be found because she was in the ladies' room reading *Double Indemnity*. When her boss finally located her, she raved about the novel and said it was "perfect" for Billy Wilder.

While the truth of its discovery is much more mundane, Joseph Sistrom, the de facto producer of *Double Indemnity* (even though he was denied that credit), was a protégé of Paramount exec William LeBaron. He was a graduate of Stanford and a devotee of crime fiction. And in early 1943, although uncredited he was effectively nominated for an Oscar for producing *Wake Island*. Without any prompting from the studio, upon the re-publication of *Double Indemnity*, Sistrom brought the novel to Wilder, and Paramount bought the rights.

Wilder loved the material and had known Cain in the early 1930s when they were both doctoring scripts for various studios. So, he wanted Cain to work with him on the screenplay. Unfortunately, Cain already had commitments at other studios, so he demurred. But as a courtesy he wrote a memo to Wilder in which he made some suggestions to get around Breen's objections.[16] In the memo, Cain noted that Breen's objections seemed to rest largely on the planning for the murder and its execution, actually raising the unlikely possibility of someone using his novel to plan an actual crime. The always amenable Cain suggested, somewhat shockingly, dumping the planning for the murder and the murder itself. And instead, Phyllis' depressed husband, who is dying of some "vague" illness and is also aware of Phyllis and Walter's adulterous ardor, commits suicide from the train to save them the trouble. Phyllis pursues collecting on her husband's accident insurance policy with the help of Walter. And the rest of the book would be the same with them turning on each other, etc. Wilder (and presumably Sistrom) thought it better to finesse Breen.

With Cain not an option, Sistrom now suggested a newer crime fiction novelist named Raymond Chandler, who had nothing but disdain for Cain's writing: He also did not think that Cain's dialogue, which Wilder wanted to maintain, would play well on the screen. In order to prove Chandler wrong—foreshadowing the contentious collaboration which would develop between the two men—Wilder had student actors come in to do a table read. This apparently convinced Wilder that Chandler was right. Cain was then called in for a meeting with Sistrom, Wilder, and Chandler, in which Wilder sadly told him about the reading and that he was sorry that they would be changing dialogue. As usual Cain was entirely unfazed, bowed out of any further consultation and left it to Chandler and Wilder to have at it.

There, however, was one more exchange regarding the adaptation. Chandler wrote to Cain, again explaining why the novella's dialogue did not work when spoken. In a written response, Cain in his own diplomatic way defended his writing style, "Your description of the vague, cloudy way the dialogue sounded when you had it tried with actors is wholly interesting, for in 'Double Indemnity' I was trying to capture some of those bellowing unrealities you get in a fever dream, and if the dialogue sounded as you say it did, quite possibly I succeeded..."[17] Like most authors he could put a spin on an aesthetic interpretation. Billy Wilder, on the other hand, could put a spin on just about anything. In terms of collegial sincerity, score one for Cain.

3.

THE MYSTERY WRITER

Was it dawn? He was shivering. He coughed, a spasm that twisted his torso. Mustard! No. He could see. Blinking he verified that his RAF uniform was still draped over the chair by the wall. On the bedside table, a dog-eared magazine: a ten-cent *Harper's Weekly* left by some former occupant of this hospital bed. "Women in Black" read the cover, a sketch of four of them, veiled, mourning, foraging for what?

The squeaky springs. Focus on that, he told himself. On the foreground of the sketch, where that sad-faced, dark-haired woman is grasping a broken carriage wheel. "Two are in the trenches. One is dead!" What he did not, could not, remember was who told him that? Who wrote that?

In his fever dream, platoon commander Raymond Chandler did not, could not, know, how long he had been here, where the shrill of a shell was replaced by the squeaky springs beneath him. He remembered the trenches, the cold, "Watch your spacing," ... the dead. There was a shrike on the wall calendar, garlands on its edges, "1918" at the top, and the tear sheet for October was visible.

What he did not, could not, remember was how he got to England. He'd lived here once—but that was years ago. Self-professed surveyor turned soldier, would-be aviator, "seasick every time the sea is rough." Why was he here, in this sanitarium, St. Leonard's on Sea? The Spanish flu. Another cough shook the memory loose. The realization that he was merely ill calmed him. He had beaten it once before ... in July. He would do it again. Otherwise, it would be a most inglorious demise.

What Air Cadet Chandler did not, could not, know, was that the war would end before he got his wings. The woman not in black, the *Harper's* writer, what was her name? Sophie...something. Addams? No, that was another essayist: "The appetite of war for human flesh. It must be satisfied, and you must be the ones to feed it." He had read her words. And he had offered his life. What more did she want? That Hull House founder from Chicago, where he was born, had not spoken of women in black.

What this native-born American turned British citizen did not, could not, know, was if he would write again. The thought of failing made him shudder. No, he'd go back to California, give up the tortured relationship with the Pascals, back to normality.

What he did not, could not, know was that his failure to become a war hero would not be his last chance at fame. That he would write again, and thousands of soldiers would read his words. His eyes closed. He went back to sleep.[1]

He dreamt of Los Angeles, of the water in mid-town lake and the Mary Clark Home for young women at 306 Loma Drive. Perhaps the women in black could come there, right across from the white stucco cottage where he lived, in the heart of

> *...a big hard-boiled city with no more personality than a paper cup. Real cities have something else, some individual bony structure under the muck. Los Angeles has Hollywood—and hates it. It ought to consider itself damn lucky. Without Hollywood it would be a mail order city. Everything in the catalogue you could get better somewhere else.*
>
> **Private detective Philip Marlowe in *The Little Sister***

Like his famous character, mystery writer Raymond Thornton Chandler spoke with the tinge of a cynic, who disdained "sentimental crap."[2] Perhaps that was because he had tried his hand at that sort of writing, as a youth, and failed. In the process of becoming an involuntary and self-taught but professional "mystery writer," he developed a signature style and a curmudgeonly outlook that draws frequent attention to itself to this day. Despite having written relatively little prose—barely two dozen short stories, eight of which were

Chandler in his RAF Cadet uniform around the time he caught the Spanish Flu.

cobbled into the earliest of his seven novels, and a few essays—after Agatha Christie or perhaps Conan Doyle, Chandler became and remains one of the most famous mystery writers in the world. Continuously in print since first published, his novels have sold millions of copies in a score of languages. And he reluctantly co-wrote the screenplay of *Double Indemnity*.[3]

Raymond Thornton Chandler was born in Chicago's south side in 1888, more than a year before Jane Addams co-founded Hull House to help women expand their opportunities in a man's world. Infant Raymond would be the only issue of a Protestant mother, Florence Thornton, only recently arrived from the old country when she met and wed Maurice Chandler, a Quaker railroad man. By the time the boy was seven, the marriage had crumbled under the weight of Maurice's alcoholism and possible cruelty, so Florence returned first to Waterford, Ireland, and then to London to live with Chandler's stern grandmother and a maiden aunt.

His uncle, head of the family firm in Ireland, wanted Chandler to qualify for a civil service post and helped get Chandler accepted as a "day boy" at Dulwich College. The young Chandler graduated then spent a traditional year abroad in France and Germany studying international law and continental life. Returning to Britain, he became a naturalized citizen in order to qualify for the civil service exam. He placed third among the six hundred applicants for a post with the Admiralty. Chandler quickly realized that being an assistant stores officer in naval supplies was not his cup of tea. Even part-time writing that led to a score of well-meaning, treacly love poems in print could not assuage his ennui. So he quit.

He wrangled a job as a reporter for the *Daily Express* but was fired,[4] so he taught part-time at Dulwich and sold essays, reviews, and poems for pennies to *The Westminster Gazette* and *Academy* literary magazine. After several years of being "holed up in Bloomsbury,"[5] Chandler claimed that he turned down an offer to write serial novels for a weekly stipend.[6] Instead, a few days before his 24th birthday, he boarded the SS Merrion in Liverpool to return to the land of his birth.[7] Why? "I had no feeling of identity with the United States, and yet I resented the kind of ignorant and snobbish criticism of Americans that was current at the time," Chandler, already a contrarian, later explained. "America seemed to call to me in some mysterious way. So, when I was 23, I managed to get a loan of £500 from my irate Uncle Ernest."[8]

On board the ocean liner, Chandler met and socialized with Los Angeles denizens Warren and Alma Lloyd, who gave him their address in the Westlake district.[8] They parted company by the gangplank on the docks. After briefly

being a clerk in St. Louis and visiting Nebraska relatives from his youth, Chandler continued to San Francisco, where he did whatever work he could find (picking fruit, clerking at Abercrombie's sports shop), rented a house, sent for his mother, and completed a night-school course in accounting. Florence's arrival found Chandler still "with a beautiful wardrobe, a public school accent, no practical gifts for earning a living, and a contempt for the natives which, I am sorry to say, has in some measure persisted to this day."[10] Apparently Chandler alternated between being a snob and resenting those who were. These mixed emotions would be carried forward into his Hollywood career.

Soon Chandler and mother made their way to the Lloyd's home, the first stop in a decades-long, peripatetic sojourn in Los Angeles that included more than a dozen different addresses, not including temporary quarters in hotels and mountain cabins.[11] When Chandler first arrived in Los Angeles, the downtown streets were only partially paved, horses and buggies were still common sights, Wilshire Boulevard in Santa Monica was a dirt track, and the only way for Hollywood stars to reach their hideaways in Malibu was by boat. Chandler settled into the Lloyd home in the same year that William Mulholland completed the Owens River Aqueduct, the still controversial project that poured millions more gallons into the city's water supply and started its progress to becoming a metropolis that would gradually expand and annex most of the adjacent communities.

Warren Lloyd, who had a doctorate from Yale, was legal counsel for several oil companies (and had also written a book on abnormal psychology). He and Alma, a sculptor and singer, regularly hosted parties for an eclectic group of friends, where discussions ranged from politics and science to the occult, and went on excursions in a convertible automobile with Chandler in the backseat next to a well-stocked picnic basket. Among Chandler's new acquaintances were the Pascals: Julian, wife Cissy, and son Gordon. In August 1917, a few months after the United States joined the "great" war, Chandler and mother were living with the Pascals. Chandler convinced Gordon to go with him to Canada (which unlike the US offered a $15 per week stipend for military families) to volunteer. Chandler's time in the trenches in spring 1918 ended when he was accepted to flight school.

Whatever he may have resolved during his hospital stays, Chandler returned to Los Angeles in 1919 and professed his love for Cissy Pascal, a woman almost twenty years older (something he did not realize for many years after they met), who divorced her husband in 1920. The Lloyd's accepted this relationship; but Florence Chandler never could, so the couple could not marry until after her death. Chandler had again secured and then quit a short-lived job (six weeks) with a newspaper (the *Los Angeles Daily Express*), before Warren Lloyd's brother arranged an accounting position at the Dabney-Johnson Oil Corporation.

Once settled into domestic life with Cissy, Chandler progressed to office manager and ultimately vice-president with a salary of over $10,000 per year, a benchmark for success. While the oil business was mostly unaffected by the start of the Great Depression, Chandler again lapsed into a funk (what early biographer Frank MacShane called "a black-Irish depression"), started socializing alone with younger colleagues from the office, and drinking heavily. "He was a loner," an office rival asserted, "At banquets at the Biltmore Hotel, Chandler was a shadowy figure, stinko drunk and hovering in the wings with a bevy of showgirls, a nuisance."[12] Drinking, womanizing, melodramatically threatening suicide, being chronically late or entirely absent from his desk on any given workday—eventually Chandler "walked out of the Bank of Italy at the corner of Olive and 7th streets for the last time, fired from his job at the Dabney Oil Company."[13] According to MacShane, Chandler thought about suing for slander but soon realized that he deserved to be sacked. "It was a disaster but typical of Chandler's resilience was his remark that the most important thing he learned from being fired was that it 'taught me not to take anything for granted.'"[14]

On a road trip to Seattle (presumably in his Chrysler Imperial 75 Roadster after having returned the company Hupmobile to Dabney), Chandler and his wife "went touring around the Northwest, where I made several ineffectual efforts to do what I had always wanted to do—write."[15] While relying on assistance from family friends to get through the loss of income, the correspondence-course accountant was soon reckoning what it would take at a penny-per-word to make a living doing what he always wanted to.

In his essay, "The Simple Art of Murder," Chandler would later theorize "the realistic style is easy to abuse: from haste, from lack of awareness, from inability to bridge the chasm that lies between what a writer would like to be able to say and what he actually knows how to say."[16] At some point, driving back to Los Angeles, Chandler may have remembered what he had been told about creating serial novels—"it was easy, you just kept on until they made you stop and then you started a new one"[17]—and decided that, if he were to eke out a living writing for pulp magazines, mysteries would be easier than science fiction.

Chandler "had to go back to the beginning and learn to write all over again." As he confided to a friend, "You'll laugh when I tell you what I write. Me, with my romantic and poetical instincts. I'm writing sensational detective fiction."[18] In researching the pulps "it struck me that some of the writing was pretty forceful and honest, even though it had its crude aspect," Chandler admitted later to one of his publishers, "I decided this might be a good way to learn to write fiction and get paid a small amount of money at the same time."[19] Chandler started the process of becoming a mystery writer by imitation. Because he wished he had "one of those facile plotting brains,"[20] he extracted the plot from a pulp piece by Erle Stanley Gardner and filled it out again with his own prose. "The Sun Also Sneezes" parodied Hemingway, but in Chandler's hierarchy of writers

> *Hammett was the ace performer, but there is nothing in his work that is not implicit in the early novels and short stories of Hemingway. Yet, for all I know, Hemingway may have learned something from Hammett as well as from writers like Dreiser, Ring Lardner, Carl Sandburg, Sherwood Anderson...a revolutionary debunking of both the language and the material of fiction had been going on for some time.[21]*

So, at age 44 Chandler found a formula with which he was comfortable and began a journey into fiction that would fill the rest of his life:

Down these mean streets a man must go who is not himself mean,
who is neither tarnished nor afraid... He talks as the man of his age
talks—that is, with rude wit, a lively sense of the grotesque, a dis-
gust for sham, and a contempt for pettiness. This man's adventure
in search of a hidden truth... I see him always in a lonely street. In
lonely rooms, puzzled but never defeated.[22]

In the early 1930s Los Angeles, mean streets and sensational stories were not hard to find. They were around every corner and on the front pages of every daily paper. "I lived many years in Los Angeles," Chandler said to Ian Fleming less than a year before his death, "but nobody in my time had tried to write about a Los Angeles background in any sort of realistic way."[23] As he tested out Marlowe prototypes in his earliest short stories, he also understood that it was his urban knight's "tender emotions" that might leave him puzzled. "Always confused," Chandler admitted to Fleming and, in that regard, "he's like me."

By the time his discussion with Fleming was broadcast in 1958, Chandler knew that many newer writers had tried, but few if any of them had captured Los Angeles and its environs with his particular style. Because almost all of his stories are written in the first person, the city is always reflected in his protagonist's eyes. Marlowe and his predecessors never fail to take note of the ironic or the absurd, the lurid or laughable details, no matter how serious the moment.

Whatever he may ultimately have thought of Hammett ("I give him everything. There were a lot of things he could not do, but what he did, he did superbly") or Hemingway ("with his eternal sleeping bag, [he] got to be pretty damn tiresome") or of Stanley Gardner who "owed nothing to them,"[24] as Chandler took his inspiration from Thomas Mallory (after whom his first character was named) and crafted a private investigator into a neo-Galahad, who was "the hero...a complete man. He must be, to use a rather weathered phrase, a man of honor—by instinct, by inevitability, without thought of it, and certainly without saying it." If that doesn't sound anything like insurance salesman Walter Huff, who became Neff, there was a contemporary writer whom Chandler believed merited only opprobrium:

*But James Cain—faugh! Everything he touches smells like a billy
goat. He is every kind of writer I detest, a* faux naïf, *a Proust in
greasy overalls....*"[25]

In 1933 Chandler slipped a typescript into a long envelope and mailed it to
Black Mask, a pulp founded in 1920 by Cain mentor H.L. Mencken, who
considered the magazine "lousy" but a generator of profits to shore up his
higher-flown literary enterprises. Of these facts Chandler was almost certainly unaware. He did know that Hammett had published extensively in
Black Mask and that its editor, Joseph T. Shaw, defended its violent and salacious content as "rendering a public service by publishing the realistic,
true-to-life, highly illuminating stories of modern crime."[26]

When Shaw opened Chandler's submission, he was dumbstruck to see
that its author had carefully spaced his typing so that the right margin appeared justified. Despite this, Shaw knew a good yarn when he read it and
paid Chandler the going rate of one cent for each its 18,000 words, ragged-
right edge or not: $180.

Now an official mystery writer, Chandler plodded on, churning out
words as fast as he could (which was not very). *Black Mask* published two
more Chandler pieces in 1934, three in 1935, and five in 1936. But while the
word count of his oeuvre grew, the money in his bank account did not. In
1938, after Shaw left *Black Mask* and Chandler had switched to *Dime Detective,* Chandler made $1,275. Not an amount below the poverty line in the
last years of the Depression, but nothing like the vast earnings of his new
friend Erle Stanley Gardner (with whom Chandler was by then frequently
corresponding) and barely ten percent of what Chandler the oil executive
had earned in his best years.

In his chosen genre, Chandler was now a name to conjure with, a name
that sold. His latest stories usually inspired the cover art for the issue in
which they appeared. Dreams of more prestigious publication, in *Collier's*
or *The Saturday Evening Post* crept into his correspondence.[27] But at some
point, Chandler realized the truth: "In America mystery story writers are
slightly below-the-salt," he told Fleming, using the British phrase for poor

61

social standing, "You can write a lousy historical novel and be treated respectfully; but a thriller writer…you starve to death for ten years before your publisher knows you're any good."[28] Despite this belief and rather than try his hand at material for "upper crust" magazines, by mid-1938 Chandler decided to start work on a novel.

But who to imitate? First-biographer MacShane quotes Chandler to the effect that Agatha Christie was "bunk" and even some of Conan Doyle was "utterly absurd, his scientific premises are utterly unreliable."[29] While never aiming for descriptive prose that was "clean and cold" or a slave to "objectivism," Chandler and Marlowe shared a need to simultaneously affirm and mock their fallen idealism and forlorn romanticism. In the end, the success of Chandler's short prose (not all that short, since every additional 100 words meant a dollar more in his check) and the knowledge that many pulp readers eagerly awaited his next fiction, must have convinced him to stick with what worked, the odd mixture of hard-boiled and lovelorn, hard-bitten and chivalric.

From Dumas and Dickens he had a sense of a larger canvas. The work and much of the novels that he admired were episodic and/or interconnecting separate but parallel events. So why not take some of his best stories and cobble them together into a longer, more complex narrative? "I had a bunch of old novelettes full of material—and it looked like pretty good material to me—and they so far as I could see, as extinct as a dodo."[30]

In an era before cutting-and-pasting, Chandler reread then rewrote. Oilman Chandler had certainly known E.L. Doheny, whose son Ned died in a murder-suicide, likely saw him at the family mansion, which inspired Gen. Winslow's abode in the 1936 story, "The Curtain." With Doheny changed from Winslow to Sternwood, Chandler doubled the length of his original to create the opening of his first novel, *The Big Sleep.*

Also using "Killer in the Rain" and sections of "Finger Man" and "Mandarin's Jade" Chandler methodically stitched together a magnum opus of 70,000 words. With hopes for a much bigger payday than a penny a word. Chandler sent his manuscript to a New York agent who sold Blanche Knopf on it as a Borzoi mystery. In a two-edged irony, publisher Alfred A. Knopf

Dorothy Fischer worked at Paramount for Raymond Chandler, "whose advice to a secretary" was published in *Strand Magazine*, April 2021: "I am only exacting in the sense that I want things right. Do not be satisfied with anything less than you want. It is never stupid to ask questions. It is only stupid to guess at the answers and take a chance on being wrong."

placed a trade advertisement heralding Chandler as the forthcoming successor to their current writers of this type of fiction: Dashiell Hammett and…James Cain.

Chandler got what he wanted…sort of. He went from being paid a penny-a-word to 20 cents a copy (10% of the $2 hardcover price), earned $2,000 (through two printings of *The Big Sleep*), and tripled his per-word income. If there were holes in the plot of his debut novel contemporary reviewers either missed or overlooked them. "As a study in depravity, the story is excellent," opined the *New York Times* reviewer, "with Marlowe standing out as almost the only fundamentally decent person in it."[31] Chandler may have felt shortchanged by that review, but the royalty checks assuaged that somewhat. "The trickiest part of your technique," he wrote to Stanley Gardner, in the midst of again cannibalizing old stories to construct his second novel, *Farewell, My Lovely,* "was…

> …*the ability to put over situations that verged on the implausible, but which in the reading seemed quite real. I hope you understand that I mean this as compliment. I have never come even near to doing it myself.… It's probably the fundamental of all rapid work, because naturally rapid work has a large measure of improvisation.*[32]

After filling up more than a hundred of the five-by-seven sheets of yellow paper that he used for first drafts, Chandler discarded those and started again. "I have never made much money out of writing. I work too slowly, throw away too much." Writing from Big Bear Lake in the fall, Chandler shared his gloom over process and results with fellow crime writer George Harmon Coxe, "I had to throw my second book away, so that leaves me with nothing to show for the last six months and possibly nothing to eat for the next six."[33]

Still in need of money (despite finally selling an "upper crust" story[34]), Chandler had no choice but to start over. Whether it was the incongruous metaphor ("a tarantula on the slice of angel food"; "a blonde to make a bishop kick a hole in a stained-glass window"); the conspicuous understatement ("All she did was take her hand out of her bag, with a gun in it. All she did

64

was point it at me and smile. All I did was nothing."); or the deft invocation of a faded femme fatale ("She looked like a woman who would have been dangerous a hundred years ago, but today was just Grade B Hollywood."), eventually Chandler used the skills he did have to overcome his self-professed technical limitations and craft a second long fiction: *Farewell, My Lovely.*

Buoyed by having sold out two printings of *The Big Sleep*, Knopf had an initial press run of 7,500 copies in October 1940. Those did not sell out. Neither did the next book which appeared almost two years later in August 1942. *The High Window*, despite another allusion to the Dohenys, was not derived from earlier stories; and in its pages Marlowe is actually called a "shop-soiled Galahad."[35]

Chandler was stoic in a letter to Blanche Knopf of October 1942: "Sorry you are feeling badly about the sales of *The High Window*. Last time you were out here, you told me 4,000 copies was the ceiling." Chandler knew this was not true, that Hammett and Cain sold a lot more than that; but all he added was perhaps, "you were just saying that to comfort a broken heart." As he neared completion of his fourth novel, which he hoped would be "livelier and better and faster, because as you know it is the pace that counts," Chandler remained both a writer and theorist of the mystery. While he may not as yet have purchased a ticket to watch the earliest examples of film noir—although, given his views on Hammett he might well have cast a gander at the latest version of *The Maltese Falcon* released a year earlier—he was keeping up with his genre: "I have just been reading a book called *Phantom Lady* by William Irish, whoever that is…but it is a swell job of writing, one that gives everything to every character, every scene and never gets scared and runs."[36] Of course, in search of "livelier and better," Chandler had already gone back to cannibalizing and used three more stories to craft *The Lady in the Lake.*

As to fiscal prospects, Chandler had already done pretty well from the sale of film rights. That past spring 20th Century-Fox had paid $3,500 for *The High Window*, or around four times the book royalties. And the previous year, RKO had paid $2,000 for *Farewell, My Lovely.* Because all rights were conveyed—a deal which Chandler later lambasted as "a contract of almost unparalleled stupidity on the part of my New York agent"[37]—RKO got two

Lurid cover of the Avon Library paperback published in 1943, while Chandler was working at Paramount.

movies (including one in which Marlowe the character finally make his first screen appearance, 1944's *Murder, My Sweet*). In fact, both studios would ultimately jettison Chandler's shop-soiled Galahad, in favor of other literary characters they already owned. The Falcon literally and figuratively took over as protagonist and slipped into the plot line of Chandler's second novel, while Mike Shayne, a private dick created by the prolific Brett Halliday, replaced Marlowe when *The High Window* became 1942's *Time To Kill*.[38]

Depressed by the events of World War II, especially the bombing of his former home city in England, Chandler waited for the publication of *Lady in the Lake*; tinkered with his to-do list, which included a Gothic romance *English Summer* ("a short, swift, tense, gorgeously written story verging on melodrama"[39]) and six or seven more sci-fi stories. He also got a copy of the paperback, "two-bit edition of *The Big Sleep*" from publisher Alfred Knopf.[40]

During the war well over a million copies of the various, small-format cheap reprints of the $2 hard-back Borzois would be sold. Those made Chandler an even more famous mystery writer, but all he got for it was chump change. Sure he had had something of a studio payday, but what RKO and Fox did to his work started Chandler on the path of resentment and ultimately led to his scathing indictment of the industry, "Writers in Hollywood," where he complained, "there is no attempt to exploit the writer as an artist of meaning. Hollywood's idea of production value is to spend a million dollars dressing up a story that any good writer would throw away." Actually those were the more restrained remarks that Chandler made, after he had called certain producers "individuals with the morals of a goat, the artistic integrity of a slot machine, and the manners of a floorwalker with delusions of grandeur."[41]

The morning of Monday, May 10, 1943, in Hollywood was sunny. The temperature would rise to 85 degrees Fahrenheit; but it was still comfortable just after 10 AM in the modest rented house at 6520 Drexel Avenue. "400 U.S. Planes Hammer Sicily Port," read the headline of the still-folded *Los Angeles Times* on the edge of his wooden desk. Sipping coffee and gazing out the window, Raymond Chandler was in his office alcove, when the phone rang. "Mr. Chandler, my name is Joseph Sistrom," said the youngish voice on the other end of the line. "I'm a producer at Paramount Pictures."

67

Ginger Rogers portraying the 12-year-old Susie helped Wilder get his first directing job.

4.

THE AUSTRIAN JOURNALIST

The round face of the short man peeked out below the brim of a baseball cap with the logo of the Hollywood Stars: it was fire-engine red with three white pinstripes running from edge to edge and crossing under the felt button on top. What he did not, could not, know, was that at some time in the future Bing Crosby, crooner of the current hit "June in January," would suggest that he invest in the minor league team. Right now, in his hand was a large envelope with a button-and-string closure on the back; on the front, a circular Columbia Pictures logo of a crowned woman holding a torch. What he did not, could not, know was if the documents inside this envelope would be enough.

An unlit Lucky Strike dangled at the left edge of his mouth, and he was fishing through the pockets of a frayed linen jacket while he stared at the sign outside the Consulado General de Estados Unidos in Mexicali. On a white sandwich board were two columns of neat sans-serif type in both English and Spanish. This was a problem. German, he knew. French, he knew. These languages, not so much. With a head shake he crossed to the battered, green 1928 DeSoto that he had parked right in front and found a matchbook from the Coconut Grove.

As he touched the flame to the tip of the Lucky, two teenage girls in uniforms—crisp blue blouses and pleated skirts, bobby sox and saddleshoes—came up the sidewalk. Dark hair in long braids were draped over their shoulders. He smiled. "Con esa sonrisa," the taller one whispered to her school mate, "Parece un duendecito." What this man who looked like a pixie, did not, could not, know was how many Austrians had already been given work visas that year. Would he seem like—he knew this word from a

Black Mask story he had muddled through by a guy named Horace McCoy—a "deadbeat" to whoever he met inside? He gave his scuffed shoes a quick rub against the back of his trouser legs, dropped the coffin nail in the gutter, and walked into the consulate.

It was the company logo, not the contents of the envelope, that sold it. The earnest young clerk noticed the image and said, "Give me your tired and your poor, huh?" He laughed at his own joke then asked the million-dollar question: "What do you do?" "I write...for," pixie man paused then thought, "scheiße...Wie heißt es Zeitung?" What the hell, he would never be a journalist again. He pointed to the Columbia Pictures letterhead: "...for movies." With that, his visa was completed and stamped. The clerk had written "Billy" with a "y" not an "ie"; but that didn't matter. It didn't matter either that Columbia Pictures had given him the gate, that despite what all the testimonial letters inside the envelope suggested, he did not presently have a writing job. What he had was a piece of paper to wave at the border guards. As he stepped out into the Mexicali afternoon, Billy pulled on the Stars cap.

What Billy (né Samuel) Wilder did not, could not, know was that in some time to come, his name would appear in gold letters inside a five-pointed star, just like the one on his cap, but repositioned on a mica-flecked sidewalk at 1751 Vine Street in Los Angeles. The De Soto's engine turned over with a whine and rattled ominously. Would it make the two miles to the border let alone all the way back to his rented room in West Hollywood? In a month it would be his 28th birthday.

What this ambitious Jewish European ex-pat, thousands of miles from his fiscal successes in Berlin and then Paris, did not, could not, know was when he would be able to buy a decent automobile.

So, I went to Mexico, to a little town that straddles the border to California. There is a wire fence. You can see right through it into the United States. If you're an American or if you have a visa, you just walk in.

Stranded émigré Georges Iscovescu in *Hold Back the Dawn*

By the time Billy Wilder co-wrote *Hold Back the Dawn* in 1941, and included that semi-autobiographical observation, it was more than six years later and he had a better car.[1] It might not have been as flashy as the Graham-Paige he owned in Germany, the 8-cylinder "Blue Streak" that he would race top-down through the Brandenburg Gate where the downdraft always threatened to blow off his trilby fedora. But the new cars Wilder bought in California were sleek and reliable and everything a successful Hollywood writer could want. Where he was and what he was doing had not likely been foreseen by the 18-year-old who dropped out of pre-law studies at the University of Vienna.

Keep in mind that for almost all of his career as a writer, Wilder's output was fiction. In that context, Wilder's personal stories, although the details were fairly consistent over decades of being a raconteur, should not always be taken at face value. Did his mother really use a nickname instead of Samuel because she so greatly admired Buffalo Bill Cody? Many biographers cite that story, but one also notes "from his mother, young Billie learned to tell a tale. You begin with the plausible and move on from there. When the actual event pales, you change it."[2]

Samuel became Bill then Billie because "his mother had had a crush on Buffalo Bill [after] she had once seen his Wild West show in Madison Square Garden."[3] Plausible? Okay. Pertinent? Ambitious young man decides to follow his parent's show-biz dreams? Fact or fiction, it made a good story, and Wilder knew that it was story, story, and then more story that made writers successful. Biographers also agree on how young Billie got his first job as a teenage journalist for the Viennese *Die Stunde*: showing up with a letter of recommendation from a high-school teacher and finding the tabloid's editor and drama critic in flagrante delicto with a secretary.[4]

Wilder was now working for the same sort of tabloids that would elevate the Snyder-Gray case into a worldwide sensation. But Vienna was smaller and staider, a place where truly sensational stories—the occasional corpse in the Danube or a raid on a brothel or gambling club notwithstanding—was not a daily event. Certainly there were 2 million inhabitants, when "Red Vienna" became semi-autonomous under the First Austrian Republic. But that was less than the population of Manhattan alone. While there were

71

Young Billie Wilder, the Austrian journalist, in 1926.

immigrants, mostly poor and sometimes violent, in postwar Vienna it was hardly the melting pot of New York's diverse boroughs.

Wilder the young journalist has been variously described as lazy, resourceful, a boot licker, and an opportunist. As a stringer, Wilder did have to hustle to get paid. Unlike his fellow Galician, New-York crime photographer Arthur "Weegee" Fellig (whose photos influenced the gritty look of docunoir), Wilder used words instead of a camera to create tales of the Viennese "naked city." When news from the criminal underworld was slow (and that seemed to be often),[5] Wilder could turn to sports stories or human interest or whatever event had a kernel that could be expanded into what passed for news. Unlike Chandler with the pulps, Wilder did not exactly write by the word. But it wasn't the same sort of job as Cain had with the *Baltimore Sun*. While Fellig had to roam the New York streets every night, speed graphic

72

in hand, makeshift darkroom in the trunk of his car, Wilder and his fellow muckrakers in the Austrian capital would drink and play pool in a café adjacent to metropolitan police headquarters, waiting for leads to be handed to them. Alternately, Wilder had an uncanny ability to obtain high-profile interviews with the Viennese elite, playwrights, composers, novelists, even psychoanalysts (that is, Alfred Adler, but Wilder constantly repeated the story of how Sigmund Freud once told him to "Beat it"[6]). It was an interview with American bandleader and "king of jazz," Paul Whiteman, that, a couple of months shy of his twentieth birthday, got him a ticket out of "red Vienna."

Although Wilder was supposed to be gone just a few days—accompanying Whiteman to Berlin and perhaps Paris and reporting on his concerts there— once settled in the glamorous Weimar capital, why go back to the boondocks of Austria? This was a real metropolis with real tabloids, and literary journals, with émigrés from all over Europe, some famous, some desperate, and a criminal underworld actually worth talking about. But why worry about that when there were abundant opportunities for Wilder to specialize in covering the American music scene in Berlin.

Still a freelancer, Wilder also did interviews and hung out with the art crowd, the theater crowd, and the movie crowd, with the likes of Marlene Dietrich and scenarist Carl Mayer. He lived like any want-to-be boulevardier. Wilder's skill on a dance floor—and at roulette tables—had helped to get him girls in Vienna and likewise Berlin. An admirer of Rex Ingram's silent epic, *Four Horsemen of the Apocalypse* (1921), Wilder would emulate the tango moves of Valentino and gave lessons, presumably without spurs and gaucho pants. And, yes, biographers agree, like Valentino, Wilder moonlighted as a taxi dancer, workings for tips. Sometimes afternoons at *thés dansants* (did they remind him of the "tango teas" staged by Valentino's character in *Four Horsemen*?), or in white tie and tails into the early morning hours.

At some point Wilder realized two things. First, freelancing was barely paying the rent on a series of cheap rooms with nosy landladies who seriously cramped his style. Second, perhaps his anecdotal approach to journalism might be better suited, and earn more money, if he turned to fiction. At this point, Wilder told yet another tall tale: in the middle of the night the concierge's daughter, who sometimes turned tricks, asked for help concealing a paying customer from her boyfriend. As Wilder hid the guy, he recognized him as a small-time movie producer. Apparently Wilder had a spec script in his back pocket. The grateful gentlemen bought it on the spot for 500 marks ($125 American).[7]

Is this really how Wilder became a professional screenwriter? Does it matter? Wilder already had lots of connections from the local cabarets. The German executives for Universal Pictures had to put together a project to be directed by Carl Laemmle's nephew Ernest. They decided it would be Wilder's first produced script *Der Teufelsreporter* (*The Daredevil Reporter*, 1929, based on actual experience?).[8] After that the only thing that held back Austrian Wilder's screenwriting in German was the first time he lacked a work visa. So, he ghostwrote for cash and joined brothers Robert (director) and Curt (co-writer) Siodmak on their micro-budget project *Menschen am Sonntag* (*People on Sunday*, released 1929).[9] Shot on actual locations in and around Berlin, it was a breakout and got Robert Siodmak and Wilder jobs at Universum-Film Aktiengesellschaft (UFA, Germany's largest studio). For the next three years, Wilder alone or with different collaborators would frequently be pacing around studio head Erich Pommer's office, pitching ideas and getting assignments. Three years and a dozen produced scripts later (two of them remade in America by Fox and Universal), Wilder no longer worried about getting rent to his landladies.[10]

Then at the beginning of 1933, German President Paul von Hindenburg appointed Adolph Hitler chancellor. The exodus of movie talent to the United States had been in progress throughout the silent era. Not just directors, writers, producers, and actors but composers, directors of photography, and production designers as well. Wilder would not be the only émigré to work on *Double Indemnity*. With the rise of the Nazi party, the need of filmmakers, particular those with Jewish backgrounds, to get to America was no longer just about making more money but literal survival.

The day after the Reichstag burned Wilder took a night train to Paris. Still an Austrian without a work permit or even a visa, he holed up at refugee central, the Ansonia Hotel—a stone's throw from the Place de l'Étoile, where other lodgers included Peter Lorre, Franz Waxman, Friedrich Hollaender (who would soon be writing songs for Bing Crosby), and ultimately his friend from UFA Walter Reisch—and soon burned through the ten $100 US bills that he had smuggled out of Germany. Where life in Berlin had been decadent, even opulent, the sojourn in Paris was relatively dismal. Wilder had no vehicle to careen around the Arc de Triomphe and no prospects for quick cash other than ghostwriting again, translating his witty German prose into inelegant French.

Wilder did write a script with two other UFA writers ensconced at the Ansonia and got backing for it. *Mauvaise Graine* (*Bad Seed*, released in 1934) was a low-budget enterprise, full of cameras mounted on moving cars, that left Wilder enervated and dissatisfied.[11] Wilder had written several musicals in Germany and "in Paris, he had written a jazzy story entitled 'Pam Pam,' about a runaway girl who took refuge in a abandoned Broadway theater."[12] What do you do, when you're in such a situation? Why, recruit some shady collaborators and stage a show. Wilder sent this to producer Joe May, who had already made it to Los Angeles and was working just south of Gower Gulch.

It's not certain if, standing on the docks in Southampton and preparing to board the Cunard line's *RMS Aquitania* in January 1934, Wilder wore a tailored suit like Raymond Chandler; but he probably had a cane and certainly a fedora. Sikov claims that there was only $11 in his pocket,[13] or $29 less than Chandler. Of course, very unlike Chandler, he had a profession and a job: $150 per week guaranteed from Columbia Pictures, which had optioned his relatively silly idea for a musical.

Once Wilder got his visa issues sorted out, as he had in Vienna, Berlin, and even Paris, he started finding work. Of course, while Joe May had saved his bacon, he had charged him room rent of $75 per week, half his salary. Back in Hollywood, he got a couple of gigs at Fox (*Lottery Lover* released in late 1934; then director May and producer Pommer used him on *Music in the Air* [1935]). At some point, he did live at the Chateau Marmont; but as per Sikov "Wilder tells a different story every time. He moved there after returning from Mexicali, he moved there in 1935, he lived there with

Peter Lorre, Lorre's apartment was somewhere else and cost $5 a week, his room was in fact the ladies room, his room was *next* to the ladies room... Whatever it was, it was cheap."[14] Wilder met scripter Oliver H.P. Garrett at a Santa Monica party, and together they sold two projects to fledgling Pioneer Pictures. Wilder got $5,000.[15]

So Wilder left the Chateau Marmont... for Europe, for Paris then Vienna, where he tried to convince his mother to come to the United States.[16] She would not agree. When he got back to Hollywood in late 1935—again the particulars are muddled by Wilder's various versions of events—he landed a $250 per week job as a staff writer at Paramount Pictures.[17]

In the course of six months Wilder moved from assignment to assignment and sometimes, encountered a tall, well-dressed man who parted his wavy hair in the middle. Charles Brackett was a monied, patrician fellow from New York, who, before working at Paramount, had written plays and sometimes reviewed theater for *The New Yorker*. Once sitting next to this man at the Brown Derby bar, Marlene Dietrich had entered and Billy had pointedly denigrated the charms of his former Unter-den-Linden sidekick.[18] Wilder almost certainly knew that this man made a lot more money than him (at $1,000 per week, four times as much to be exact) and was near the top of the roster of Paramount writers. But that did not deter him from crude remarks and cracking wise. In mid-August, Wilder's familiarity with the work of Parisian playwright, Alfred Savoir (né Poznański)—in particular his hit 1921 play *La Huitième Femme de Barbe-Bleue (Bluebeard's Eighth Wife)*—brought him into a meeting about a screenplay version for star Greta Garbo and studio director Ernst Lubitsch. His new co-writer was none other than Charles Brackett.[19] This project for Lubitsch was the first of fourteen script collaborations between Wilder and Brackett interrupted only by *Double Indemnity*.[20]

"We had nothing in common writing," Wilder realized quite early on. "He would tell me many stories, and I told him many stories. It was not like Mr. Raymond Chandler. We did get along. We just never saw each other for dinner. We never did that."[21] On their first full day together Brackett wrote: "Worked with Billy Wilder, who paces constantly, has over extravagant ideas, but is stimulating. He has the blasé quality I have missed. He has humor—a kind of humor that sparks with mine."[22] Some time later, he added a lengthy appendix to his initial comments, from which it is clear Wilder did tell him many stories:

> *To examine him as he was then: 32 years old, a slim young fellow with a merry face, particularly the upper half of it, but from the brisk nose up it was the face of a naughty cupid. Born some place in Poland [" half-an-hour from Vienna," he used to say, "by telegraph."] he'd gone to Berlin, he'd been a dancer for hire at fashionable restaurants and he'd written an article about his experiences in that capacity. Because he was Jewish and had an acute instinct, he had slipped out of Germany as Hitler began to rise.[23]*

Brackett continues his brief bio by disparaging certain of Wilder's earlier work ("*Music in the Air* was a real abortion.") and adds yet another variation on the tales of the Chateau Marmont. By early September, Brackett was refining his assessment: "Billy is a hard, conscientious worker, without a very sensitive ear for dialogue, but a beautiful constructionist. He's extremely stubborn, which makes for trying work sessions. They're stimulating…but Billy can't stand a line he hasn't worked on…almost driven mad by his niggling passion for changing words."[24] Wilder had his own issues "For Christ's sake, what is this?" Wilder exploded when Lubitsch expressed regret for disquieting Brackett. "He apologizes to you! You and he will be making a baby together before the picture is through!"[25] By November, Wilder was making fun of Brackett's earlier work but attending a screening of *Champagne Waltz* (1937) with Brackett took the wind out of his sails.

Eventually work on *Bluebeard's Eighth Wife* ended without Wilder and Brackett ever coming to blows. In an afterword to a difficult day Brackett delineated his view on their key to success: "As I know ideas I suggest will be rejected with violence, I rarely put forth any," to which he added later, "This was before I learned the routine with this temperamental partner. The thing to do was to suggest an idea, have it torn apart and despised. In a few days it would be apt to turn up, slightly changed, as Wilder's idea. Once I got adjusted to that way of working, our lives were simpler."[26] Wilder's reflection was less analytical: "Whenever I worked with somebody *more* than once, that tells you. I worked with Brackett twenty years…it was all very, very peaceful. There was no jumping around on tables and couches."[27]

Wilder flanked by Charles Brackett, left, and director Mitchell Leisen, right, a shot that gives the lie (at least slightly) to Wilder's claim of being banned from the set by Leisen.

In December, Wilder's option was picked up by the studio. Having tweaked *The Big Broadcast of 1938* (work that was uncredited), the "team" was put on *Midnight* (1939) for producer Arthur Hornblow and director Mitchell Leisen, the man who, for all the wrong reasons, would lead Wilder back to the director's chair. "I became a director because so many of our scripts had been screwed up." Wilder's last iteration of this open secret was for Cameron Crowe: "Leisen was the worst one. Mitch Leisen!" because he had let an actor talk him into ruining a great scene with a cockroach.[28] Ultimately Wilder endured three pictures with Leisen, all of which were commercial successes. Sans cockroach, the screenplay for *Hold Back the Dawn* had been nominated for an Academy Award. As had been their second job for Lubitsch on loan-out to MGM: *Ninotchka* (1939), that could also be considered the pair's first *succès d'estime*.

When Wilder and Brackett were approached about a third loan-out (they had also been to Universal to tweak a Deanna Durbin screenplay), this time for Sam Goldwyn (*Ball of Fire*, 1941), "Billy agreed," according to Wilder biographer Maurice Zolotow, "provided he could be at director Howard Hawks' side during the filming. He was going to learn how a master directed films."[29] It was Hawks who, unlike Leisen on *Hold Back the Dawn*, and even without a clause in the loan-out, would likely have allowed Wilder to be discreetly on set. In fact, Hawks took credit for helping the blocked writers re-envision the arc of Wilder's original treatment. Back from a fishing trip with Hemingway, Hawks was told "'We don't know what it's about.' I said, 'It's Snow White and the Seven Dwarfs,' and Billy said, 'We'll be done in a couple of weeks!'"[30] As to the shooting, "I was there all the time, the whole picture," Wilder recalled to Crowe, but did not admit to considering Hawks a master. "I just listened how to say 'Action,' how to say, 'Cut,' how to say, 'Print number seven.'"[31] There has never been a question about Wilder's role model for directing. "For many years, I had that sign on my wall: HOW WOULD LUBITSCH DO IT? What kind of track would Lubitsch be on? How could he make this look natural? He was my influence as a director"[32]

It was over the course of the last Leisen picture and with the spring 1941 box-office success of *The Lady Eve*—the third feature of Preston

Stanwyck met Wilder while he shadowed director Howard Hawks on *Ball of Fire*. Wearing the outfit for the visit to Neff's apartment, Stanwyck confers with Wilder on the *Double Indemnity* set.

Sturges, "the first writer who became a director" at Paramount in Wilder's recollection—that Wilder firmly decided to press his case for becoming a director. Wilder returned to the writer's building with a new plan. Zolotow reports Brackett's leeriness at this prospect and paints a vivid picture of their secretary frequently cowering outside the door at the sound of screaming, hurled ashtrays, and capsized lamps (but no mention of jumping on couches or broken flutes).[33]

Wilder had learned enough of studio politics to know that despite their acquiescence the executives hoped for his failure. His suspicions were confirmed by reports from his "spy"—per Zolotow, long before he got those copies of *Liberty* magazine from him, Wilder had recruited Joe Sistrom for studio espionage work. So Wilder and Brackett (whose first diary entry about it was not until mid-fall 1941[34]) played the development of *The Major and the Minor* close to the vest. The entry was about a planned lunch with Ginger Rogers, who had beaten out both Davis and Hepburn at the Academy Award ceremony that past February and whose agent now also represented Billy Wilder.

80

"Hell, no," was Ginger Rogers' reply when Zolotow asked her if she had been pressured to give Wilder a leg up, "I didn't do it to help anybody. I did it because it was one hell of a good script and I knew that Charles Brackett and Wilder were the best writers in the picture business and they had written one hell of a part for me."[35] Whatever the full extent of her reasons, with Rogers aboard, there was no revoking the green light.

Wilder's oft-repeated story of pulling up next to Ray Milland at a red light and pitching him is probably true.

Not even Pearl Harbor could change the green light for Wilder's directorial debut (in America). Brackett was the producer (credited as an "associate") and at just over $925,000 ($175,000 of that for Rogers and presumably with the same overhead cushion that Paramount put on the similar *Double Indemnity* budget), there was enough time and money. It would be nothing like *Mauvaise Graine*.[36] The budget was more than adequate to the task. When Wilder confessed his nervousness to Lubitsch before the start of shooting, the unofficial mentor recruited a roster of eminent émigré directors (and Preston Sturges) to act as cheerleaders on day 1.[37] Fortunately for Wilder he had editor Doane Harrison (whose work on the three Leisen pictures he had admired) on the set every day to help with the shot selection and to counteract the pandemonium caused by the day one visitors.

The Major and the Minor grossed $2.5 million. With that result, Wilder knew he was good for at least two more bites of the directorial apple. With Brackett as producer, the team again got the cast and crew they wanted for the next picture, *Five Graves to Cairo*. Doane Harrison was again the cutter. Plus, Wilder had coaxed Sturges regular John F. Seitz on board as Director of Photography. Finally, on Lubitsch's recommendation thanks to his work on *To Be or Not To Be* (1942), Brackett and Wilder set long-time Alexander Korda composer Miklós Rózsa for the score.[38] The war movie was a tough shoot; but the full team had performed extraordinarily well. What would be next?

On May 11, 1943, in his fourth-floor office in the Paramount writer's building, Billy Wilder was pacing, swishing his Malacca cane, ready to scream in frustration. Brackett had left him high and dry...and at the worst time. Their story about fighting the Germans in North Africa, *Five Graves*

81

to Cairo, would be released before the end of the month; but Field Marshall Rommel had gone back to Germany weeks ago and everyone who picked up a newspaper knew that what was left of the Afrika Corps would surrender any day. Who would want to see his dated war movie? It would certainly be a flop.

His shoelace was untied. He moved the checked sweater vest that he had peeled off earlier because it was too hot off the arm of the chair across from him, put his foot up, and fixed the shoe. On the table between the two chairs were a stack of *Liberty* magazines. He straightened those, hung the vest on the hat rack by the door, and paced again. He needed to get this new project into gear, now, not later. It had to get made, and it had to be good, no, better than that, it had to be great.

5.

THE MOVIE: A FANCY PIECE OF HOMICIDE

As he came out of the writers building, the courtyard was hot, unexpectedly so for a spring day. And humid: moisture condensed on his Windsor eyeglasses. As he started to walk around to 4th Street and along the executive offices, he fumbled for a handkerchief. Not finding one, he wiped the lenses with his tie. What this perspiring, young, dark-haired man did not, could not, know was how much hotter it would get inside that building in the coming weeks... not just the temperature.

On the Rommel movie, he had never been out on location, all he did was look at numbers and keep the studio updated. Plus, Charlie Brackett had been a buffer with Wilder. Now it was just him, named producer on a million-dollar movie. Buddy DeSylva was making good on his promise after his credit on *Wake Island* got torpedoed by Paramount. Four nominations, four! Buddy knew. He could have gone to Fox with Bill LeBaron, Bill would never welch on a deal. But this project was better. What he did not, could not, know was that New York would again put the kibosh on his credit demand.

Just before he reached the Bronson Gate, he checked his watch. He noticed that one of his Stanford cuff links had almost worked itself loose again. He had to fix that, or it might be lost. He glanced north: no sign of a green 1932 Dodge in the visitor spaces by the wardrobe building. Where had this odd duck wandered off to? Billy was already getting annoyed, being petty. And it didn't help he'd beat him the last time they played bridge. He had to start throwing hands... but subtly.

He waited for the gate guard to write a pass for the young blonde driving a red Cadillac Series 62 convertible. Nice car. Nice blonde, whoever she was. How would his dad handle this? He had worked with difficult people. For God's sake, he'd managed production for DeMille on *King of Kings*. He could still remember being a teenaged extra on that silent epic at Iverson Ranch. That was where he realized this was the business he wanted to be in. His father had heard stories about Billy from director Allan Dwan, who called him "the fake-tourist-guide twerp from Berlin that tried to screw my wife." Could that be true? He would call his father, ask for advice, but that wasn't possible as he was in England, fighting fascism firsthand by producing patriotic pictures for RKO British.

He stood back as the Cadillac roared onto the lot. The guard told him his visitor had not parked where instructed, but kept going up to Stage 4 then turned right and disappeared. Head thrown back in exasperation, he pulled off his jacket and headed north. "That's the guy!" The guard was pointing at a middle-aged, sandy-haired man in a tweed jacket coming around the wardrobe building.

"Hello!" He waved as he called out, "Are you Mr. Chandler?" What he did not, could not, know was that the frumpy looking guy nodding yes and heading his way had his own bad temperament, that he could write a mean memorandum and hold grudges. No, this will all work out, Joe Sistrom told himself. What he did not, could not, know was that almost everything would.

This Dietrichson business. It's murder. And murders don't come any neater. As fancy a piece of homicide as anyone ever ran into. Smart, tricky, almost perfect, but—I think Papa has it all figured out, figured out and wrapped up in tissue paper with pink ribbons on it.

Insurance claims manager Barton Keyes in *Double Indemnity*

It was awkward. Chandler was standing in front of two movie men, young men, neither of them born in the last century, unlike him. He did give them a brief precis of his career arc, his dipsomania and reinvention of himself in

84

middle age. Wilder saved his ballroom dancing stories for later. But he did not have to feign enthusiasm for Chandler's prose. Joe had given him novels (several possibilities were mentioned), and he had read one in a single sitting. He kissed the tips of his fingers then opened them to indicate that he had savored the novel's flavor. Decades later Wilder still recalled:

> By God, a kind of lightning struck on every page. How often do you read a description of a character that says he had hair growing out of his ear long enough to catch a moth? Not many people write like that. And the dialogue was good, the dialogue was sharp.[1]

Did Chandler know *Double Indemnity,* Wilder asked as he cast an eye towards the stack of *Liberty* magazines that Sistrom had brought him just days ago. Chandler had read it, certainly, and quoted himself as regards the smell of billy goat in Cain's work. Now Wilder glanced hard at Sistrom with a look that asked, "Did you know this?" Joe shrugged, "No." Chandler also knew about Snyder-Gray. The origins of the story were news to Wilder. Sistrom remembered joking about the more salacious details as an adolescent. He had seen the picture of Ruth dying in the chair. If Wilder had seen it, he could not remember.

Then Chandler asked: "Why not get Jim Cain?" Under contract to another studio. And Wilder's regular collaborator, Charles Brackett, did not like the material. Chandler was candid. He could not afford to be picky. Give him a sample screenplay, a thousand dollars, and he would be back in a week with a draft. Now Sistrom shot Wilder a look that said, "Let's see how this goes." Chandler left with a copy of *Hold Back the Dawn* (presumably with cockroach scene).[2]

"If I was casting a man to play an accountant, I would cast Chandler."[3] There are various reports of what else Wilder may have said to Sistrom about Chandler's avuncular aspect (tweed coat with leather patches on the elbows, dress shirt with old-school tie) or low energy or why they were waiting a week for his draft. Were they already pinching pennies? In some versions, Wilder and Sistrom immediately pressed Chandler to accept a weekly deal. Per Maurice Zolotow, Chandler said "I must have a minimum of $150 per week." But why would Sistrom then say, "We propose to pay you $750 per week." This is not what an old-school producer would do, especially since there were still a lot of staff writers making much less than said amount per week at Paramount. Sure, that was the minimum they would have had to pay Cain, probably more. Chandler may have been undervaluing himself, but why not offer $250 or $300, save a few dollars to spend on gift baskets for the stars? Of course, Zolotow was the Wilder biographer who thought Chandler's "favorite refreshment" was Old Forrester and not Crown Royal.[4] In fact, if Wilder told this story to Zolotow, it was around the same time he told another interviewer, Ivan Moffat, about Chandler that "like so many former alcoholics, he was on the wagon."[5]

Chandler biographer Frank MacShane agrees regarding the $750 per week (for not 10 but 13–14 per Wilder to Moffat—weeks) and notes "a sum of amazing magnitude for a man who had been living for a decade on a few thousand dollars per year."[6] Chandler "must have felt as if he had hit the jackpot" notes most recent biographer Tom Williams.[7] Was that actually the deal? Chandler worked for considerably more than 10 or 13 or 14 weeks, which would have been a gross of $9,750 (or close to $175,000 today). The studio's final cost report is very specific. In an era of 6-day workweeks, Chandler actually received $350 per week for 161 days of work from May 12 through November 20, 1943. Then (as a bonus for a job well done?) he got a raise to $750 per week for the last four days of shooting. Total compensation was $9,891.66.[8]

Is it likelier that Chandler left to produce a draft and then returned in a week on the promise of a minimum of $1,000? Or did he agree to start work the next day (as the studio cost report records)? The paper trail is incomplete. Sistrom might have retroactively fixed May 12 as the first workday for Chandler. All that is clear is that, first, many years after his review of *Machinal*, Charles Brackett had no interest in working on another "racy" fiction based on Snyder-Gray. So when Brackett left the field two months earlier in mid-March, Sistrom had picked up the ball and was still running with it. By mid-May there were plenty of other items for Wilder and Sistrom to fret over besides fine points of Chandler's deal. The budget to make the movie would be up to $1 million; but the unresolved issue of Joe Breen had nothing to do with money.

It is clear in hindsight that the film noir movement to that point, and in specific ways culminating with *Double Indemnity*, had subtly but substantially chipped away at the power of the Hays office over the depiction of crime and criminals. Not that gangsters or gunsels fully reverted to the tommy-guns blasting out of car windows from the early 1930s, but consider Paramount's 1942 remake of *The Glass Key* adapted from Hammett's novel. "We'll have a couple of drinks," mob-muscle Jeff (William Bendix) whispers to Ed Beaumont (Alan Ladd), "and then I'll knock your teeth out." Of course, despite a brutal beating, in which his character is bounced "off the walls in a little room upstairs that's too small to fall down in," Ladd keeps his teeth.

Before he got his first screenwriting gig, Chandler himself had wondered why the studios diminished the violence but augmented the sexual innuendo when they adapted his work. In fact, by 1943 movies like *The Glass Key* (Paramount), *The Maltese Falcon* (Warners), *The Shanghai Gesture* (UA—1941), *Johnny Eager* (MGM—1941), and *I Wake Up Screaming* (Fox— 1941) had already moved the needle on sex and violence and had brought criminal protagonists and crooked cops and women of easy virtue back to the screen with a force almost matching the pre-Code (1934) films of gangsters and liberated women.

Many writers have suggested that it was the arrival of World War II that finally softened the position of Joe Breen and his team of blue noses, that in light of the atrocities being committed across the globe, the world would not end if a married couple had a double bed in the room where they slept. Except that double beds were still forbidden. Nothing changed about the motion picture code after Pearl Harbor except that more rules were added to prohibit content that was anti-war, pro-Axis etc. Not that the studios needed these simple new realities codified for them. Wilder may have scoffed at the recutting of *Mauvaise Graine* for release in the United States because it told viewers how to steal cars. On May 11, 1943, Wilder could well have asked Sistrom what had changed on that issue and all the others that might derail this project. Had it all begun less than two months before?

87

What day exactly had Joe Sistrom brought in the copies of *Liberty* magazine featuring Cain's scandalous *Double Indemnity*, when had Wilder read them in a single sitting and decided, "yes, this what I want to do"? That's the day he must have mentioned it to Brackett. Was that March 15? It was the day they announced the new "meat rationing." After Chandler left with nothing resolved, did Wilder ask himself, "What had Charlie said?" Sure, Cain was coarse; but Charlie was no prude. He certainly did not bring up billy goats. But Charlie talked to Buddy, who put the kibosh on it one day then said it was okay the next. March 15. Now Wilder remembered what happened on that date: the goddamned letter from Joe Breen.[9]

Exactly what Brackett said to Wilder on March 16 will never be known. Did he tell Wilder "it was disgusting. He would not write it,"[10] or that "it was such a distasteful book" that Wilder would have to make it without him.[11] Brackett recalls that on March 16, "Billy was having a touch of claustrophobia at being tied down to working with me, so I told him to go ahead with Joe [Sistrom...then]. Buddy De Sylva nixed it, saying it was none of Joe's business to suggest such a thing."[12] The likelier cause of the Tuesday "nixing" would be receipt and discussion of Joseph Breen's letter, which was dated March 15, by the Paramount executives. But by Thursday, to Brackett's chagrin, the project was back on:

> *Buddy telephoned me to say that Joe was to do* Double Indemnity *with Billy. I had thought I'd be depressed by the news but as the day wore on I felt vastly relieved by it. Gravely doubt that I can ever bring myself to work with Billy again. At the moment the idea of doing so takes all the joy out of life.*[13]

Had Brackett expressed his disgust too vociferously? Wilder did not mention that to Ivan Moffat, just that "Charles Brackett was off on some other thing, so it just worked out that I was free."[14] In his thoughtful monograph on *Double Indemnity,* Richard Schickel throws out more alternate dates and numbers by having Chandler say, "Gentlemen, I have no agent but I am not cheap, I'll tell you right now that this screenplay is going to cost you $750, and you can have it a week from Friday."[15] After the inconclusive first meeting with Chandler, could Wilder have been thinking that he should have cajoled Brackett into coming aboard? Too late now. He hadn't seen him, except for icy looks in the corridor, since Brackett pitched that broad who was too old.[16]

Chandler did return the following Monday or Tuesday with around 80 (or 85 or 65) pages of screenplay. Again stories differ about the particulars. Did Wilder leaf through it on the spot, then throw it at his prospective co-writer's head, while shouting, "This is shit, Mr. Chandler!" As usual, Zolotow's version is, as Sikov calls it, "saltier."[17] Apparently none of these Chandler script pages was scorched by lightning, but Wilder's comments to Moffat were certainly more sedate:

> It was eighty pages of technical drivel. And we said, "All right, relax, Mr. Chandler, you will be working with Mr. Wilder." When he repeated [what] he wanted, we said "None of that thousand dollar shit. You are going to get $750." And he said, "750, I will not work for 750." We said, "No, relax, 750 a week." And he said, "Oh, really, then it only goes 2 or 3 weeks?" And we said, "No, fourteen weeks. You don't know how scripts are written."[18]

It's unlikely that Chandler relaxed again before November 26, 1943—the completion of shooting the movie and his last day on the project—if then. At least by that date he certainly did know how scripts were written or, as he put it to his British publisher Hamish Hamilton, "to work with Billy Wilder on *Double Indemnity* was an agonizing experience and has probably shortened my life, but I learned from it about as much about screenwriting as I am capable of learning, which is not very much. I was under contract to Paramount and did several pictures for them."[19]

At some point, Harold Norling Swanson, aka H.N. Swanson or "Swanie" to clients and friends—the same agent who had sent over the typescript of the reprint of Cain's novel in *Three of A Kind*—came to represent Chandler. How that happened is not completely clear. Some chroniclers say that Sistrom (or someone at the studio) contacted him to get a line on where

Chandler might be found. Even likelier would be someone calling him to check on Cain's availability.

The consensus, however, is that whether or not it was follow-up or initial contact, in a moment of extraordinary producorial *largesse*, when Chandler said he had no agent for screenplays (not the purview of Sydney Sanders), Joe Sistrom hooked the mystery writer up with Swanie. "Chandler doesn't know a thing about screenplay writing but it doesn't matter," he told Swanson on the telephone. "He knows the kind of people Cain wrote about. He's eager to try his hand at the material and would take the two or three hundred a week the studio would probably offer him. Will you be his agent and get him a proper deal here?"[20]

Swanson was one of the best-known reps of literary Hollywood, whose clients besides Cain included sometime screenwriters William Faulkner and F. Scott Fitzgerald and high-earning, hard-boilers such as Cornell Woolrich, Frank Gruber, and Steve Fisher (who would replace Chandler after he gave up on adapting *Lady in the Lake* at MGM—1947). Given Chandler's residual annoyance at the measly fees Sanders had gotten from RKO and Fox, he made Swanson his only agent in 1946, after Warner Bros. had made *The Big Sleep*.[21] Initially though, it would appear that, if Swanson did arrange formal terms of employment, all he got was $50 more per week than the top number Sistrom mentioned.

Screenplay

After being hurled at Chandler's head, where did those 80 pages that he brought in the next week (probably on the 18th of May) end up? In the office wastebasket? There is no mention of his being given a copy of the novel earlier; but, unless he, too, had a set of *Liberty* magazines in the small, living-room bookshelves at 6520 Drexel Avenue (or a copy from Knopf, unlikely given his comments regarding Cain), where else would he get the source work? According to MacShane "Wilder knew that Chandler was unfamiliar with film writing, so when they met for their first conference, he suggested that each of them take the text of *Double Indemnity* home over the weekend. On Monday each would come back with a sample treatment, over which they would work together." Rather than work initially in Wilder's space, MacShane further notes that "Chandler was nervous and ill at ease...in the Writers Building at Paramount, known as the Campus because of its cloistered courtyard (to others the Tower of Babel as it housed so many foreign writers exiled from Europe) each room had bare walls, plain office chairs, desk, and a single telephone. Chandler was assigned to one, where he began to work."[22]

The earliest scripted scenes that exist for *Double Indemnity* bear only Chandler's name and are dated May 24, 1943 (a Wednesday).[23] Was this Chandler's first revision, working alone in that small office and dutifully removing all the "technical drivel"? Had he also familiarized himself with the details of the Breen letter, which questioned whether the content of *Double Indemnity* would meet with the Hays code standards? It was clear that neither Sistrom nor Wilder yet had a firm idea of how to work around that, other than to keep the truth from Breen. Was Chandler expected to solve this problem? "As for the dialogue," MacShane notes, "Chandler and Wilder first wanted to use as much of the original as possible, but they became aware that something was peculiar...when they got some actors to do a scene right out of the book, they discovered that it sounded, as Chandler put it, like 'a bad high school play. The dialogue oversaid everything and when spoken sounded quite colorless and tame.'"[24]

"They"? While it is unlikely that Chandler or even Wilder (who was not producing his own projects) knew how much Paramount was paying Cain for the rights, it made perfect sense to use as much Cain as possible, a process that must have been helpful for Wilder—as a charter member of the Tower of Babel—when he adapted the Savoir play (*La Huitième Femme de Barbe-Bleue*) in his first joint work with Brackett.[25] At some point early on, it was clearly Chandler who made his case against the novel's dialogue. "They therefore had to write new dialogue that would stand up to dramatic presentation," MacShane concludes. "Wilder has acknowledged that Chandler deserves most of the credit for this work."[26]

91

The first of seven yellow pages dated May 24—less than a week after he ducked to miss being hit by what Wilder threw, and barely 10 work days after Chandler was officially hired—reads with underlined all caps: "<u>D.I.</u>" and "<u>TEST SCENE</u>." Many details of it are telling (and contain no jargon), starting with: "The scene is the living room of the Nordlinger [sic] house. The room is empty. The front door bell rings. Phyllis Nordlinger enters and crosses the room to the door. She is everything you want, dressed casually in slacks or house pajamas or something on that order. She opens the door to a youngish man who carries a briefcase."

Chandler's test scene then starts the dialogue between PHYLLIS and the MAN who is quickly revealed to be HUFF. It covers the events of Cain's first two chapters, that became separate scenes in the movie. *She* has asked him to come by; and they sit. "He is very correct in every manner except for his eyes, which are bold." The initial banter is more Chandler-esque but nothing striking. These are two ostensibly ordinary people, so HUFF: "Lovely place you have here." PHYLLIS: "It is nice, isn't it?" HUFF: "And lovely people in it." PHYLLIS: "You think so." A parenthetical for her adds "(Smiles, says nothing)" Ho-hum.

Cain makes no secret of what's coming in the novel. Huff talks of "Glendale...three new truck drivers...company bond...renewal over in Hollywoodland"—but it only takes 38 words on page 1 to get to "House of Death, that you've been reading about in the papers." How might Cain have explained this explicit opening? Would he have said, okay, it's not in the Snyder-family home in Queens; but think about it, sir or madam, perusing this story of mine in *Liberty* magazine. What's going to happen? Didn't the cover art tip you off? Don't you realize this story is not about what's going to happen but how it happens. That is going to take a while. Oh, yeah, if you're a writer's secretary at some studio, Fox or Paramount, maybe, you're going to be in that bathroom for a while.

Whatever Cain intended and novice that he may have been, Chandler eliminates Huff's moment at the front door with an unnamed "servant" and has "Mrs. Nordlinder" herself answer the door. (He meant "Nordlinger," or rather "Nirdlinger"; and we mean attention to detail and spelling are important, too, Mr. Chandler.) Chandler's possible explanation: so, I had Huff give what's-her-name a little leer, nothing like a Tex Avery cartoon. How is this excrement, Mr. Wilder? It's a movie, not a novel, so we wait until page 2 to get to the accident insurance and then a quick switch. We don't need more chitchat about the automobile club (boring), just one last line to subtly hint (make that to hint subtly, an old-school boy like Chandler would never split an infinitive) at her darker motives: "My life's a specialty in boredom, if anyone should ask you." They should call this an example of the Bovary complex, or is that too literary? Anyway, why did you circle that, Mr. Wilder (okay, I'll call you "Billy")? And I don't agree with what you wrote on page three.

Was it Wilder who circled various lines in the test scene? The handwritten note is certainly his.[27] Apparently there was no objection on the director's part to Chandler shamelessly cribbing from *Now, Voyager* by having Huff light two cigarettes like Paul Henreid did for Bette Davis. Probably Wilder was thinking: so, you've seen some movies, Ray, but this is not how a good setup works. You hold back a little longer. That stuff top of page three about how he doesn't "eat, drink, sleep and dream" insurance, yeah, it's good, it works. He complains a little about the grind, but then he's ready: what can I sell you? But right away you have her say, "I'm not in the least, interested in automobile insurance, Mr. Huff. Not in the least." What? That is definitely a "No!" I should have used two exclamation points. Three! What did I write at this point? "Huff goes into details. Phyllis no attraction and into accident insurance." Balance, always. Remember, Ray, we will fix all this together, we have the time it will take, that 7-to-11-page-per-day-minimum output that the studio expects is bullshit. It does not apply to us.

Test scene page three continues with talk of the dangers of the oil field, some of the details of which made it into the movie. Chandler has Huff "(smiling)" at her breathless example of a casing line that "whipped through the air and barely missed his head." In the movie, of course, this is what put the Foreman in the hospital and has wifey "worried sick." HUFF: "It might have taken his head clean off at the neck." PHYLLIS: "That amuses you, Mr. Huff." Wilder only circled one more line in the test scene at the top of page six, but it was a doozy. Phyllis (very slowly and deeply) declaims: "I'm so completely unhappy. My life is dust and ashes in my mouth, every day of it. A husband like an ice-filmed stone. A void, a terrible emptiness." While laying this on heavily, in a memo 10 days later, Chandler pondered whether details from the novel—"Huff wants to score off Keyes and lets Keyes know that he has scored off him" or "Wants to clear Sacchetti for Lola's sake"—would play in the film.

What Chandler's first pass initially removes from the movie is the sense of fate, an unseen hand that brings all the elements into alignment, by having this would-be black widow call in the insurance guy (a la Ruth Snyder). "I forget their names at the moment, the mutual friends, I mean," says Mrs. Nirdlinger on page 1, "but that's why I asked for you personally. To come out here I mean." Is Chandler implying that some gal pal told her Huff would handle her need for secret insurance? That's where Wilder should have first written, "No!" The unforeseen is what underlies and sustains the suspense in the story and the movie. Sure, most readers and viewers knew what was coming. Because of that they needed moments of particular tension throughout, moments like Huff/Neff stepping out on the rear of the observation car and discovering somebody's there. The sense of fate, not knowing the moment exactly when something is coming, underlies the entire narration and gets underscored in instances, like not realizing murder could smell like honeysuckle. It is explicit at times in the novel and never more so than when in the movie Neff muses about how "maybe those fates they say watch over you had gotten together and broken his leg to give me a way out." Moments later, the phone rings and it's on again.

Without question, Chandler's first pass also puts it all out there a bit too quickly and clearly. But a lot of the lines on page 6 of the May 24 test scene are actually in the movie. On page 5, even if it's fully subconscious, Chandler clearly gives Phyllis another moment to channel Mrs. Snyder's portrait of husband Albert. PHYLLIS: "He'd kill me if he even knew I'd talked to you about it." HUFF: "Well, I'll be darned." PHYLLIS: (Not quite brokenly but with emotion) "Oh, he's such a miserable man he makes everybody about him miserable. Sometimes I think— I think—" Ignoring that some of Huff's lines are a bit feeble (none more so than "I'll be darned"), in this early draft, once he gets Mrs. Nordlinger's drift, hears her Bovary-esque lament, the light goes on for Huff.

Cain has Huff pointedly react to the words "accident insurance" on his novella's page five. The salesman gets back "in the car bawling myself out for being a fool just because a woman had given me one sidelong look"[28] In their first movie scene, Mrs. Dietrichson does say, "Accident insurance" but Neff is too focused on her anklet to react with anything other than a smile. In Chandler's test combination of scenes, Huff/Neff's immediate attraction is similarly indicated. It is a full 20 minutes into *Double Indemnity* the movie before the look on Fred MacMurray's face matched what Chandler suggested on his page six.

In the actual movie, all the almost identical lines are in Neff's second visit. They are rearranged slightly in this side-by-side to match where they appear in the test scene:

Billy Wilder and Raymond Chandler hard at work in a fourth floor office of the Campus. Notice Wilder's bemused expression and his fedora perched nearby.

May 24 Test Scene – Walter Huff meets Phyllis Nerdlinger	Movie – Walter Neff returns to Phyllis Dietrichson's living room
P: A casing line broke and the loose end whipped through the air and barely missed his head…	P: The other day a casing line snapped and caught the fore-man…[Not in the September 23, 1943, draft screenplay]
P: So I was wondering if it would be at all possible to write that insurance for him…without his knowing it.	P: Could I get an accident policy for him without bothering him at all?
H: Maybe a crown block would fall on him…Sometimes they have to have a little help before they fall. They just can't make it on their own.	N: Then if some dark wet night that crown block did fall on him… Only sometimes it can't quite make it on its own, it has to have a little help.
H: You want to knock him off, don't you baby.	N: Look, baby, you can't get away with it. You want to knock him off, don't you?
P: That's horrible.	P: That's a horrible thing to say.
H: And you'd need help, wouldn't you, baby. (laughs brutally) And I look like that kind of sucker to you, do I? That's the way I look to you, is it? I look like a guy who would walk into a good looking dame's front door and say, "How do you do, I sell accident insurance on husbands, lady, how about some—without his knowing it, of course, and once we're all set with it—for a small extra charge, I help you collect on that insurance.	N: Who'd you think I was anyway. A guy that walks into a good look-ing dame's front parlor and says, "Good afternoon, I sell accident insurance on husbands. You got one that's been around too long. Somebody you'd like to turn into a little hard cash. Just give me a smile and I'll help you collect." Boy, what a dope you must think I am. [September 23 script: "I must look like to you."]

P: I think you're ghastly.

H: I think you're swell—as long as I'm not your husband.

P: Get the hell out of here.

H: You bet I'll get the hell out of here. I don't do things the dumb way. You bet I'll get the hell out of here!

P: I think you're rotten.

N: I think you're swell. So long as I'm not your husband.

P: Get out of here.

N: You bet I'll get out of here, baby. I'll get out of here but quick.

What is remarkable about the test scene is that in a very short time, Chandler alone or with some slight Wilder input, came up with a considerable amount of dialogue that was ultimately spoken by the actors. Besides introducing Huff/Neff's frequent use of "baby" (of which there are more than a score of iterations in the finished film), the tone of both the lead characters is already quite different from Cain. When it was finalized then staged, the angles, shot selection, and performance accomplished what Wilder clearly wanted from his first note on the May 24 draft.

The consensus of biographers is that the first six weeks of joint effort was spent on story, and that little if any of Cain's suggestions—such as Mr. Nirdlinger/Dietrichson's convenient and Zola-esque self-immolation—were considered. Brackett's diary for June 11 notes that "Billy began actual writing on his *Double Indemnity*, though as yet they have no actor to play the male lead."[29] There is no other date that contradicts this.

On June 1 Chandler made "notes on climaxes and scenes," a sort of "beat-sheet" that indicated a progression through all the sequences or "acts" (which was not yet an industry-standard term for parts of screenplays): "(1) moment of decision, (2) murder, (3) Keyes says "murder," (4) decision to kill Phyllis, and (5) discovery she feels that way, too." Chandler questioned the narrative complexities of Cain, such as Huff getting a new check from his intended victim proffering a partial cash refund under the smokescreen of evading company rules and auditors.[30] Two pages of prose in the novel that is mostly about Huff's smugly describing ingenuity and his anticipation that Nirdlinger would be delighted at being handed a double sawbuck.

Perhaps by this time, Chandler and/or Wilder had already heard producer Sistrom's admonition (as cited by Richard Schickel) that "all characters in B pictures are too smart"[31]; and this was no B-budget movie with B-budget killers chasing some measly payday. Were the writers aware that Cain had reduced the $45,000/90,000 payout for Albert Snyder's misadventure to $25,000/50,000? Of course, Cain likely realized that, thanks to the depression, when he was writing the original, the actual numbers in the Snyder policy might seem too large. In fact, it was not until 1943 that $90,000 had returned almost exactly to its 1927 real value.[32] So the screenwriters kicked it up to "$50,000 capital sum" that would double to $100,000, or just slightly more than the $97,000 total proceeds on Mr. Snyder, over which Prudential had successfully demurred.[33]

The next day, there is a draft of four scenes from Sequence A that includes a much less overt first meeting between Huff and Phyllis (with Nettie the maid), the signing of the policies, and Neff's apartment. By the June 14th revised test scene, Cain's first-person prose is transformed into voice-over narration with observations such as Keyes being a "sourfaced, vinegar-mouthed sucker." And the first iteration of what Neff did not get (money or girl) is already there, as is the chilling term "morgue job." The next day (June 15) Wilder's name appears at the top of a more finished draft with the Gorlopis confrontation in Keyes' office very close to the final version.

Three weeks later, on August 6, Brackett confirms that the collaborators have finished the first act. "Billy and [Raymond] Chandler called me into consultation this morning. They are in Second Act trouble and I was of very little use."[34] The final draft screenplay has five sequences ("A" through "E") and runs 137 pages. The "first act" could be as little as the 40 pages of Sequence A or a third of the script—44 pages—or some other point, but the pace is slow. Even with some paid time off for Independence Day, 30 to 40 work days must have been spent on Act One. Brackett consults again on August 11: "I helped Billy and Ray Chandler a little (Billy is in a phase of turning to me for help, having no reliance on Ray, etc.).[35]

Whenever it began in full earnest, much has been written about the strained process that became more intense from the first day that Chandler took a seat in Wilder's spacious office. Some biographers suggest that Chandler's memo to Sistrom came just four or five weeks in. Wilder told Moffat "one day after about the first three weeks, I remember, Mr. Chandler did not show up." Brackett's chronology is more precise, and it belies that statement. Unfortunately, neither Wilder nor Chandler kept a contemporaneous log of their squabbling. But as Brackett's diary reveals, there was plenty of that in his work with Wilder. It was the success of what they did hammer out together, plus the fact that both Wilder and Chandler achieved a greater level of fame than Brackett, that attracted the attention of future chroniclers. There was even an off-Broadway comedy about it titled *Billy and Ray*. The problem with the show was that, like the actual events must have been, neither critics nor theatergoers found that short-lived reenactment very funny.[36] This is what Brackett wrote on September 14:

Raymond Chandler had failed to appear. When Billy spoke to him he said he was talking to his agent about something Billy would learn in due course. Joe appeared, talking with Chandler over the phone, went to see him, came back and reported that Chandler bitterly resented Billy's treatment of him but that Joe had managed to straighten it out. Billy was completely mystified and when I pointed out that his manners were at times "brusque," denied it. Joe and I yelled with laughter at that and in due time Chandler appeared.[37]

Given how many weeks had passed and how close September 14 was to the start of shooting, there are two possibilities as to what truly happened. Either (a) Chandler went AWOL a second time or (b) Brackett has the date all wrong. The description is a pretty good match for other versions. So perhaps Wilder first told Brackett about the spat on that September date.

Did the stress actually shorten Chandler's life? He died at age 70. Despite being quirky and irascible Wilder got dealt an additional 25 years and made it to 95. What is certain is that during and after working with Chandler, Wilder put out a lot more ink about it. His kindest comments were made to Moffat (for inclusion in a book about Chandler, after all): "He would kind of growl. He was a very difficult man...bad tempered, kind of acid, sour, grouchy—I don't know. There was something about him." But Wilder muses, "I much preferred that to somebody who is light of foot, graceful, full of jokes, but totally incompetent, you know. Give me a collaborator like Chandler any day."[38] Two decades later the comments to Crowe were less charitable: "The anger you know...you forget about it. I cannot forgive Hitler but I certainly can forgive Mr. Leisen and Mr. Chandler. But then...there was a lot of Hitler in Chandler...in the way he talked behind my back."[39]

The complaints in Chandler's memo to Joe Sistrom may have seemed petty to Wilder. Chandler filled the office with pipe smoke, so how was "For Christ's sake, Ray, open a window" out of line. Okay, he did not always say, "Please." Yes he took frequent bathroom breaks (who wouldn't to get away from Chandler for a couple of minutes?). He talked to girls on the phone, but Chandler timed him? "One of them took 15 minutes...and he was just outraged. He could not take it, because he was impotent, I guess. Yeah, I had the stick, [the Malacca cane] and I had three martinis before lunch."[40] Brackett did not like the cane either, but not even Chandler complained of Wilder's liquor before lunch. During and after was another matter. In the end Sistrom apologized for Wilder, then, per Wilder "I apologized. I will never talk. I will never drink in your presence, and so on. And we finished the script."[41]

What did happen in September, likely as the first revised version was being typed was (per Brackett) "Billy and Ray in an ecstasy of torture at composing a foreword to satisfy the Hays Office about *Double Indemnity*."[42] Obviously tortured and somewhat imprecise presentations that were created by the studio, the subterfuge with Breen, succeeded in getting the screenplay cleared. That event was perilously close to the start of shooting for Paramount Pictures "PROD. #PF-134," the date of which is indisputable: The final, white shooting script is dated September 25, 1943 (a Saturday). Day One of principal photography was Monday, September 27, 1943.

Remarkably Brackett's last note about the screenwriting in his diary is for November 1 (a Monday), on what was the beginning of Week 6 and the 30th day of shooting. It reads:

> *Spent the morning with Willie Wilder and Joe Sistrom and Ray Chandler.... Billy asked me to read a scene he and Ray Chandler had written. I found it heavy and false and said so to Chandler and agreed to come back for discussion of it tonight.... After dinner went back to the studio and discussed the double murder scene with Billy, Ray and Joe. They overruled me on most points but will change it a little, I hope.[43]*

The "double murder-scene," that is when Neff and Phyllis shoot each other in the Dietrichson living room, was scheduled for Thursday (and was Stanwyck's last day of work). Since "Willie," at least, had to be on the set at some time that day, it must have been a long day for the director.

What, if any, last-minute changes were made? Almost none. As per the existing screenplay Phyllis comes down the stairs, leaves the door ajar and extinguishes the lights. In the living room, two lamps, one by the goldfish bowl and another by the desk, are extinguished. The action line calls for a glint of something metallic, but it is clearly a chrome revolver. Not a silhouette but a clear shadow on the wall. The sound of a car door is heard as she lights a cigarette. Small changes certainly not recommended by Brackett.

As to the dialogue, as usual in performance MacMurray changed a word or two and added more "baby's" at the beginning on script pages 104 and 105 while Stanwyck was almost exactly per script. Perhaps understanding the menace of the moment, she dropped the first two "Walter's" on page 106. The third, to get him to turn around before she shoots, is gone, too, either not shot or cut in post. She, or writers for absolute clarity, adds "When I couldn't fire that second shot" to her moment of realization on page 107. Again, unlikely a Brackett idea. His input having been ignored, his note

101

when invited to view the scene that Sunday (November 8) is predictable: "Saw the rushes on *Double Indemnity* when Joe saw them and found them a little monotonous in their single note of brutality."[44]

The Hays Office

Even after they agreed to the terms of "The Code to Govern the Making of Motion Pictures" in 1930, for members of the Motion Picture Producers and Distributors of America (MPPDA, starting 1945 just MPAA for Motion Picture Association of America) compliance remained voluntary. As is widely known, there were both pre-Code *and* pre-Code-Enforcement movies released from 1922 through 1934. The issue in the silent era was twofold. Besides the Arbuckle case—the unofficial Hollywood representative in the pre-Snyder-Gray sweepstakes for crime of the century—there were other screenland scandals: the still unsolved murder of William Desmond Taylor, director for Paramount pre-cursor Famous Players-Lasky; the death of FP-L star Wallace Reid from opioid addiction; and the mysterious demise of producer Thomas Ince on William Randolph Hearst's yacht. Was it a burst appendix or a misdirected bullet meant for Charlie Chaplin, purported paramour of Hearst mistress Marion Davies?

None of these and lesser scandals actually hurt ticket sales, especially in the cities. However, the resolve of local censors in the American hinterlands to rein in wayward Hollywood was reinforced. There was a very real economic impact when cities, counties, or even states adopted their own rules and prohibited screenings in their jurisdictions. In the silent era, making cleaned-up versions for either pockets of prudish America or overseas was easily done at minimal expense. Re-editing sound movies became a little more cumbersome and costly.

When Joe Breen got hired by the Production Code Administration and serious enforcement began, association members could still shoot whatever movie they wanted. But it was the Hays Office that administered the Code Seal. Like most of the major studios Paramount had its own chain of theaters; and without the seal replicated somewhere on every print, none of

Hollywood's Morality Czar Joseph Breen looking quite self-satisfied about the job he was doing overseeing content for the PCA.

those houses could screen a movie. Nor could any of the D's in the MPPDA distribute the film. Throughout the code era (and even early in the era of the ratings system) independent, low-budget producers, purveyors of product like *Reefer Madness* (1936) or *Escort Girl* (aka *Scarlet Virgin*, 1941) trumpeted their refusal to conform, restricted their releases to "specialty" theaters, and still made a few dollars. That was never an option for Paramount or its peers.

Most of Breen's March 15, 1943, letter to Luigi Luraschi, the head of the "Domestic and Foreign Censorship Department" at Paramount, was retyped word-for-word from what was sent to Louis Mayer in 1935 (everything found in end note 13 for Chapter Two). In other words, "Go ahead and make this into a movie, Louis or Luigi, just don't expect us to give you a Seal of Approval on it." Hence the power of the Hays Office to control exactly what got shot. The difference this time was that Wilder (and Sistrom) convinced Buddy DeSylva that they could deliver a moneymaker that would push the envelope but ultimately get approved. Was the studio deterred by the March 15 letter?

On the same day that Chandler's test scene was completed, a March 24 trade release announced the movie to be produced by Sistrom and directed by Wilder from a screenplay he would write with...Cain.[45] This info likely came from Wilder/Sistrom (see details in Casting below) after Chandler was hired and was accepted by administrators at Paramount who were not yet paying close attention to this project. As the script developed the clearance folks at Paramount were concerned with legal matters not code compliance. There was an insurance agent in the Midwest somewhere named Huff. So Walter Neff was born. This all became so tedious for Wilder that in early August, after changing Nino Sachetti to Zachette, he took the time to write a pointedly mocking (and ethnically insulting) interoffice communication to Luraschi, in which he proposed all last names be changed to those of sundry Paramount executives and concluded, "You are driving us mad, but really, Viva Il Duce!"[46]

The actual preface for the Hays Office born of an ecstasy of torture per Brackett is not in the archive at the Academy Library. Brackett purportedly, like Cain, had early on written out some suggestions about how to mollify Breen. Nothing in his diaries details that. Richard Schickel suggests that the most that came down from the offices of Luraschi or Breen were "nitpicking: Be sure Phyllis' towel fully covers her...[not] too many details about the disposition of the murdered corpse. Eliminate a line in which Walter tells Phyllis not to handle the insurance policy of her husband unless she was wearing gloves."[47] If gloves were ever mentioned they are gone from the moment when Neff drops the policy in her purse at the market; and the line in the final script is still pointed but sufficiently vague: "You never touched it or saw it, understand?" Bristling at the 1940s mansplaining (just as Cain's character did), the reply from Phyllis is equally pointed: "I'm not a fool."

The week before principal photography began, there was a table read at Paramount with the cast. Were Wilder and Chandler alarmed by the rumor that Joe Breen himself might attend the final draft reading on Thursday the 23rd of September? Was that true? Did Sistrom and Bill Dozier, head of the story department, do a hasty re-edit of the screenplay to be read for Breen? On September 21, Luraschi sent a memo to Breen, but all that was attached were "Sequences 'A' through 'C' of Yellow Script and Outline of Balance of Sequence 'D'." At this point, of course, six days before start of production, the screenplay was complete; but apparently studio executives opted not to send it all to the Code office.

Wilder on the upper landing of the interior of Cain's "House of Death" uses his infamous Malacca cane to direct Stanwyck, or perhaps merely remind her that the towel must never rise about the knees.

On the 24th Breen replied with six specific requests, including the finger-print reference, the knee-length towel, and less than "flimsy house pajamas." On "Page 47: Please omit the underlined words in the line, 'to park your south end'"; regarding the corpse dump, "we strongly urge that you fade out after they take the body from the car"; and lastly "Page 74: censor boards will probably delete the references to specific poisons in Keyes' speech. We sug-gest you omit this particular sequence entirely." In the September 25 draft (which seems 12 to 15 pages longer than what ever Breen saw), the finger-prints are gone, it's "park your pants" [page 59], the poisons are listed by type with proper names [page 91]. However, while the screenplay indicates that inside a rug "the corpse is not seen," it still ends up "lying beside the tracks, face down." [page 76]. In the movie itself, when Neff hauls the body out of the driver-side suicide door of the La Salle sedan, the arm of Dietrichson's photo double is visible. The shot of the dragging is tight on Neff; but since actor Tom Powers had already finished in picture, Dietrichson's face could not be seen. Embodied by the photo double, that is dead Dietrichson on the tracks.

On the second day of shooting (the 28th), Breen got revisions and back came (on the 30th, the company's fourth day in the House set on Stage 8) a thumb's up: "We have read the incomplete white script dated September 25, 1943 and are happy to report that this material as far as it goes, seems to meet the requirements of the production code."[48] With piecemeal scripts still going back and forth, before Breen's partial approval, on Monday September 27, 1943, on Stage 8 Nettie (not Belle, as in the novella, where Nettie was Huff's secretary), performed by 45-year-old Betty Farrington, reluctantly ad-mitted Walter Neff (of the Pacific All Risk, not Huff of the General Fidelity of California, and certainly not Ashfield of the Prudential), personified by the just-turned-35-year-old actor and real-estate investor Fred MacMurray, to the home of the Dietrichsons (not the Nirdlingers and not the "House of Death," merely of the future planning thereof). As she escorted him into the living room, Nettie added the somber note (spoken by one who appeared to know from experience) that "they keep the liquor locked up." A concept that Breen must have certainly not always approved.

106

Despite what Breen may have preferred, Dietrichson's body is left lying face down on the tracks.

Actors

Wilder told Ivan Moffat that "*Double Indemnity* was extraordinarily diffi-cult to cast because, in those days, for a big star to play a murderer or a murderess—though Barbara Stanwyck instantly knew that it was a great, and she volunteered—was nearly impossible."[49] Stanwyck was certainly a big star, the highest paid woman in any field of endeavor in 1943 America. Did she actually volunteer? Noting that he would be writing with Cain, Wilder

107

sent "the script" (a copy of the novella with notes?) to her agents, Zeppo Marx and Allan Miller, on March 24. Why no mention of Chandler, who some time on the same day dropped his test scene on Wilder's desk? Because there was no "script" other than Cain's prose that Paramount had purchased?

The real question, given that he had been on the set of *Ball of Fire*, so that Stanwyck was not just someone he nodded to in the commissary, was had Wilder already approached her? Was her being "very interested" if not actually committed, as Ginger Rogers had been to *The Major and the Minor*, the name attachment needed by DeSylva for him to give the go-ahead that Brackett records on March 18? Did Stanwyck help override Breen's stern warning? Other details have been suggested. Stanwyck didn't want to consider doing the part initially, so it was sent in the back way via one of her confidants, her studio hairdresser (Hollis Barnes). The consensus is that when Stanwyck vacillated, Wilder had to hold her feet to the fire, at one point chiding her by asking, "Are you a mouse or an actress?" At some point early in the process, Stanwyck was firmly on board.[50]

The casting of Huff/Neff took a while longer. Although he was under contract to Paramount, Alan Ladd did not see himself as "a smart insurance salesman." Ultimately neither did Wilder. Plus, it was clear that the United States Army might soon have a part for Ladd in uniform that he could not refuse. "Everybody turned me down," Wilder told our late colleague Robert Porfirio, "I tried up and down the street, believe me. Nobody would do it, they didn't want to play this unsympathetic guy."[51] Did Wilder send the synopsis of the yet unfinished script to every agent in town, as he later asserted many times? Given the consistency of the George Raft details—he didn't read scripts, tell it to him and, "When do we have the lapel?"[52]—that offer was probably made and declined.

There were other Paramount contract leading men—Wilder had worked with Ray Milland and freelancer Franchot Tone—but except for Brian Donlevy (too rough) none are on the "approached-to-star list," which variously included Gregory Peck (too young), Fredric March (too old), Spencer Tracy (at MGM and too strong unless opposite Hepburn). One has to wonder when that mass submission to agencies took place? Was it early, before Stanwyck was attached? What agent would immediately pass if she were involved? There was someone very eager to portray Huff/Neff. "Dick Powell. He told me," said Wilder, "'I'll do it for nothing.' He knew he had to get out of those silly musical things. He came to my office to sell me."[53] Wilder was unsold, while noting this was before Powell played Marlowe in *Murder, My Sweet*.

At that point, where was Fred MacMurray on the list? Had he, as Wilder often recalled been at or near the top since the beginning or was he the only name without a line through it? According to Zolotow (who did speak to MacMurray but does sometimes exaggerate), Wilder "badgered him every day—every single day, according to MacMurray. He badgered him in the commissary, in his dressing room, at home."[54]

One wonders how Chandler felt every time Wilder ran out to badger MacMurray? Did Wilder not mention he would reteam with Stanwyck, his co-star on Paramount's *Remember the Night* (1940) directed by Wilder's chum Mitchell Leisen? "He said 'Look, I'm a saxophone player, I'm making my comedies with Claudette Colbert. What do you want?'"[55] At this time MacMurray, who was a moneymaker for the studio with and without Colbert, was in contract negations. Is it true that his agent told him to use the threat of accepting the *Double Indemnity* lead as a ploy? Would production head Frank Freeman, unhappy with this sort of crime movie and smug new director Wilder, actually cave on a pay raise and tell him not to do the movie? If that were true, it certainly did not work. Or was it the 50th time Wilder asked (make that badgered) him with the promise "Believe me it's going to be rewarding. And it's not that difficult to do."[56]

It could have been any of those reasons. It could even have been the money. By then, MacMurray was a very successful investor in Los Angeles real estate and a salary equivalent to $1.75 million dollars in today's money could add a choice property to his portfolio. Actually, thinking of it as $100,000, which was his minimum payment for *Double Indemnity*, those 1943 dollars probably buy more. After all, Neff speculates that the multi-level, Spanish-style Dietrichson home in the hills above Hollywood would set somebody back $30,000 (or $525,000 today, but let's not get into what that house would cost now).[57] Whatever the actual reason(s) for MacMurray

"Missy" Stanwyck and "Bud" MacMurray enjoy some ice tea brewed by a prop master in the replica of the Spanish-style house on Paramount's Stages 8/9.

to nod yes: "He did it. He didn't want to do it. He didn't want to be murdered. He didn't want to be a murderer,"[58] but he signed on. At that point, did anyone realize that actors whose nicknames were "Missy" and "Bud" were about to portray those facsimiles of criminals of the century "Momsie" and "Bud"? Probably not.

Edward G. Robinson did not want to be third-billed; but his character was neither murdered nor a murderer. He liked the part and perhaps he realized, never having been a romantic leading man and now 46 years old, that a good part and good pay—on a weekly basis of $12,500 per week with 8 weeks guaranteed (that is paid whether he actually worked that long or not), he was the highest paid actor, highest paid person working in any capacity, on the movie—was not be to be sneezed at. He would be above the title on the same card, probably on his own line, so why not?[59] Like Wilder, he was a serious art collector and $100,000 would buy a nice French tableau (let's not get into today's money on this either).

Even though these three leads would consume a large chunk of his budget (more than 40% of the "direct costs"), Wilder, Sistrom, and the studio execs (even Frank Freeman) knew that it was worth it. The featured parts, chosen from Paramount stock players, would cost around $1,250 per week for one or two weeks. Since that was the case why not make a special deal or two. Who actually suggested paying Howard Hughes a flat $5,000 for the services of Mona Freeman for Lola—she had no actual credits at that point— is not clear; but it was certainly okay with Wilder. Until it wasn't.

Numbers

As several biographers have reported the budget of *Double Indemnity* was $980,000 or just over 17 million in contemporary dollars. Then, as now, the summary of a budget was called a top sheet, which was divided by a mid-page line. Above it, were the "creative" costs: writing (story and screenplay), producing, directing, and performing (stars and featured players always, with bits and extras sometimes excluded). Below that line was everything else, physical production costs, then editorial including music. These were the Direct Costs ($740,000 in the *Double Indemnity* budget), to which were added overhead, special insurance, etc. This budgeting and accounting system that relied on department heads went back to the silent era (invented in the 1920s by producer Thomas Ince to curtail profligate spending) and the rule of thumb for decades, after the star system and actor salaries had grown, was a 60/40 ratio between the direct costs for ATL (above-the-line) and BTL (below). A larger ATL was not catastrophic as long as the higher prices paid (for rights to best-selling novels or actors with proven box-office appeal, few directors or producers promised impact in that regard) were a reasonable risk.

Then, as now, studios were owned by shareholders, who elected a board of directors (often based in New York not Hollywood), to whom production executives were answerable. Enough movies were made in any given year that a flop or two would not plunge the corporate enterprise into the red. But bad decisions could have consequences. As most ATL people were under contract and not profit participants, a few large successes could cover a score of studio breakevens and occasional miscues.

The overhead charges varied (it was 32.5% at Paramount in 1943); but those covered the salaries of executives and the operating staff, the cost of the physical plant and its myriad contents. And, of course, until the 1948 Paramount consent decree, most studios also had their own chain of theaters.[60] Of the reams of paperwork generated by Paramount bean counters for *Double Indemnity*, we have mostly relied on the cost report of June 17, 1944, which was effectively the final such recap of real numbers. Also of interest was the budget estimate of August 4, 1943, a "Quick Figure" from the Budget Bureau that totaled $1,005,000. It was based on only 30 pages of script dated July 26, 1943, and was for 42 days with a start date of August 16.[61] Remarkably it was slightly higher than the final budget number; but pretty much on the money vis-à-vis the final costs. On direct costs of $755,272 this estimate has a 57/43 ATL/BTL ratio. The actual direct costs in mid-June 1944 were lower: $726,823.02. The final ratio: 61/39.

The budget bureau's quick figure reflects the $100,000 to each of the three stars (so all of whom must have been set by the end of July when this estimation began). As detailed in the final cost report Barbara Stanwyck and Fred MacMurray were both guaranteed $10,000 per for ten weeks or 60 days (Saturdays were workdays in 1943 Hollywood). MacMurray ended up working 61 days and got $1,666 extra, making him the movie's highest earner in the final cost report. Stanwyck only worked 35 days. At $2,083.33 per day (for 48 days guaranteed), Robinson only worked 37 of his 48 guaranteed days (from Day 10 through Day 46).

The amounts paid to Cain ($15,000, long set by the estimate) and Chandler ($9,892) have already been noted. Some commentators/biographers have suggested that Wilder got close to the same amount as the lead cast.

Not really. Not that what he did earn was peanuts. Like many writers re-cently turned director, Wilder was still willing to take less than top dollar for calling the shots on set. He made $43,916.67 as a writer, for 24 weeks of work the first 8.2 at $1,500 per then $2,000 for the next 15.8.[62] He also made $2,000 per week as director: $26,000.[63] His total compensation of $69,916.67 was $1,233,075.45 in current money. Not bad for a young man from Austria who had gotten off a boat in New York less than 10 years before.

The rest of the cast—with none other than Mona Freeman, budgeted for more than $2,500—barely added $20,000 to the $301,666 for the three leads. Rounding out the ATL were Joe Sistrom (whose $21,582.22 is hardly the round number one might expect on a "Per Picture Basis") and Frank Waldman as a writer for $900 at $150 per week for 66 days starting on November 29, a week after shooting finished. Yes, this also does not add up (beginning to wonder about those Paramount accountants) but more importantly what did Frank Waldman, who had no known credits at this point, do?

There were a few high earners below-the-line as well. In the last pre-production budget of September 25 (on which Buddy DeSylva and studio production manager George Bertholon signed off), Costume Designer Edith Head has a fee of $3,000 for the picture. Director of Photography John Seitz would be paid $550 per week to a maximum of $5,300. At that point, composer Miklós Rózsa was contracted for $2,500. $600 each was allo-cated for staff process and effects cameraman Farciot Edouart and Gordon Jennings with exact days to be determined. Nobody else made as much as $200 ($3,500 today) per week. Except for first assistant director C. Clifford "Buddy" Coleman ($159), Unit Production Manager Hugh Brown ($173), and dialogue director Jack Gage ($150), no one made more than $150 ($2,645).

Lastly this approved budget contained some detailed costs. Among them were $4,695 for the gas chamber set (out of an overall $90,000 esti-mated for set construction and dressing, which was a considerable sum, the equivalent of $1.6 million today) and over $2,500 for Phyllis outfits. If that does not sound like much, four of the ensembles (hat and/or bag included as appropriate) were $400 or more, which is more than $7,000 today. The "bath towel and slippers" alone were $40 then or $700 now.[64] Two suits and eight shirts for Keyes were only $450. And at that point Walter's wardrobe would come out of stock.

Locations and Sets

Many commentators have focused on the use of Los Angeles as the backdrop for the movie. Cain had long ago moved true crime events from Queens to California. Wilder found Chandler's use of the colorful landscape as a background for Marlowe's exploits most appropriate. The mystery writer's dialogue was "good and sharp" but "Cain did not have that kind of sting in his dialogue. And I must say Chandler's great strength was a descriptive one. There are few people who can get the flavor of California."[65]

Despite what you may have read on the Internet Movie Database, Wikipedia, or on various tour sites touting maps to the noir locations of Los Angeles, very little of *Double Indemnity* was actually shot off the Paramount lot. Certainly the opening montage of a coupe (not yet identified as Neff's) racing back to an office building was set on actual city streets. Wilder himself directed MOS (that is, without sound recording) pre-production units on two early mornings in August. The first shot of the movie was filmed on the 14th day of the month[66] and looks north up 5th Street past Olive Street.

Light glints off trolley rails, and three smudge pots delineated a road repair site. Momentarily the flame from a welder's torch lights up his protective mask and a sign for the Los Angeles Railway Corp. Maintenance Dept. Another worker with a lamp waves at the car, which veers screen right and swerves past. Perhaps Wilder got the idea for this when he went out on the 4th with a small crew of two stunt drivers, and a few extras to shoot Neff's car running a traffic light and nearly colliding with a newspaper truck at 6th and Olive.[67] After the coupe pulls over in the fifth shot of the film, MacMurray exits the car on stage during week seven of the main schedule.

It is a long-demolished network of urban streets and building facades (modeled after New York City and Boston) at the rear of the lot which acts as

The opening shot of the movie on location in downtown Los Angeles.

the setting for most of the night exteriors, sometimes combined with shots of actual locations and/or process photography. Neff agrees to give Lola (Jean Heather) a ride to "Vermont and Franklin." They converse inside his car on the process stage, then he drops her on New York Street to meet Nino Zachette (Byron Barr), although there are two MOS shots. One is staged as the point-of-view from inside the car. A second unit shot is of Byron Barr standing in front of Newson Drugs at Hollywood and Western Boulevards. A second angle takes him to Neff's car, where Jean Heather is a passenger and a door frame blocks the view of the face of whoever is behind the wheel, a photo double for MacMurray who drives off at the end. The dialogue is on a process stage, where the window lettering for "fountain lunch" is lowered to match the actual street.

While it actually existed in downtown Los Angeles, La Golondrina Café was also on New York Street. Of course, Neff and Lola do visit an overlook to the Hollywood by way of a fairly obvious process screen. In special cinematographer Farciot Edouart, Paramount had one of the foremost specialists in process work, which for the most part (as in all the shots of Neff driving, the murder car, etc.) works quite well.

Police were hired to guard the food used as set dressing and to pose for this publicity shot.

On Day 14 (October 12), which was mainly devoted to scenes in Norton's office, a second unit got an establishing image of Jerry's Market—not in Los Feliz but across the street at 5330 Melrose—and "ins-and-outs": including Stanwyck as Phyllis approaching the open-air stands by the sidewalk. Her entry into the market cuts to an interior on Stage 11 that was shot on Day 24 (October 25). There are several angles to choose from in the photos distributed to newspapers and magazines of Wilder and his two stars posed in that stage set with some off-duty Los Angeles police officers, ostensibly there to make sure no member of the cast (such as day player Constance Purdy) or crew walked off with any of the hard-to-find, rationed foodstuffs on the set. Most of the packages were empty; but it was a successful publicity stunt by Paramount.

There are only three practical (or real) locations in which more than one or two shots of principal photography with speaking cast took place. One was the underground parking garage at the El Royale Apartments (less than a mile from the studio) that was shot on Day 46 (November 8). Neff's departure and return by the fire stairs were also done there.[68] The ground level exteriors of Neff's apartment were a bit farther away (two and a half miles), just north of Hollywood Boulevard in a mixed block of homes and rentals on Kingsley Drive. MacMurray starts for the auto ramp at the El Royale and emerges at the other location, where he takes "the walk of a dead man": a single panning shot follows him past the canopied front walk, where he pauses for an apprehensive glance backward, then south into the darkness.[69]

The masquerade continues as Phyllis smooths the way for Neff to board the train while posing as her injured husband.

Because of the war (and a year and half after the total blackout during the "Battle of Los Angeles") there were still restrictions on lighting at night. At the beginning of Week 4 (October 18) there was a 7 PM call for the first of two nights at the train station where the blue-suited "Mr. Dietrichson" is to board and then fall off "the ten-fifteen from Glendale." Whether it was light problems, ease of access (it is never simple to turn trains into action props on working urban rail lines), or some other reason, the actual filming was around the Burbank Southern Pacific station, six miles to the northwest. The brightest item in the shot as the Dietrichson sedan pulls in is the prop sign reading "Glendale." Two nights was enough time for the arrival, jump from the observation deck, meeting Phyllis and the body drop, but not the rest of the sequence. Thursday was a turnaround day back to regular hours and the next week on Days 28 and 29 two passenger cars were set up on Stage 6/7 for the rest of the sequence.[70]

The only shots of the actual "Dietrichson house" made during principal photography were on Day 50 (November 24), the last day and the Wednesday before Thanksgiving, so that non-contract crew would be laid off before the holiday. MacMurray did one "drive-in" and one "out," at the place that matched Cain's description most closely: "It was just a Spanish house, like all the rest of them in California, with white walls, red tile roof...The garage was under the house, the first floor was over that, and the rest of it was spilled up the hill any way they could get it in. You climbed some stone steps to the front door, so I parked the car and went up there."[71]

The house is on Quebec Drive in the Hollywood Hills. There is also a day-for-night pull out of Dietrichson leaving for the Glendale station with photo doubles. Then the MOS unit moved to the bowling alley, which contrary to what the narration says, is not at "Third and Western" but Santa Monica and La Cienega Boulevard. Neff "rolled a few lines," and purportedly MacMurray had five strikes in a row (although in the single shot he leaves himself the 2-10 pins to pick up a spare). Then Wilder challenged him to hit another. MacMurray threw his shoulder out. It didn't matter. The actor was "done in picture." At some point, other MOS night exteriors were picked

The actual location that the filmmakers found for Cain's "House of Death" is still on Quebec Drive in the Hollywood Hills and looking exactly the same except for a single garage door.

up, such as the sedan turning off a two-lane avenue in the murder alleyway and (again with photo doubles, on December 8) Phyllis dropping Walter "a block from his apartment house."

On July 19, Joe Sistrom, Wilder, Assistant Director Coleman, location manager Norman Lacey, and a still man (possibly Ed Henderson, who worked during principal photography or someone else) took the train to San Francisco for an overnight visit to San Quentin. To cover scouting costs for the gas chamber Sistrom had pulled a $700 travel voucher. In August the same group rode the rails east to Arizona, which had a very similar execution venue in the state prison just south of Tucson. It never was the plan to shoot Sequence E (pages 135 to 137 in the September 25 draft) on a distant location, merely to see for themselves what the venues and their surrounding corridors looked like. There is also studio file of a response to queries titled "Official Data on San Quentin Executions." It answers the question of whether there was one chair or two. Grim details follow such as "the body of the executed man is left in the gas chamber until about noon."[72]

Was this sequence ever seen outside of a studio screening room? Brackett does not mention it in his entries after seeing a first assembly of the entire movie (on December 2) or attending "the first sneak" on January 28. There is no definitive indication whether or not the gas chamber scene was included on either of these dates. Neither of the trade reviews at the April preview screening in Westwood mention it. Again not definitive. It was certainly shot on Day 44 (November 17). When was it cut? That remains an open question.

Several questionable assertions have since emerged. One claims that when the final scene in the insurance office was shot, it was so powerful that Wilder decided the gas chamber scene was not needed. Or that Wilder watched it in dailies or cut together and after seeing the powerfully forlorn performances of his leading men on the screen and said, "It's too sad!" At the point, even Wilder himself sometimes thought a new ending was conceived and the insurance office doorway re-shot. "I performed a major surgery on the end of *Double Indemnity*. I had an ending about twenty minutes long…the gas chamber. Then after I built the whole thing, I saw it was unnecessary. I found a scene where he collapses, and in the distance you already hear the sirens, so you know what the outcome is going to be." (See that shot on page 174.)

Was the execution scene, as is sometimes asserted, only in there to satisfy the Code's need to see criminals punished, ignoring the fact that Neff

The Dictaphone scenes end, and the movie returns to real time for the end of the trolley ride.

lies gravely wounded with the cops on the way and has recorded his confession in great detail. The prospect of capital punishment has just been mentioned again, when Keyes suggests a doctor: "What for? So I can walk under my own power into that gas chamber in San Quentin?" Collapsed in that doorway, Neff's prospects for long-term survival are quite dim because, now or later, he is going to die. If Wilder never intended to use it, why actually spend money to scout and then shoot it? If the studio felt it had to be in the script so that the punishment for murder was actually seen, why something this elaborate?

To be clear, it is unlikely that Wilder or his editors could get twenty minutes of running time out of three script pages, no matter that it had been "done with minute precision. I had the priest from San Quentin. I had the warden. I had the doctor, and everything was absolutely perfect. I had the

121

gas chamber with the pellets dropping and the bucket and the fumes, and outside is Eddie Robinson watching."[73] The Hays Office did not need "minute precision" or the elaborate details Wilder and Chandler wrote out; an actual, simple throwaway scene would have been sufficient. Joe Breen was not being copied on requests for travel vouchers or production reports or shown dailies. Still Wilder himself said that only afterwards did he realize "it was unnecessary."

Nice stories. But none of them hold up based on either the September 25 script or the shooting schedule. Regarding the latter (why-shoot-it?) first, it makes fiscal sense that Stanwyck and all the cast except MacMurray and Robinson were finished in picture before Day 44. Yes, Stanwyck, like her co-stars, was effectively on a flat deal. But the principles of scheduling, then as now, have both practical and aesthetic components. Of course, the movie was not shot in continuity or exactly in script order. As much as possible both sets and supporting cast were "shot out," that is finished as soon as possible. But Stanwyck's last scene was when Phyllis is shot. C.C. Coleman knew that both director and actor expected there would be no more workdays for Phyllis after she died. The same aesthetic proprieties apply to Neff's execution. Granted MacMurray drove up to the house and went bowling after his character succumbed but there was no more heavy lifting performance-wise.

As to the script, it could not be clearer. Wilder never "found" the last scene in the insurance office. It was shot exactly as written (and before the art department even built the gas chamber): after "I love you, too" Neff "fumbles...gets out a match, tries to strike it, but is too weak. Keyes takes the match out of his hand, strikes it for him, and lights his cigarette."

FADE OUT

THE END

Then after several blank lines: "(See following pages for alternate ending)"

Page 134A gives Neff a few more words: "At the end of that...trolley line...just as I get off...you'll be there...to say goodbye...will you, Keyes."

Except for a guard asking witnesses to vacate the chamber, the writers fill page one with all the details they got from the location shot and the official date. Not until page two does the Warden "turn to executioner and nod." Scene E-7 reads:

INT GAS CHAMBER – MED. SHOT

CAMERA IS SHOOTING ABOVE Neff's head (just out of shot), toward spectators standing outside the gas chamber, Keyes in the center. Gas floats into the scene between CAMERA and spectators. Keyes, unable to watch, looks away.

When did Wilder actually realize that it was too much and/or just not needed? Does it matter? On the last page, as Keyes starts for the door, puts a cigar in his mouth and "stops, with a look of horror on his face." Did Wilder have to tell Robinson that the prison would leave the body of the guy who used to

Keyes and a score of other witnesses, none of whom are there for a best friend, mill around the gas chamber.

light his matches in the death chamber until noon? That was probably not required for an actor like him to sell the moment, forget the cigar and walk away "slowly, stiffly, his head bent, a forlorn and lowly man."

Maurice Zolotow also reports many of these "alternate facts." A final addition is the tale of Buddy DeSylva complaining about tossing the alternate ending because the gas chamber reconstruction cost so much. In fact, scouting, building the set, and shooting the scene did not carry any extraordinary price tag, certainly nothing like the $100,000 to 150,000 (the highest number as per Wilder to Zolotow) that is often asserted. Really? Did it never occur to anyone citing this number to ask: how could one set possibly cost over 15% of the total budget?

If that had been the case, whenever he approached Wilder (possibly at the January 28 sneak preview) DeSylva might well have balked at consigning such costly celluloid to the waste bin. But the executive producer certainly had an idea of what the gas chamber in the scene actually cost; and hadn't—from a very different perspective—no less than Joe Breen asserted what Wilder was thinking now: "the details of the execution seem unduly gruesome...and will certainly be deleted by the censor boards."[74]

As to the actual cost, using photographs and the description in the script written after the scout, art director Hal Pereira and set decorator Bert Granger did need time and money to create the detailed replica on a sound stage. And the budgeted amount we noted above was exceeded. Final cost is recorded at $6,607 ($6,301 for construction and $306 for dressing).

Per the production reports there were seven named parts for the first day, two for the second. Although most of them did not speak, presuming they were paid as voice actors and not "silent bit" extras, the cost even with some overtime would not exceed $500. 14 to 20 assorted extras in somber suits and hats would cost around $300. The prorated cost of the crew, equipment, stage rental, etc., would equal around $1,500. Add in the travel voucher and the actual cost was still under $10,000 or, as we said in the Prologue, slightly more than 45 times what it cost to execute Momsie and Bud ($9,607 divided by $200 is 48).

Design and Photography

As was the case at most studios, the head of the art department, German-born Hans Dreier (who started at UFA in the silent era and came to America at the urging of Ernst Lubitsch) had the top credit as Art Director. The hands-on work was done by his colleague (and eventual successor) 38-year-old Hal Pereira. His "Dietrichson home," one set with red-tiled entryway, stairs and landing with wrought-iron railing, adjacent to a living room with dark wood accents, was closely modeled on the actual interiors of the house on Quebec Drive; but none of it was shot there. Two portions of the house exterior, the doorway where Walter and Phyllis reiterate their pledge to go "straight down the line" and the garage and adjacent steps, were also replicated on the studio lot.

With its wraparound balcony overlooking rows of desks on the floor below, the two levels of the Pacific All Risk Insurance Agency, as well as its

A wraparound balcony overlooks rows of desks on the floor below.

street level lobby, elevator, and interior offices for Neff, Keyes, and Norton, were the art department's largest and most complex construction project (and the most significant chunk of the $100,000 detail in the cost report spent to build and dress sets). Its design was certainly affected by director Wilder's admiration for the office floor in King Vidor's *The Crowd* (1927) with a layout and Beaux-Art style typical of early 20th-century American design. None of the interiors were shot in any practical location (as is sometimes claimed by Zolotow and others).[75]

While no practical interiors were filmed at the apartment building on Kingsley Drive, the main room, kitchen, and corridor of Neff's apartment were much like those inside that building. There is no particular resemblance, as is often claimed, to any of the cramped spaces that Wilder had actually occupied at the Chateau Marmont or (beyond its actual fire stairs) to the El Royale, although all three buildings came into service in 1929. The most obvious quirk of Neff's apartment is its front door, which opens out into the corridor. Was the atypicality of how it was hung that apparent to a viewer in 1944? It was not noted on any of the preview cards. Nor is it likely to strike someone watching Neff turn from his rain-spattered window and cross to open the door for Phyllis' first visit.

As the door opens out, light flashes off its wood surface to reflect into the room and Stanwyck's raincoat-clad figure, hair and shoulders backlit, is revealed in the corridor. Neff blocks her, until four lines are exchanged and 10 seconds pass, then he steps back to let her enter. It seems perfectly natural. Obviously if Neff's door was like most apartments of that era (or any era) and opened into the main room, the suspense gag that has Phyllis hiding behind it when Keyes leaves would not be possible.[76]

As noted before, a substantial amount was allocated for Phyllis' wardrobe (only dresses in the budget, which in two instances become trousers and a pantsuit), and the actual wardrobe costs were slightly over budget overall. Whatever the outfits cost, Stanwyck appreciated Edith Head's design decisions.

"You knew Edith would really help to give you your character for the audience," Stanwyck later asserted. "What people don't know is that she

Is this Edith Head showing Stanwyck "how to feel cheap" or show off her legs (or both)?

helped give me my character…helped me to *feel* cheap." According to Head, "The clothes shouldn't call too much attention to themselves or be too cheap, but Barbara Stanwyck's figure had to show. No one had greater legs."[77]

In her survey of noir fashion, Kimberly Truhler asserts that "*Double Indemnity* continues to be a reference for fashion designers…Whether influencing other films or inspiring fashion, *Double Indemnity* is all about style, straight down the line."[78] If as Head confirmed the "clothes weren't off the rack. 'Cheap' [context ours] clothes can be more important than the most elaborate costumes."[79] Design decisions should be simple, under-stated but true to character. For example, as Truhler notes, Phyllis changes from a towel into a "pale blue summer dress"—it is unclear why the script for a black-and-white movie indicates a color; perhaps because Cain has her in "blue pajamas"—then goes upscale "for Neff's next visit, Wilder directed the costume to be 'a gay print dress with a wide sash over her hips.' [script page 22] Head reinterpreted this as a long-sleeved, floor-length gown with a floral print bodice and solid skirt. This dress in particular, with its dropped waist in the back, shows off Edith's technique for correcting Stanwyck's long torso."[80]

There are no wardrobe indications in the script "when Phyllis first visits Walter at his apartment, she wears a pale cardigan sweater worn backward— a style popular in the 1940s—black trousers, and belted camel's hair coat. It seems a strategic move on Phyllis' part, downshifting into a more innocent ensemble to try to reel Walter back in," Truhler aptly suggests and continues, "The sweater is subtle but still overtly sexy, revealing her bra beneath it. The cardigan caused such a commotion that even during filming in 1943, Hollywood gossip columnist Sidney Skolsky said to Stanwyck, 'But the sweater. The sweater! (see it on page 131). How did the Hays Office ever let that get by?' "[81] In an earlier visual analysis we reproduced a posed photo of Stanwyck in that cardigan and a black skirt and noted that "Stanwyck's pose, costuming, and expression speak volumes about her personification of the conniving and murderous Phyllis."[82]

The script did have particular stipulations for the scene of Neff's second visit, where Wilder starts tight on Stanwyck's feet, when "she comes down the stairs her high heels clicking on the tiles. The anklet glistens on her leg as she moves." In the vernacular of the time, a married woman who wore an ankle bracelet might be signaling to men that although married, she was available. There is no anklet in Cain (just banter about the freckles on the face of Phyllis). Besides its possible ready-to-party message, the writers use it to introduce Mrs. Dietrichson's first name and make that a point to banter about (Neff: "I'd like to drive it around the block a few times").

Truhler had previously noted that "Phyllis is superficial and wants to be seen as a wealthy woman. Some of this is accomplished by adorning

Stanwyck crosses her legs better to display that "honey of an anklet," the fetish that drew Neff in.

Stanwyck in stunning Joseff of Hollywood jewelry, in particular a gold anklet with Phyllis' name engraved on it."[83] Both Stanwyck and Head certainly understood the implications of the anklet. As Truhler notes, when she first appears in the towel the script does call for Phyllis to have the item "on her left ankle." Whether it was forgotten by the set costumer, it is not there. Had some later biographer pointed this out to Wilder, he might have claimed Neff couldn't have seen if from where he stood and/ or it was purposefully held back until Phyllis is dressed and skips down the stairs in her white stockings and slippers. Nor is it recorded if anyone ever asked Wilder about the wedding ring on Neff's hand, and whether it had some subtle meaning. The only reason, it would appear, was simply because neither Fred MacMurray nor the prop master remembered to remove it on the first day of shooting. Some have noticed another ostensible continuity mistake: Neff's hat, which Phyllis visits him that evening to return, is not left behind. That would certainly be a more egregious error. Except that it's not.[84]

On one issue, Wilder was often questioned and repeatedly vacillated: the coiffure. Stanwyck's brown hair is covered by a blonde wig, that was actually obtained from Warner Bros. stock and had been placed on Marlene Dietrich's head in the movie *Manpower* (1941). Why exactly was that wig used? There is no indication of hair color in the script, although Cain did say "dusty blonde hair." What is certain, as chronicled by dozens of writers, is that at some point executive producer Buddy DeSylva remarked, "We paid for Barbara Stanwyck, and we got George Washington" or words to that effect. It is clear in an era when "A" pictures often included day-for-night shooting and process photography, a not always seamless and sometimes clunky methodology audiences readily accepted. Wilder went from lamenting not being able to afford process photography in his car-theft movie *Mauvaise Graine* to confessing to Bob Porfirio that "the whole thing is that we now go out of the studio because we cannot fool the audience so easily anymore, because they know how it is, they know every goddamned thing. You cannot cheat them anymore."[85] But didn't the wig look fine in 1943?

From the 1980s on, Wilder would explain that he wanted that wig. In 1986, Otto Friedrich quotes the director: "I wanted her to look as sleazy as possible."[86] You can read the same in Zolotow, Lally, Sikov, etc. Per Truhler "the director took it further with an over-the-top bleach-blonde wig. Stanwyck didn't find the wig to be an issue; she was accustomed to wearing them."[87] But sometimes, before all these books, Wilder had a very different take on DeSylva's comment, as he confessed to Bob Porfirio in 1975:

Stanwyck in the sweater that shocked Sidney Skolsky and modeling the wig taken from Marlene Dietrich in *Manpower*. A daring choice but it got the desired effect (Buddy DeSylva notwithstanding).

Mistake there. Big mistake. I wanted her blonde. Blondes have more fun...and I wanted an ice-cold look like that. But it was a mistake. I was the first one to see the mistake after we were shooting. But when the picture is half-finished, after I shot for four weeks with Stanwyck, I can't say, "Tomorrow you ain't going to be wearing the blonde wig." I'm stuck...I can't reshoot four weeks of stuff. I'm totally stuck. Fortunately it did not hurt the picture. But it was too thick, we were not very clever about wig-making. But now if someone says, "My god, that wig. It looked phony," I answer "You noticed that? That was my intention. I wanted the phoniness in the girl, bad taste, phony wig." That is how I get out of it.[88]

In the simpler days of the silent era, directors of photography were just "first cameramen,"[89] Even by the 1940s in Hollywood, many directors still relied on directors of photography to decide all the details of any given shot—not just lighting but camera placement, framing, moving, etc.—while he or she (in a few instances at least) focused on the actors and their performance.[90] Clearly Wilder had already made many decisions about specific shots in the writing stage. While not over-burdened with such indications, Wilder had a basic approach that was refined on the set.

As on his last feature, the key collaborators were Doane Harrison and the director of photography he met on *Five Graves to Cairo* and would use twice more after *Double Indemnity,* John F. Seitz, "a very old man." Wilder joked to Crowe, "only 51 at the time and had done pictures with Valentino."[91] While he had worked closely with director Rex Ingram on several features (including the early Valentino *Four Horsemen of the Apocalypse*), Seitz had been a contract DP on scores of features at Fox and MGM before moving to Paramount in 1940, where Seitz shot the early film noir *This Gun for Hire* (1942). Like most old-school cameramen, Seitz believed that shot decisions "would depend on what the scene was, the mood. By the time of shooting, we generally had a pretty good idea of the mood we wanted. There was a lot of night work in *This Gun for Hire* and we just kept that style throughout. You know, I saw *Double Indemnity* the other night, and it's almost a perfect picture."[92]

Seitz and Wilder certainly agreed on first principles. "Johnny Seitz was a great cameraman. And he was fearless," Wilder continued to Bob Porfirio about the final scene in the house, "That was beautiful. Johnny was brilliant."[93] But even in the context of the noir style, "We had to be realistic. You had to believe in the situation or the characters or all was lost." Wilder related to Crowe:

That was the approach. No phony setups. I tried for a very realistic picture—a few little tricks, but not too tricky. I had a few shots in mind between MacMurray and Robinson, and they happened at the beginning and the end. Everything was meant to support the realism of the story. I had worked with the cameraman before and I trusted him. We used a little mezzo light when Stanwyck comes to see MacMurray in the apartment—this is when he makes up his mind to commit murder.[94]

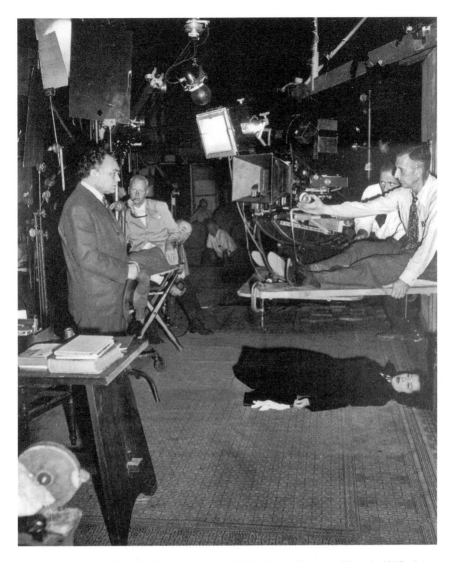

An even older John F. Seitz lines up a shot in *Night Has a Thousand Eyes* in 1947 of star Edward G. Robinson. Co-star Gail Russell is on the floor. Director John Farrow is in the high chair to the left.

One little trick "was a very specific thing. I told Seitz that whenever I came into a house, there was always dust in the air. I asked him, 'Could you get that effect?' And he could."[95] All that took was a sprinkle of "pixie dust" (fine metal particles) and a wisp or two from an effects smoker to define shafts of light. While not all the lighting and shot selections in *Double Indemnity* may be uncontestably "perfect" or "beautiful" or "brilliant," none are phony and most are powerfully effective.

Shooting

Principal photography began Monday September 27, 1943, with the first scenes at the Dietrichson home. It was a short day for Stanwyck (who made her initial appearance wrapped in a towel at the top of the stairs); but around eight hours for Fred MacMurray, who wandered around the living room "still stuffy from last night's cigars" after the disgruntled Nettie ushered him in. It's unclear whether dialogue director Jack Gage or script supervisor Nancy Lee read aloud the narration so that MacMurray could time his leisurely amble around the sets.

Editor Doane Harrison was certainly there watching over Wilder's shoulder. The presence or absence of John Berry, assigned to shadow Wilder by the studio's director-training program, is not recorded. Nor is it certain if Chandler was there (probably) or on the fourth floor of the Campus tweaking future scenes. After nine setups, everybody packed up and went home. The film went to the lab for processing to be synchronized in editorial with the materials from the sound department for a screening of dailies on Day 2. Neff's second suit No. 1 was hung in MacMurray's dressing room for the next morning, while the day one threads went to wardrobe to be cleaned and pressed. Most every other item stayed where it was on a locked Stage 8.

The next day's work still resonates in the history of motion pictures. Wilder, Chandler, and the two leads must have had an inkling from the table read the week before of just how well the second dialogue scene between Walter and Phyllis would go. Not everyone may remember "there's a speed limit in this state: 45 miles per hour"[96]; but "How fast was I going, officer?" and "I'd say about 90"—how many times have those lines of dialogue been alluded to or replicated outright?

Then in Week 2 there was the performance, or rather the appearance, of Mona Freeman. Imagine how Wilder might have related his reaction after watching dailies of Scenes B1 and B2 in the Dietrichson living room to Maurice Zolotow: "She looked like she was 12-years-old. They told me she'd be 17 when we shot her. 17, my ass! Half-price ticket on the train, like in *Major and the Minor*, no problem whatsoever for Miss Mona Freeman, because she really did look like she was twelve!"[97] Did Joe Sistrom or anyone else think this? Given how fast the call got made (and despite that it meant losing more than a day's work), the production report for Day 10 (October 6) shows Mona Freeman as "N.C." (not called) and finished on the next day. Presumably Wilder must have met and thoroughly satisfied himself about how easily contract player Jean Heather could have gotten a half-price train ticket before he allowed her to step into the part of Lola.

At some point—the likeliest would be Day 38 of Week 7 in which scene A33, the walk to Keyes' office is listed—the cameo of sourpuss Raymond Chandler, parked on his south end outside of Keyes' office as Neff walks past, was shot. Chandler glances up diffidently at the passing MacMurray, and in the blink of an eye his bit is over. Why did he perform a cameo? It could be that Wilder noticed the bench was empty and yelled, "Ray, grab that magazine and sit down there." (Make that "Ray, please...") Except there is a publicity still of a smiling Chandler, sitting there and chatting with MacMurray, as makeup is applied to his pale writer's hands. So it wasn't completely impromptu, seconds before cameras rolled.

Apprentice director and John Houseman protégé John Berry also appeared as the last man off the elevator when Keyes tells Neff he has discovered the "somebody else." Berry was just 26 at the time—years away from directing the noir films *Tension* (1949) and *He Ran All the Way* (1951), then troubles with the House Unamerican Activities Committee (HUAC), decades in exile in France, a gig with the blacklist-exploiting King Brothers, all before finally returning to Paramount 35 years later for *The Bad News Bears Go to Japan*. Did the studio get anything from Mona Freeman for the $5,000 ($88,000 today) that it paid Howard Hughes? Did she appear as an extra? Was she one of the five women who exit the Pacific Building, as Neff hands

135

Seated outside Keyes' office, Chandler is on-screen quite briefly.

Keyes a match for that cheap cigar? Not likely. Probably she just went back to high school.

There is another, oft-cited event that would have transpired on Day 11. That's when Wilder went to his car to drive to lunch at the Brown Derby, and his engine wouldn't start. After he tried the starter button again and again, thoughts of a three-olive martini were replaced by a great idea. He ran back to the process stage and stopped the crew from changing the set just in time by yelling: Get the actors back, we're going to shoot it a different way! Some nit-picking: on the day inside the sedan with rear projection, would they not have shot the scheduled killing before the aftermath of dumping the body? And how much of a reset would have been happening on the process stage? Also, could Wilder really get to the Brown Derby, have lunch, and get back in less than an hour?[98]

None of those questions matter, because it's just another nice story. What matters—Breen's repeated reservations notwithstanding—is that the scene in the car after the body has been dumped, when it's time to drive

136

The murderers after they almost didn't get away...because of car problems for which the automobile club could not be called.

away, but the engine won't start, that scene B-67 is fully detailed on page 77 of the September 25 script. The writers used short sentences to evoke the intended emotional intensity: "The starter grinds but the motor doesn't catch. She tries again. It still doesn't catch. Neff looks at her. She tries a third time. The starter barely turns over. The battery is very low." That's the end of the first paragraph of dialogue-less description. The second paragraph goes on for 11 lines.

Something did happen when this scene was shot, in a single take and more or less in the exact manner that Wilder and Chandler had envisioned. Whatever story he may have heard about the scene from Wilder, Mr. Zolotow did realize the entire action was "in the script. Phyllis cannot start the car." He then segues to what he heard from Neff himself:

And now let us see what took place when co-author Wilder became director Wilder. Fred MacMurray remembers how surprised he was that this turned out to be "the most successful scene in the picture. I remember we did it on a process stage with rear projection for the trees, you know, the scenery behind us. Barbara and I sat in this dummy car. Just a car seat. No dashboard. No ignition key to turn. We fake it, pantomimed it. When I changed places with her and turned the key, I remember I was doing it fast and Billy kept saying 'Make it last a little longer,' and I finally yelled, 'For Chrissake, Billy, it's not going to hold that long." And he said, "Make it longer!" And he was right. It held—that was how much the audience was involved with the story.[99]

The single take on the process stage when the car won't start. The scene runs for forty seconds before the car starts. There is no record of how much—if and when he ever saw the movie—Joe Breen might have been on the edge of his seat and rooting for that engine to turn over, for the adulterous killers not to be caught, not here, not yet. Of course, he had presumably read the script (or were his memos to Lucaschi based on notes from some researcher) and would probably have remembered that eventually the car would start.

Principal photography had originally been scheduled (and budgeted) for 7 weeks (42 days). Without any significant uptick in estimated cost, a week was added and 47 days of filming plus that "turnaround" day were plotted out. The only significant hiccup, the only one of the "mistakes" to which Wilder later admitted had to be corrected and that cost extra time, was the recasting. So there was a Week 9 with MacMurray (the only one of the stars still on payroll, Stanwyck and Robinson having finished in less than their guaranteed periods) recording the narration in Neff's office on Days 48 and 49 then finally, actually, "run up there for this auto renewal on Los Feliz."

The Dictaphone scenes are shot in long takes; the cut in the last is when Neff notices Keyes is there. After the wounded man manages to get the machine set up and sit down, the first dictation is shot tight on the actor. Later there are some camera moves, a dolly in and out. "According to Billy," Ed Sikov relates, "According to Billy, MacMurray was 'a notorious line muffer [but] he got so interested he never missed one.' This is a slight exaggeration on Billy's part. In fact, when filming his initial Dictaphone scene, MacMurray kept blowing his lines. It was a long speech in a single take, and MacMurray couldn't manage to get it all out without flubbing something along the way."[100] Did this happen? If it did, MacMurray ultimately got that monologue, got all of them, in one piece.

Wilder had most likely seen the actual house, not just Pereira's replication, before. But at some point, probably exhausted but exultant on the last day of a long shoot, something new did come into his mind. Exactly as scripted, Neff's coupe drives past children playing in the street and parks in the garage apron while an ice-cream truck passes. Originally Neff's voice-over said that he smelled the honeysuckle on the way up to the house. No, that was for later. Maybe Wilder did not hurry back to the lot, to the Campus, at the end of that day. At some point with or without Chandler, with or without thinking about what Cain had written, but certainly remembering the house, new narration—not what was in the September 25 draft through any yellow, blue, green, or pink pages up through "11/27/43"—was written: "It was one of those California Spanish houses everyone was nuts about 10 or 15 years ago. This one must have cost somebody about $30,000, that is if he ever finished paying for it."

By the fourth dictation scene, the blood stain has grown considerably.

The last day with MacMurray at the house and then bowling alley[101] was the third over schedule. Despite this and all the other issues, wigs, "she looks twelve-years-old," doors opening out, the movie was in the can for what would turn out to be less than had been budgeted. There were a couple of film problems and that pickup unit in early December, but all those included in that Final Production Cost report that indicated *Double Indemnity* was $50,191.38 in the black. That is not an insignificant sum ($885,193 today); but apparently no one—not Wilder or Sistrom or Doane Harrison or Johnny Seitz—got a cash bonus or anything more than a pat on the back (if that) from Paramount.

Post-Production

Brackett's December 2nd entry in his diary indicates—with a touch of *schadenfreude*—that "at 2 o'clock went with Billy, Joe, Doane [Harrison] and Lee [Hall, assistant editor] and Ray to see *Double Indemnity*, which I enjoyed very much, rather the more because while a good picture, it is not a great one, being extremely one-noteish and rather drab than tragic [sic]. I think it will have a success d'estime or de shock, but doubt that it will be much of a money-maker. The direction is uneven and some of the writing extremely poor, and my black heart sang like a bird."[102] It might have been, barely a week after shooting wrapped, that the assembly of scenes was a little rough or ragged, perhaps with temp music cues, if any, but no Miklós Rózsa underscore. But, still, what movie was Brackett watching? What is remarkable, and not noted by Brackett, is how quickly this cut was assembled. One has to presume that after being on set during the day, Doane Harrison went to the cutting room for detailed consult with Lee Hall, who worked a night shift. However, it was done.

As promised, Wilder hired Miklós Rózsa for the music early on, despite negative feedback from Paramount's preeminent composer, Victor Young, on the score for *Five Graves*.[103] Per Rózsa on *Double Indemnity* "Billy has the idea of using a restless string figure (as in the opening of Schubert's *Unfinished Symphony*) to reflect the conspiratorial activities of the two lovers against the husband; it was a good idea and I happily accepted it."[104]

Again there were issues with the studio in the person of its musical director, Louis Lipstone. As the composer explained to Bob Porfirio in 1977, "In my case...so-called film noir was a natural fit. *Double Indemnity* was the first film which I did in this film noir style...not standard Hollywood. When we started to record, [Lipstone] could hear this was not that, this was brutal music, and he hated it."[105] Eventually, fed up with Lipstone's muttering, "Billy Wilder finally turned to him and snapped, 'You may be surprised to hear that I *love* it.'"[106] According to Rózsa, after the man who was technically his boss stormed out, he rode down in the car with him before the first preview in Long Beach, "miles way, so that the press didn't cover it, because the film was not completely finished."[107] After the screening Rózsa apprehensively approached DeSylva, who Lipstone believed would hate the music. Instead Lipstone's creative boss thought "it was exactly the sort of dissonant, hard-hitting score the film needed. The only criticism he had: there wasn't enough of it."[108]

141

Composer Miklós Rózsa (left) with the staid and musically conservative Louis Lipstone, Paramount musical director.

On December 15, Paramount received an "Analysis Chart" for its "Melodrama-Horror" feature from the office of PCA staffers Geoffrey Shurlock and T.A. Lynch, which recapped the movie's content from particular Code perspectives. "RR Tracks" (where the body was dumped) was typed in for "Locale of Note." No gas chamber was in the list of settings. Had Breen's December 1 memorandum already caused it to be removed? The analysis continues: three "prominent" leads are typed in, "Insurance Salesman, Oil Man's Wife (?!), and Claims Manager," all straight (as opposed to comic) but the top-two "unsympathetic" characterization. Only one minor "profession" of interest is marked with an "X": no Doctor or Journalist but "Lawyer(s)," which must refer to the three men leaving Norton's office, whose characterization is "Indiff[erent]." There are no public officials or religious workers, but under "Races or Nationals" "Colored" and "Mexicans" (again? Could L. Greenhouse have mistaken the name Gorlopis—a Greek-named character portrayed by an Italian—as "Gorlopez"?[110]) are added. The bottom of the form has one last list of events that might be problems. Not liquor. In this reviewer's opinion, the bourbon at Neff's is "incidental drinking," and "little" has the X-mark for amount. The "Type of Crime" is Murder; the "No. killings" is Two; and the "Other Violence" is Gunshots. But on the line for Fate of Criminal(s) is typed: "One killed – One apprehended." No mention of a cyanide cure for miscreant Neff. No "X" either in spaces next to "ADULTERY" or "ILLICIT SEX"—a curious omission. Finally the detailed synopsis, typed up in two, single-space pages concludes with: "Neff tries to escape but collapses from loss of blood. Keyes telephones for a police ambulance."[109]

While it is still not certain from this artifact whether Brackett saw the gas chamber on December 2, it is pretty clear the PCA reviewer did not. On December 18, Luraschi received a copy of MPPDA code certificate number 9717 that was added at the bottom of the penultimate main title card. It is also pretty clear that, contrary to some reports, the gas chamber scene was not in the public sneak preview of January 28, 1944. Charles Brackett was clearly in a different mind-set (more supportive than jealous of long-time partner Wilder) as he drove to Long Beach on that date:

143

Dined and hurried to the first sneak of Double Indemnity *and, as edited and scored, it is an absolute knockout of a picture, the most flawless bit of picture technique imaginable. The awful giggling-kind audience was held spellbound and those who knew pictures were set back on their heels and I am to report in myself a kind of rejoicing that it was such a superb thing. The cards weren't as hearty as some we've had and it may not have the superficial audience appeal, but it's a* success d'estime *of the most esteemful kind.[111]*

6.

THE MOVIE: THE TOP SHELF

It's simple. There's Double Indemnity *and there's everything else. Nothing is as twisted and dismal and perfect, so why not just begin and end any explanation of film noir there. You want to know what the elements of film noir are, you just saw them.*[1]

I s it that simple? In some ways, yes. Whatever variations (and there are a few) from the actual facts of its making that Richard Schickel might have included in his 1992 monograph, his comment above is spot on. In the end it is not about how any movie came to be. It's about the movie itself. Of course, if it were really that simple, no one would ever dispute such assertions as "perfect" or "sensational" or "masterpiece."

> **I don't see why they always have to put what**
> **I want on the top shelf**
> Unnamed Woman with a Child in Jerry's Market

Exactly where *Double Indemnity* sits on the shelf of fine films (or perfect pictures or magnificent movies) has been a shifting question since before its release. Charles Brackett, the man who knew the true crime, found its rehash in *Machinal* monotonous, and hated the novel—he couldn't make up his mind in a single viewing. He went from "one notish" and "extremely poor" the first time he saw it to "absolute knockout" and "superb," the next.

Few would deny that Double Indemnity *is a definitive film noir and one of the most influential movies in Hollywood history.*

In his 1998 essay on "The Death Chamber,"[2] James Naremore starts off well enough. *Double Indemnity* is top shelf. Then, unlike Dietrichson's corpse, he goes off the rails. Of course, after a remark like the one cited above, a "but" often follows, "a contrary view."[3] Of course, Naremore is not a trade reviewer or an industry professional, he is a detached observer, a well-credentialed historian of cinema. In the aftermath of its release *Double Indemnity* inspired a slew of reactions. As we will detail in a bit, it made a dollar or two, got some good press, and turned out better than even some involved in its creation ever expected.

What did Fred MacMurray or Barbara Stanwyck think when they first saw a one-sheet of the characters they had somewhat reluctantly embodied, in a clinch and staring into each other's eyes against a pink background? And how about that tag line: "From the Moment they met it was Murder!" If they thought perhaps that they should have listened to the little man inside telling them not to take this part, they soon found out how wrong they were. "When I meet fans," Stanwyck later affirmed, "more of them want to talk about *Double Indemnity* than any other work I've done."[4] So when did it become more than a successful, somewhat idiosyncratic movie, that many people loved, and a few hated? How did its shelf life get extended, how did it become a classic? Again, we would allege, the answer is the movie itself.

Putting aside questions about the rise of film noir, there is no question that *Double Indemnity* occupies a pivotal position in that film movement, which as noted before had already incorporated criminal characters, sex, and violence into its earliest examples. Imagine suddenly seeing the first wave of film noir all at once. That is exactly what happened in Europe after the end of World War II. So, what did Nino Frank—who along with Jean-Pierre Chartier was one of the guys who invented the term film noir in 1946—think:

We rediscover this hardness, this misogyny, in Double Indemnity. *There is no mystery here, we know everything from the beginning,*

146

and we follow the preparation for the crime, its execution, and its aftermath... Consequently our interest is focused on the charac- ters, and the narrative unfolds with a striking clarity that is sus- tained throughout. This is because the director, Billy Wilder, has done more than merely transpose the narrative structure offered by the James Cain novel from which the film is adapted. He started by creating, with Raymond Chandler, a peremptorily precise script, which deftly details the motives and reactions of its characters. The direction is a faithful rendering of this script.[5]

More than seventy-five years later, for us, it's hard to quibble with that, or with Frank's excited conclusions that "these noir films no longer have any common ground with run-of-the-mill police dramas. Above all, don't make me say that the future belongs to crime movies told in the first person."[6]

It took a while for the term to cross the Atlantic (over two decades more than it took the postwar prints of the movies to arrive in France); but eventu- ally English-language writers started in on defining the bigger picture. The authors of *Hollywood in the Forties*, used a translation of the term, when they classified *Double Indemnity* as a prime example of the style of "Black Cinema": "The sound of 'Tangerine' floating from a radio down the street, as the lovers enter their death cling in the shuttered room in *Double Indemnity*. Chinese checkers played on long pre-television evenings by people who hate each other's guts."[7]

By 1972 Tom Flinn was writing about "the three faces of film noir" and noting the difference between "Mary Astor hiding her Machiavellian de- signs behind a mask of gentility in *The Maltese Falcon* [and] Barbara Stan- wyck in *Double Indemnity*, a tougher, less bourgeois breed"[8] of fatal woman. In that same year, Paul Schrader wrote effusively: "*Double Indemnity* was the first film which played film noir for what it essentially was: small-time, unredeemed, unheroic. The Wilder/Chandler *Double Indemnity* provided a bridge to the post-war phase of film noir. The unflinching noir vision of *Dou- ble Indemnity* came as a shock in 1944. Three years later, however, *Dou- ble Indemnity*'s were dropping off the studio assembly line."[9] Or as our late

As Phyllis tells Neff, "It sounds wonderful. Just strangers beside you. You don't know them. You don't hate them. You don't have to sit across the table and smile…"

colleague Art Lyons put it "It was not until *Double Indemnity* in 1944 that noir production really took off and soon the studios were cranking out *Double Indemnity*s by the dozen."[10]

In his groundbreaking early essay, "Paint It Black: The Family Tree of Film Noir," English critic Raymond Durgnat is one of the first (published in 1970, two years before Flinn or Schrader) to use the French term for the noir movement. The analysis delineates nine keys to noir narratives, after initial mention of *Double Indemnity* in section 4, "Privates Eyes and Adventurers," which Durgnat dubs the "poetic core of film noir."[11] As Durgnat certainly knew, the "private dick" and the police detective are far less featured as lead characters than one might assume in the noir canon. The poetry emanates from a handful of protagonists, created mostly by Chandler and Hammett, who do appear in key films. On the tree's branch 5, "Middle-class Murder," Durgnat situates *Double Indemnity*, while noting that *"Double Indemnity* is perhaps the central film noir, not only for its atmospheric power, but as a junction of major themes, combining the vamp (Barbara Stanwyck), the morally weak murderer (Fred MacMurray) and the investigator (Edward G. Robinson). The murderer sells insurance. The investigator checks on claims. If the latter is incorruptible, he is unromantically so; only his cruel Calvinist energy distinguishes his 'justice' from meanness."[12]

Investigation and fear of the investigator are the principal convolutors of the plot of *Double Indemnity*. One could also argue from the family tree perspective that *Double Indemnity* has blossoms on more branches than any other noir, as many as six of Durgnat's nine. There is an element of social criticism in the crime (Durgnat's no. 1), because it is a middle-class murder and its nonconforming characters test the fabric of bourgeois normality. While Neff and Phyllis never become, as Cain's characters do, a fugitve couple "on the run" (Durgnat 3), there are moments mid-movie when the audience might wonder if they will end up fleeing together. There are clearly an investigator (Durgnat 4) and a middle-class murder (Durgnat 5). While the couple's initial sexual engagement may appear straightforward, the abnormal twists that are later revealed add components of both sexual pathology (Durgnat 7) and psychopathy (Durgnat 8). Without them the nuances of Stanwyck's performance are missed, and Phyllis Dietrichson cannot become the enduring archetype of the femme fatale.

In our own deconstructions of the classic period, we have spun off Durgnat's approach several times. In *Film Noir The Encyclopedia* major limbs and minor branches of a family tree are implied when we wrote:

From its very titles, the noir cycle uses boldface and continually points that deadly finger. Its figures are the Accused, Abandoned,

Cornered, Framed, Railroaded, Convicted, Caged, *and* Desperate. *A character menaced by an* Act of Violence *makes a* Journey Into Fear *or lives* Between Midnight and Dawn, Somewhere in the Night, On Dangerous Ground *and does so in isolation:* I Walk Alone, In a Lonely Place. *There are certain characters, like Walter Neff in* Double Indemnity, *whose behavior is more classically existential because he understands from the beginning that he need not have chosen, as is metaphorically explained to him, to board a "trolley" for "a one-way trip and the last stop is the cemetery."[13]*

How many titles apply to Walter? He fears being accused and convicted, which makes him feel cornered and desperate. His act of violence committed between midnight and dawn began his journey into fear and left him somewhere in the night on dangerous ground, walking alone and, much like the doomed Judd Gray, incapable of hearing his own footsteps. It was our publisher who called the original edition of the book "An Encyclopedic Reference to the American Style," and a key to its definition was the prototypical journey of Neff and Phyllis to the end of the line.

Some years later in *Film Noir*[14] we distilled ten narrative motifs from the Durgnat model. We used *Double Indemnity* as the key example of the section, The Perfect Crime; but again it crosses over into many other branches: the fatalistic nightmare, male violence, women in film noir, the private eye (Keyes is an investigator), and darkness and corruption. Finally, in analyzing *The Noir Style* we used just six key titles for chapters: Out of the Past, Night and the City, Deadly Is the Female, the Dark Mirror, the Reckless Moment, and Night Has a Thousand Eyes. How many of those might apply to *Double Indemnity*? In terms of its characters, setting, and visualizations? One could say all six.

About the shot in the market, we noted in the "Out of the Past" section: "The visual tension of everyday items and extraordinary events is a frequent ironic motif in film noir. The supermarket scene from *Double Indemnity* is a perfect example. When Neff and Phyllis cannot chance having a private rendez-vous observed, they arrange to be in the same aisle of a local market.

150

The last meeting at Jerry's Market: Phyllis is determined, so Neff has reason to worry.

The meticulously ordered array of packaged goods as well as the sign for 'quality foods' are unrelentingly mundane and easily read as symbols of the ordinary and ordered world in which most people live. For Phyllis, the sunglasses shield her eyes and her possible hidden motives from Neff. His expression is telling, glancing over despairingly at her as she looks straight ahead. Trapped, almost completely enveloped in the two dimensions of the frame, these killers are discomfited not by their guilt but by their fear of discovery, dependent on each other's nerve but uncertain if they can count on it."[15]

Or in "Deadly Is the Female," we analyzed the posed anklet shot in the Dietrichson living room: "Phyllis Dietrichson is playful and threatening at the same time. She reclines comfortably in an armchair, all smiles, no stress or tension in her face, arms are extended on each side of the chair as if inviting

151

A posed shot referencing the angle. A staging in which Neff actually touches Phyllis' leg would be problematic for Joe Breen.

an embrace. From one hand a cigarette dangles. Her left foot juts out stiffly towards Walter Neff. On it is a 'honey of an anklet.' While Phyllis is in white and fully lit, Walter is in shadows, lessening his visual position in the shot, perched on the edge literally of an upholstered arm and figuratively of disaster. His face is cut ominously by venetian blind shadows, and even the wall behind him is brighter. His expression is one of surprise as he gazes at the extended limb. The momentary dynamics of their relationship is summed up in this pose. Phyllis continually challenges the cynical Walter who, fascinated by her hard edge and overt eroticism, will soon agree to follow her down 'straight down the line' to murder and betrayal. Their kinship is expressed in the matching dangling cigarettes, hers in her left hand, his in his right."[16]

Durgnat and Schrader were among the earliest English-language critics to define film noir as a movement not a genre, something that could use theme and style to bend other genres into noir. The seminal piece by Lowell Peterson and Janey Place was the first analysis of the film noir through its visual motifs. While an overview, it did pointedly isolate one moment, Neff with Phyllis behind the door, where "direct, undiffused lighting of Barbara Stanwyck in *Double Indemnity* creates a hard-edged, mask-like surface beauty. By comparison, 'hard-boiled' Fred MacMurray seems soft and vulnerable."[17]

This is what we said about the shot selected by Peterson and Place in *The Noir Style*: "The door in this well-known image from *Double Indemnity* acts as a literal and figurative barrier. It shields Phyllis Dietrichson from the prying eyes of Keyes, the insurance investigator who has come to see agent Walter Neff and at whom (off frame somewhere) Neff apprehensively directs his gaze. While she hides behind it, seeming much smaller in the frame in relation to the anxious Neff in the near foreground, her expression is more impassive. Place and Peterson remark about Stanwyck's 'a hard-edged, mask-like surface beauty…by comparison [Neff] seems soft and vulnerable.' The flat lighting does distinguish Phyllis' smooth features from the modeling on Neff's face. Still in two dimensions there is a strange visual conjunction between them, even as the door separates them, for Neff's shadow on the door blends in with Phyllis' figure so that it seems like he is joined to her left shoulder. The door may symbolize the barrier of mistrust between these two lovers and conspirators while Phyllis, the temptress in the recess behind Neff, may also personify the criminal lurking inside him that she awakened. It is clear that the smaller Phyllis has dominance in this reckless relationship."[18]

Finally, we perceived a figurative "dark mirror" when Keyes stands outside the gas chamber (reproduced in the Prologue on pages 4-5): "Edward G. Robinson is on the other side of the dark mirror as Keyes in *Double Indemnity*. In this scene cut from the final release of the film, Walter Neff awaits execution, at the 'end of the line' of the criminal journey on which he embarked with femme fatale Phyllis Dietrichson. Here the drab gray comes from the exterior walls of the execution chamber, as the overhead light on Neff turns his eyes into black pools and models the cheek, so in his last moments his visage almost becomes a skull-like death mask. The foreground rail, which Keyes clutches, creates a darker gray line that separates Keyes. The bolts around the airtight window through which Neff is visible are the grotesque ornamentation of a noir frame. For Keyes, anguished over his protégé's fate, that frame encircles both a picture of death and a mirror, into which he cannot gaze, of his anguish."[19]

"The slow but inexorable advance of the man on crutches."

In his seminal essay of the 1970s, "No Way Out: Existential Motifs in Film Noir," Bob Porfirio found the earliest of "when doomed men like Walter Neff in *Double Indemnity* (Fred MacMurray) or Al Roberts in *Detour* (Tom Neal) withdraw to a darkened office or a small diner, they are reminiscent of the older waiter in Hemingway's 'A Clean, Well-lighted Place.' They can use the quiet and solitude to try to order their lives; to carve an aesthetic order out of the diffuse materials of existence."[20]

After diverse writers initially grappled with the impact of *Double Indemnity* on the noir movement through the 1970s (the first edition of *Film Noir The Encyclopedia* appeared in late 1979), revisionists began to appear. In 1983 French critic Marc Vernet appreciated the movie's opening: "Finally, the slow but inexorable advance of the man on crutches, which illustrates the title sequence of *Double Indemnity*, recalls the determinedness of *The Enforcer* and provides a preview of the character who will avenge himself without pity."[21] Okay, so far. Then it gets a little heavy and obscure: "The ending of *Double Indemnity* is exemplary in this respect. Here the woman is condemned, which is to say rendered evil and pushed aside, for having confused the difference between good and evil or between love and the desire for power; in short, for having transgressed the categories of the heroes' personal code."[22] Hard to tell what "personal code," other than "Don't get caught," was brought into the deal. Let's change "power" to "money," Vernet's point remains murky.

Perhaps Vernet could not reconcile a straightforward dramatization of fatal instincts and deadly consequences in a Hollywood movie. After all this is the guy who threw a Gallic sniff in the direction of film noir when he called it "the triumph of European artists even as it presents American actors."[23] Aside from its remarkably unembarrassed Eurocentric bias, such a statement completely ignores Paul Schrader's warning that "there is a danger of over-emphasizing the German influence in Hollywood."[24] It is among the first of frequent and ongoing attempts both to break down the "myth" of film noir and to relocate its origins, to de-Americanize it. What becomes of a movie like *Double Indemnity* in the process of deconstructing film noir, claiming it only exists after the fact, that "the French invented film noir,"[25] that its makers did not know what they were doing. Opinions may differ (as we will continue to illustrate), but facts are facts. *Double Indemnity* exists. Film Noir exists. Moving on.

As to different takes on the same thing, in his 1979 dissertation, Robert Porfirio found a bit more depth than Vernet in the title sequence:

This film begins with Miklós Rózsa's score immediately behind the Paramount logographic and its major motifs continue through the credit titles, which are superimposed over the shadow of a man on crutches walking toward the camera position. This background is as expressionistic as that in The Maltese Falcon *but the surface naturalism of the shadow itself (which bears a marked physical resemblance to actor Fred MacMurray) makes it a non-diegetic index of Walter Neff's later impersonation of the murdered Mr. Dietrichson.*

156

And Rózsa's title score segues quickly into the frenetic background of the film's opening shot (a car careening through the streets of downtown Los Angeles), suturing the title sequence more closely to the diegesis.[26]

At about the same time as our friend Bob was crafting his analysis, the late feminist film theoretician Claire Johnston was also addressing this "suturing":

The title sequence sets the film under the mark of castration: the silhouette of a male figure in hat and overcoat walks towards the camera on crutches. In the next sequence we see Walter Neff, injured and bleeding, entering the offices of his insurance company to begin his "confession" to Keyes...As symbolic father, Keyes' unshakeable access to the truth, to knowledge, resides in his phallic attribute, his "little man," which "ties knots in his stomach" enabling him to spot a phoney claim instantly.[27]

The implication for Johnston and her oedipal underpinning to the Keyes/Neff dynamic, is that beating the system of rules and laws is beating Dad. There is also, Johnston continues, "the repressed homosexual desire of Neff for the idealized father." Is it clear that the father/son aspect of the relationship has a sexual component? Does "I love you, too" take it that far?

Placing any film noir in its social context, by indicating "the male universe of the insurance business," does reflect one key reality of movie making in 1943. Consider for a moment, how L. Greenhouse, whether that was a man or a woman, identified the main characters in his/her analysis chart: their professions for the men, "Oil Man's wife," for Phyllis. Still, while Neff's own little man is clearly filling his larger head with ideas from the first view of the towel-clad Phyllis to what that "honey of an anklet" might mean, does the "contemplation of the female form" always evoke "castration anxiety for the male"?[28] In an article on the film, Sheri Chinen Biesen has a somewhat different take:

Who does he really love?

An extraordinary visual style and a dark ominous abyss surrounds the viewer to convey the film's brooding existential milieu, even from the opening credits of Double Indemnity. *It starts with a menacing silhouette of a man limping on crutches who moves forward to visually swallow the screen until it goes completely black. The black screen in* Double Indemnity *shifts to the murky, late night streets of the noir "urban jungle" of Los Angeles on July 16, 1938. The suspenseful strains of Miklós Rózsa's riveting music score blares a heightened sense of tension and turmoil when the shadowy,*

158

nocturnal expanse is pierced by the stark headlights of a car as it zigzags and nearly collides with other vehicles.[29]

Whatever is in the silhouette, menace, a hobbled man, or the patriarchy limping forward, the evocation is, as Biesen puts it, a "shadowy exemplar of noir visual style."

Some male commentators do buy into Johnston's structure. Keyes "dislikes Phyllis the moment he sees her, perceiving her as in some way a threat to his own relationship with Walter. He is offended by Phyllis' obvious sexuality. Clearly there is a strong connection between the two men...Phyllis is a figure of Machiavellian evil, chilling and reptilian, a castrating Eve in a nightmare inversion of the Garden of Eden myth."[30] An interesting reading, especially since Keyes' raised eyebrow and pointed expression of disdain seem focused on Norton, and once that doofus starts "running with the ball," there is no shot of Keyes for several moments. Insert one of those frowns into the anklet exchange of Neff handing the veiled blonde a glass of water, and you might have something. But Wilder did not do that. If anything, Keyes would not mind echoing Phyllis, "I don't like you, Mr. Norton," and slamming the door on his own way out of the large office. Sure, once the little man tells Keyes that the dame did it, he does not speak of Phyllis with respect, anymore than he did with that other cheater, Gorlopis.

What is seldom discussed is Keyes' own alienation from middle-class values and normal relationships. Cut from the movie is his taunting of Gorlopis about different recipes, for dinner and for insurance claims: "Let's say you came up here to tell me how to make meat loaf. That's all. If you came up here to make an insurance claim, I'd have to turn you over to the law. They'd put you in jail. No wife—no kids...and no meat loaf, Gorlopis!"[31] Keyes is dyspeptic about life: The cause, as always, is his "little man." He came close to marriage once to an unnamed fiancée; but it is Neff who decides "she was a tramp from a long line of tramps." Keyes may think that Neff's current "Margie" drinks out the bottle; but Phyllis took his bourbon in a glass. Keyes does respect the social order in an almost fetishistic manner. There are subtle threats everywhere, the noir underworld that permeates the films in the movement. Does the fetish extend to matches, or is it true that "they always explode in my pockets"? What are the odds?

Putting castration anxieties aside, it may be that when writers venture into such territory, among the figures in the carpet (or the academic big heads looming like the moai of Rapa Nui behind any essay where plot becomes diegesis) are the likes of semiotician Christian Metz and psychologist Jacques Lacan. These folks have a slightly more convoluted view of how movies work. Except, of course, that the first-person storytellers in both novel and film are not Jamesian characters fixated on finding out secret meanings.

Briefly back to basics: no movies work without the audience for whom they are made. Phenomenology aside (if a movie gets made and no one ever sees it, is it really a movie?), you could ask who made *Double Indemnity*? Is Billy Wilder its auteur? Or would the author be Paramount Pictures through its diverse employees. As a work for hire and in terms of copyright, Paramount owns the product (or, at least, it did until it sold the old titles in its library to Universal, which has somewhat indelicately and anachronistically slapped its own logo at the head of the movie). We believe it has been demonstrated so far that the answer, the search for a maker, is not quite so simple. But in order to discuss the impact of *Double Indemnity* as a work of fiction, and let's say of art, also, it is necessary to presume some "one" made it, that there is an "intentionality" behind everything we see in the movie. With that in mind, a few more examples from a feminist perspective follow.

"Film noir is a male fantasy," asserts Janey Place in *Women in Film Noir*, and in "*Double Indemnity* Phyllis' legs (with a gold anklet significantly bearing her name) dominate Walter's and our own memory of her as the camera follows her descent down the stairs, framing only her heels and silk-stockinged calves."[32]

Writing in the same anthology about a "Woman's Place," Sylvia Harvey extends the shared perspective, in which suspension of disbelief means that narrator Neff stages the scenes for the viewers. "The family home in *Double Indemnity* is the place where three people who hate each other [the artificial domestic unit of Phyllis, Dietrichson, and Lola] spend endless

"It is only under Neff's gaze that her legs become the focal point."

boring evenings together. The husband does not merely not notice his wife, he ignores her sexually; so that it is only under Neff's gaze that her legs become the focal point of both the room as Neff sees it and the composition of the frame."[33]

Twenty years later in "Lounge Time," Vivian Sobchack embraces the perspective of chronotype created by Russian theorist Mikhail Bakhtin, that "locality serves as the starting point for the creative imagination. But this is not a piece of human history...this is a piece of historical time condensed in space."[34] In these terms, "The suburban house into which Phyllis Dietrichson invites insurance agent Walter Neff is merely a house: its furniture plain, its decorations sparse and impersonal, motel-like. It doesn't look lived in.

Indeed, its interior decoration is best described in a line of dialogue offered by a character about a house in a later film noir, *The Big Heat* (1953): 'Hey, I like this. Early nothing.'"[35]

Another two decades later, Imogen Sara Smith adds refinements: "the classic California Spanish-style house with its ersatz historicism stands for the false promise of success that leads people to lie, cheat, and kill. Phyllis Dietrichson has murdered to get her dream home, and now is ready to murder again to escape it. The dark, somber furnishings—Turkish carpets, heavy carved chairs and wrought-iron banisters, thick drapes—and the dim, dusty lighting in these interiors create the sense of a suffocating tomb. Phyllis complains that her husband keeps her shut up, 'on a leash so tight I can't breathe.' A pall of inert boredom hangs in the air of the living room; goldfish circle in a small bowl on the piano. Stanwyck appreciated the power of these sets, recalling, 'You could smell that death was in the air. You understood why she wanted to get out of there, away, no matter how.'"[36]

There are no temporary milieus in *Double Indemnity*, just "normal" home and work locations (the Dietrichson house, which is a workplace for Neff, his apartment, and the offices of Pacific All Risk). Some commentators yet to be discussed have put a spin on the work milieu, but for Sobchack the other places just don't fit into "lounge time." Unlike the true crime from which it sprang, there are no bars or hotels. The film may be "linked irrevocably to noir but poses problems to its particular urban iconography... which does not evoke Phyllis Dietrichson, pushing a shopping cart up and down the aisles of a supermarket, wearing dark glasses and planning the murder of her husband with Walter Neff over canned goods."[37]

Phyllis does not actually push a shopping cart, but the point is apt. Brief moments at the drive-in and bowling alley notwithstanding, the market is a public place rife with atypical resonances. How many of their fellow shoppers are having similar discussions? Surely the underlying irony of middle-class murder is simple: that it is middle class, not arising out of a desperate need for money or part of an ongoing criminal enterprise. Fatality or mischance is as much at play for Neff as it is for Lucia Harper in *Reckless Moment* (1949) or Chris Cross in *Scarlet Street*—1944 (or Robinson's hapless professor in *Woman in the Window,* also 1944). Neff and Cross get embroiled so deeply that eventually the only way out is to kill the woman who has enmeshed them.

In her essay, "What Is This Thing Called Noir," Linda Brookover addresses two poses seen above including the market scene: "Fred MacMurray's sneer as Walter Neff and Barbara Stanwyck's brazen, square-shouldered sexuality are keys to their outlook in *Double Indemnity.* Their underlying emotional estrangement is reinforced by the staging. Two typical moments are found in the scene stills of the couple side-by-side in a market but not facing each other or her hiding behind his apartment door. How would the audience have perceived them if they had acted and been posed this way throughout the film?"[38]

One of the enduring ironies of Double Indemnity, *which is arguably one of the most important noir films of the classic period, is the casting of its principals. In a credit block of stars that included Fred MacMurray, Barbara Stanwyck, and Edward G. Robinson, how many viewers not already familiar with the plot from James M. Cain's novel would have expected the star of* Little Caesar *to be the only good guy? The tough-talking, sometimes shady characters portrayed by Barbara Stanwyck in* The Lady Eve, Meet John Doe, *and* Ball of Fire *were not exactly shrinking violets (what heroine of Howard Hawks or Preston Sturges could be); but compared to Phyllis Dietrichson they were choir girls. And long before portraying the craven second mate in* The Caine Mutiny, *Fred MacMurray was more likely to be trading jibes with Claudette Colbert than tossing bodies on train tracks.*[39]

The issue of audience expectation raised by Elizabeth Ward in her article, "The Camouflaged Femme Fatale," aptly asks the question: is not any character nuanced before the fact by the past roles of its actor? Does this not make it easier for the audience to identify with the criminal couple than with "the old crouch" who defends the rules. This is also why performance

163

usually trumps milieu in terms of diegetic impact, how the meanderings of the movie's plot are redirected in conformance with, or contrary to, what the genre or casting (and in fairness the trailers and ad art used in the marketing) initially suggest to the viewer.

For Biesen style, angle and lighting, trumps décor. Night lighting from the car in the streets to the office provides stark "contrast to the first images of his flashback memory—his initial approach to Phyllis' house in broad daylight as kids play outside on a sunny afternoon—before entering her house splintered by venetian blinds...visual bars of entrapment splintering over Neff to suggest his doom. He is shown in a position of helplessness: he looks up at her, shot with an extreme power angle and backlit, so that she is visually ablaze and cinematically fetishized by his gaze as she is scantily clad in a towel standing at the top of the stairs towering over and peering down at him."[40]

In *Rethinking the Femme Fatale in Film Noir*, Julie Grossman takes issue with the commentator who called Phyllis a "reptilian, castrating Eve" and also asserts "the immutable noir logic that a 'femme fatale' cannot be humanized: see Barbara Stanwyck in *Double Indemnity*."[41]

The "immutability" of noir logic is dependent upon a false assertion of the fixedness of the "femme fatale." Indeed I want to contest this claim [and] also want to point out [that] very few "femme fatales" really fit the strict model of evil, opaque woman, who "cannot be humanized," which explains why Phyllis Dietrichson becomes canonized as the prototype."[42]

As Grossman later elaborates, like certain male characters in Victorian literature (and in Cain), "Like Jude [the obscure], Walter Neff is seduced not just by a woman, Phyllis Dietrichson as the 'femme fatale,' but also the homosocial fantasy that he can compete with Keyes ('It's something I had been thinking about for years')."[43] *Double Indemnity*'s main characters are all vertices in a complex triangle of emotions. Elisabeth Bronfen concludes that Neff participates in this "triangulation of desire...not because he wants the

Another triangulation: the oppressive and clueless husband Mr. Dietrichson, looking back at this fate.

money or the women, as he claims in his voice-over confession. Instead, he has been obsessed with finding a way to trick his company and prove that he is cleverer at fraud" than Keyes is in detecting it.[44]

A few commentators have grappled with the subject/object tension in *Double Indemnity*, "*Double Indemnity* dramatizes this distancing from and yet reflection of ordinary experience. Narrator of the flashback in which he is the principal character, Walter is both the subject and object of the resulting narrative." As Barton Palmer continues, there are two faces of Neff in both "the experiencing-I and the narrating-I" and in the split between professional agent and murderous scammer, and he "fills both roles simultaneously until he reconciles a third self—confessed murderer—that reconciles them."[45] One might note, however, that the "confessed murderer" is the second self (the first rides the elevator) to appear. Does this third self influence how the events related in flashback are portrayed? Was Phyllis, as Neff recollects her and presents her to the moviegoer, ablaze and fetishized?

Clearly within his role as narrator and over the course of the movie, Neff's inclinations toward Phyllis can shift from physical attraction to murderous repulsion. Those parallel the movement Palmer cites, from "law-abiding citizen [to] cold-blooded murderer." Almost all of the movies' scenes are effectively first person (significant exceptions are to come), in that the viewer only sees what Neff saw. But whatever his conscious or unconsciousness thoughts may have been in the moment (anxieties or lack of them included), however Phyllis objectively appeared on that balcony, and in every subsequent encounter, every detail is filtered through Neff's memory. For Jay Telotte, "*Double Indemnity* does more than simply trace out the consequences of an impulse that finds its source in a mysterious, unknowable force: desire impelled by an alluring enigma, Phyllis eventually proves no more enigmatic than Walter, and even less able to deceive Keyes; meanwhile Walter's voice-over makes him seem less mysterious."[46]

"Having Neff recite the past events [means] that the plot resolution is known from the outset," notes Claire Johnston, "The first person narration presents itself as a 'confession' which reveals the truth of the narrative of events [and] it purports to provide the knowledge of how things really happened."[47] In a movie, scenes on the screen do more than "purport." Absent a contrary indication what is seen is true. Of course, there can be flashback lies or flashbacks from two or more perspectives where events differ; but the conventions of expression in motion pictures, then and now, do not presume that any character's recollection is faulty. As already noted, what is known when any movie begins varies from viewer to viewer. But that does not mean "the plot resolution is known from the outset." As early as 1944, standard expectations had already been refined for a noir film. The ad art and the trailer played with and against those expectations. Could not someone who had bought a ticket based on previews *and* having read the novel, expect the first-person, the scheme, the crime, ending in Cain's double suicide? Except, of course, this movie is not a discovered manuscript. Neff is not dead at the end.

Many commentators presume Neff's death. Schickel says "dead," Johnston, J.P. Telotte, Phillip Sipiora, and others, say "dying." Is he really dying? He can't make it to the elevator that "somebody moved a couple of miles away"; but help is on the way. And, however ruefully he takes a puff of the cigarette that Keyes lights for him, it is reasonable to presume this will not be his last coffin nail. These commentators may opine from any perspective, may discover vectors in which Neff's relationship is "open" with Keyes, "closed" with Phyllis, or vice versa. Neff can be Oedipus or Jason or Aegisthus or Adam. Phyllis can be Eve or Clytemnestra or Medea or Jocasta, and the Erinyes (guess those furious sisters, who *were* born of castration, would be embodied by Keyes) can nip at their heels from beginning to end. But in this drama, Sam Gorlopis is the only Greek character, ancient or modern.

On the one hand, the trailer is remarkably explicit. "It's MURDER!" says a graphic enlarging over the scene of the body on the tracks until if fills the frame. Next a large chunk of the opening Dictaphone scene that gives the full who, what, when, and why. Not clear enough? Well, how about seeing the couple clinch on the couch, after which a stentorian trailer voice intones: "From the moment they met it was murder." Then let's hear from Keyes: "A murder's never perfect. It always comes apart sooner or later." That's just the first minute. Next how about a piece of the corridor scene—who cares about undercutting the suspense—just to make it clear. Want all the details? Then come see "Paramount's SHOCKING...SUSPENSE-FILLED MASTERPIECE OF *LOVE...AND MURDER!*" Did we make it clear, it's about murder...and some love. We don't have the exact term for it, but you will certainly agree that it's classic something. On the other hand, as many commentators have also said, what is held back is the how. So, epistemology aside, the "how" is the key to *Double Indemnity.*

While most writers agree "how" is the focus of the narration, both Neff's tone and his elisions are also significant. At the very beginning of his discussion of *Double Indemnity* Gerd Gemünden cites an anomaly:

The modern Medea, Phyllis hides the revolver, as she waits for her wayfaring lover Walter.

The sequence between Neff's departure from the Dietrichson home and his arrival at his apartment building uses only a few seconds of screen time, and at most represents a couple of hours of Neff's afternoon, thus leaving much of the time between his brief mid-afternoon visit with Phyllis and a sunset in May unaccounted for. This omission by the narrator stands in contrast to his otherwise meticulous efforts toward situating his story within precise

168

temporal and spatial coordinates; it suggests that Neff either no longer remembers his precise whereabouts this afternoon, or that he may even have been unaware of the passage of time. The image of displacement and alienation which the anonymous locales visited by Neff evoke is thus reinforced by the unhinging of the subjectivity of the narrating voice which so far has been anchoring the tale unfolding in front of us.[48]

Like several other writers before, Gemünden later quotes Jerry Wald's glib comment about the impact of *Double Indemnity*'s structure: "From now on every picture I make will be done in flashback."[49]

First- or third-person flashbacks did become a notable trend in film noir. Besides Wald's adaptation of Cain's *Mildred Pierce* (1945), other notable examples were the Keyes-like insurance investigator in *The Killers* (1946), *Out of the Past*, and the multiplicity of voices in *Brute Force* (both 1947). Obviously, the major utility of such a structure, especially in a complex narrative with many characters, is ease of scene selection, presenting the viewer only what the character flashes back to. More importantly, what it does in *Double Indemnity* and other key noirs is permit ironic introspection by or about a doomed figure. To quote another adulterous and criminal conspirator's narration five years later: "From the start, it all went one way. It was in the cards, or it was fate, or a jinx or whatever you wanna call it—but right from the start" (Steve Thompson in *Criss Cross*—1949). As the wounded Neff lurches into his office building, from the start there is no question that it already has gone wrong. Was that a surprise for more viewers then or now (particularly those whose expectations have not been tuned up by a host's introduction)? And did/does it matter?

Put aside his inference of the "invention" of noir by French critics (to which we will return below), for James Naremore, exterior contexts and alternate endings supersede the literal how and express "the theme of industrialized dehumanization…the tendency of modern society to turn workers into zombies or robots."[50] He cites the influence of the Weimar Republic on the sets, especially the empty desks in the dark space below, devoid of its "mechanized" employees, when Neff returns to the office. In film noir, shots such as that are not about the symbolic transformation of workers into drudges (*The Crowd*), sheep (*Modern Times*), or zombies (were zombies that much of a trend in 1943?[51]). It might be better to say (as per Biesen's notion of "dark abyss") that what is reinforced by this staging is Neff's sense of isolation, out of synch with his normal presence in that space, wounded as he passes it with only a slender guardrail preventing him from stumbling and tumbling down into that darkness below.

Certainly, Wilder was an admirer of director King Vidor's *The Crowd* (1927) and familiar with Weimar aesthetics, German expressionism, etc. On the symbolic montages of Chaplin's *Modern Times* (1936), he was silent. Unlike his contemporary Otto Preminger, Wilder might not have called such high-flown interpretations about film sets "nonsense."[52] What he did say to Bob Porfirio back in 1975 was "It is not that I am tossing up and down in my bed like Goethe conceiving art, and wind is playing in my hair, and I plan it all out to the last detail. No. It's happenstance."[53]

Naremore moves to search for "behavioral conformity" in other settings, such as "the big store [that] makes them anonymous, invisible to other shoppers" is "the most surreal mechanical reproduction."[54] But the store is, by any normal standard, small; and the plotters are hardly invisible since they keep blocking access for those actually shopping, whose only complaint ("Why do they have to put what I want on the top shelf?") is minor bleating from someone irritated by false conventions.

For Naremore, Neff's escape after the disturbing suggestions from Phyllis are also telling. He "bowls along in an enormous bowling alley" with its "identical lanes."[55] Whatever its size, this venue does offer the distraction of regulated, physical endeavor, "get my mind thinking about something else for a while," anything but Phyllis. Of course, in the single angle, Neff is in lane five, it hardly seems enormous, and there are others present, a couple of pinsetters and three bowlers including a female extra who, like Phyllis, sports a floral print top. Ominously as Neff and that woman bend towards each other to take new balls from the rack, there is a dissolve to a night exterior so that the last few frames that the viewer sees of the alley are enveloped

Neff about to make himself useful to an actual shopper (Constance Purdy, holding child's hand) and get the item off the top shelf.

in blackness, then superimposed headlights sweep by, evoking the dark pull of the noir underworld and the inevitability of Phyllis appearing again. As William Robertson puts it, "Suddenly, in this otherwise murky tale of passion and murder flashes the image of Fred hurling a bowling ball down the hardwood with what can only be called balletic grace...Bowling is a bright beacon of chuckleheaded salvation burning the dark existential American

171

night, which noir characters can either follow to safety or spurn."[56] The later drive-in café is a process shot, a flattened and dematerialized physical reality into which Neff, sitting in his car, literally in another time and place, cannot escape.

As it would be for Steve Thompson and later narrators in noir, there is no question that fate is in play for Walter in one of the classic period's earliest productions. If it were not already subconsciously clear to the viewer, it is explicitly mentioned in an office voice-over, the fulcrum point of the entire movie: "Maybe those fates they say watch over you had gotten together to give me a way out." Of course, even as he says this, Neff knows what's coming: the determinative telephone call from Phyllis that locks in his destiny. Perhaps the most compelling of several possible reasons for Neff to reject the job Keyes offers him in that scene is not completely clear—the freedom of sales, the ill-gotten money and/or the woman—but the fate in play is not "mechanical" destiny, not the context of *Metropolis* (1927) but more akin to such other Lang movies as *Der Müde Tod* (1921) or even the ironically titled *You Only Live Once* (1937).

Finally Naremore writes about the "death chamber," as if he had actually seen the sequence (and later suggests that might be an option, except that it has long vanished from the Paramount film vaults); but it's clear he has not read the sequence in the script carefully in suggesting that a doctor enters the chamber (a suicidal act) rather than "listens on a stethoscope connected with the outlet in the wall the gas chamber."[57] As already detailed, the sequence was not shot "at considerable expense," its cost being close to what was budgeted at an early stage on a movie that came in well below its final budget. It is clear to us that the lost scene is not Keyes' lonely walk, but the irony of fishing for matches in his vest pocket. That may be crushing for Keyes but nothing in this scene "would [clearly] have thrown a shadow over everything that preceded it." It is far likelier that after the moment of transference with Keyes matching Neff, that fumbling in a vest pocket would be a false coda, needless embellishment of a statement already made more simply and powerfully in its focus in the end on Neff's mischance and Keyes' rueful triumph. Or as Jesse Schlotterbeck puts it:

I disagree with James Naremore's argument that Double Indemnity *would be a stronger film with its omitted conclusion, in which Walter Neff is executed in a gas chamber. In the film, as it was released, Walter simply accepts a cigarette from his boss, Keyes, in the hallway of the insurance building where he recorded his confession and accepts the fact that he will either die before trial or die in jail. These moments are days away when the final shot fades out, and yet the scene's haunting quality comes from the suggestion of entrapment, death, and violence that are to follow rather than shown on-screen.*[58]

In the end it does not matter why Sequence E is gone, whether it was Breen's vacillation—punishment of criminals, yes, per his March memo, BUT not in an "unduly gruesome" manner per his December 1 memo, sent after the scene was shot—or the fact that Wilder never intended to use this alternate scene. Nor does it matter what Wilder said to Ivan Moffat that one of the "best scenes that I have ever shot in my whole life was the execution of Fred MacMurray in *Double Indemnity.*" If he really thought that, and he still never appended it to the movie, even for a preview—why not? Was it because, as Wilder continued to Moffat, "But then the scene was unnecessary. We ended it when he collapses and you hear, in the distance, the sound of the ambulance or the police car."[59] You decide.

Somehow, Naremore concludes that without the death chamber, *Double Indemnity* is a "lighter entertainment" than the novel. Should either work be viewed through comparisons such as this? What Cain did in prose, what the various creative contributors did on the film, have been there to read and to view for 80 years or more. Distinctions made by such serious writers as Graham Greene notwithstanding—are *A Gun for Hire* and *Brighton Rock* mere entertainments?—the form of cinema that the French first described as noir may be more akin to Greene's "thrillers" but are hardly light. From its true crime roots to its Zola-esque mores, *Double Indemnity* (with or without the excised ending) follows a line from American naturalist literature through the powerfully visual metaphors in the heart of darkness that is film noir.

"Closer than that, Walter." The script and actual final scene of the movie, despite the alternate ending having been shot. Wilder: "In the distance you already hear the sirens, so you know what the outcome is going to be."

One could agree that later noir films—*Scarlet Street, Out of the Past* (1947), *Criss Cross*, or *Gun Crazy* (1950)—are as powerfully grim in their conclusions but, from even before film noir got its official name, *Double Indemnity* would have been and remains at the top of any list of darkest of the dark (or, if one prefers, *les plus noirs du noir*).

As regards Naremore's comparison with Cain, the movie substitutes the novel's purer sociopathy for a Phyllis that is less insane and more conflicted, a reach back past Cain to Ruth Snyder and her middle-class murder. Which is why, where Huff and Phyllis Nirdlinger were a car wreck waiting to happen, Neff and Mrs. Dietrichson are less explicitly so. It may be too fine a distinction to say an encounter can be fateful without being deterministic but that is the line along which the movie's narration walks. That is why Cain's murder might smell of "billy goat" (as Chandler claimed) but the movie's scheme has the scent of honeysuckle, why its sense of doom is not mechanistic but merely cheerless, situated in that bleak landscape of ostensible normality where at any moment the power of a noir underworld that lies beneath the surface can reach up and drag the unwary down to hell.

And, of course, the filmmakers all realized at every stage that the last layer through which a touch of sociopathy might be added was performance. The script says that while Dietrichson's neck is being broken, "Phyllis drives on and never turns her head. She stares straight in front of her. Her teeth are clenched." Compare that to the scene that Schlotterbeck describes:

The struggle between the two men is left entirely off-screen. Instead, a long-take close-up of Phyllis's face shows her determined and cold expression. Bright lights from passing cars occasionally flash across her face. The viewer looks for a sign of some emotion; a hint of a smirk appears as the shot dissolves, but just barely. The drama of this close-up is expressed more by what is not shown rather than what is. Mr. Dietrichson is brutally strangled in off-screen space. Whatever Mrs. Dietrichson's thoughts or feelings as this happened, too, are mostly withheld in Stanywck's icy performance. This, the climactic murder scene from Billy Wilder's Double Indemnity, *is clearly violent and disturbing yet also works within recognizable limits. The scene could be said to typify one of the most fascinating aspects of noirs: the fact that film noirs are considered particularly violent, brutal films and that, also, the entire noir cycle occurs under a fully active and enforced censorship code.*[60]

Perhaps what continues to make *Double Indemnity* still relevant, as a movie and a film noir, 80 years later is the ongoing interest from critical commentators at every level. Yes, some of the observations are a trifle facile, even off-the-mark. "Phyllis is the avaricious but romantic cipher, we know only what we see of her in the moment—the plotting against Mr. Dietrichson, of her presumed desire for Walter, of her possession of a gun in the end."[61] To make the important distinction, however filtered, there are times that we do see her in the moment that are theoretically beyond the scope of the narration. The two most obvious, non-subjective moments are approaching Neff's apartment while he is inside and preparing the house, including putting the revolver under the chair cushion (impossible to miss even in the dimmed light given the intensity of Rózsa's cue). In the moment, those are not known to Neff; but after he is shot, he can fill in the gap of where the gun must have been.

The only triangulation of the three leads.

176

Does she fear Keyes will suddenly shout, "I see you hiding there, you murderess!"? Or does she sense that male bonding?

While Neff may not see her arriving for the scene with Keyes in Neff's apartment, Phyllis has telephoned Neff. He knows she is "coming up"; but MacMurray restricts the character's anxiety with occasional eyes glancing right while Keyes is suffering indigestion in his living room. The most telling of the objective moments are like the one Jesse Schlotterbeck describes, an expression on the face of Stanwyck as Phyllis that Neff can never see. Immediately after Keyes leaves, inside the apartment, the script suggests that Neff and Phyllis are facing each other. But Wilder stages it differently. Phyllis is behind him, her mouth and chin covered by his shoulder for parts of her comments about being pulled apart.

177

Whose idea was this staging? Absent an indication to the contrary (from the actors), one must presume that it was Wilder. As regards what is seen during Dietrichson's killing, Wilder did cite his interest in off-screen murder as inspired by Fritz Lang's *M*.[62] The killing is scripted as "CLOSEUP - PHYLLIS' FACE ONLY."[63] The other aspect, the reaction from Phyllis, was that something she brought to the table or also Wilder's idea? Inside the apartment with Keyes, the script indicates "another long pause, agonizing for Neff." Was it MacMurray's idea to downplay the agony or Wilder's or both? The "triangulation" of the three leads in the corridor is the only time all of them are ever alone in the same shot. They are, in fact, all in a four shot with Norton in his office, but Keyes and Neff have their backs to the camera. Tellingly in that shot, in the two dimensions of the frame, Keyes separates Neff from Phyllis. In the corridor, Neff and the door separate Phyllis from Keyes. Not in the script but added? The cigar bit. In that regard "The idea," Wilder said a few times, "was to write a love story between the two men and a sexual involvement with the woman."[64]

Even before that interview, he elaborated to Bob Porfirio, "I tried to work with that because I was fully aware that the greatest love story in American pictures was never Clark Gable and Vivien Leigh, or with Joan Crawford and Lana Turner. It was Clark Gable and Spencer Tracy. You get that thing working, and I knew that this thing was going to work. I was right; but I could have been wrong, too."[65] With the cigar bit added in the corridor, even as Phyllis is right there, Neff and Keyes have their affectionate interchange. There are no close-ups indicated for this scene; but Wilder shot and inserted one of Phyllis behind the door, that he cuts in smack in the middle of the cigar being lit.

Can Phyllis even see what's going on? Is that anxious expression on Stanwyck's face about straining to hear? Does she fear Keyes will suddenly shout, "I see you hiding there, you murderess!"? Or does she sense that male bonding? And, of course, inside the apartment, as a still-agitated Neff stands there with his back to her, in a long take, the camera dollies in slowly, constricting the frame. Finally, Phyllis has to force him to turn and face her then accuses him: "You don't really care whether we see each other or not." His reply, "Shut up, baby." Who does he really love?

As she stands behind him, Phyllis realizes Walter is afraid.

What is cut and what is added are for the most part far less obvious than the missing death chamber. For example, shot but discarded was a moment in his office where Neff "slowly crosses to the water cooler" with a blood-stained handkerchief and is interrupted by a janitor. So none of the cuts back to Neff narrating are interrupted until Keyes arrives. Whether made on the set or in the editing room, it is possible that Doane Harrison participated in such decisions. Does it matter? It is reasonable to assume that all such decisions were in line with Wilder's overall vision for the movie. Wilder also talked about style choices with Bob Porfirio:

You said Preminger took issue with you about Expressionism... when you used a key concept: looking for patterns. Now, you must understand that a man who makes movies and certainly somebody like myself that makes all kinds of movies, works in different styles. Have you seen a lot of Expressionist paintings? That was my milieu for a while in the 1930s. Berlin was that kind of town, like living in the set from an early gangster picture.[66]

One of the reasons that Richard Schickel gives for the importance of *Double Indemnity* is its authority. From where does that spring? Its diegetic or narrative voice has diverse roots, true crime, Cain's spin on the story, Chandler's crafting of dialogue, etc. In terms of film noir, Wilder added:

> *If you give ten directors the same scene, the same set, the same cameraman, it's still going to come out differently. Certainly,* Caligari *had a style that you would call film noir. But I would also think* Oedipus *is a play noir, right? [Georges] Simenon has written many novels that you would call "roman noir." I think Zola as well has a lot of these dark elements. The question is whether you have a catharsis at the end. In what category would you put, for instance, King Vidor's* The Crowd? *Is that "naturalistic" or noir? There is no big overall theme of my oeuvre, I say that laughingly because what is it? You're trying to make as good and as entertaining a picture as you possibly can. If you have any kind of style, the discerning members of the audience will detect it.*[67]

How does the noir style function in *Double Indemnity* and overall? We have addressed that question before: Here is a list of eight motion pictures released over a period of just 18 months from May 1947 through November 1948: *Framed, Brute Force, The Unsuspected, Out of the Past, Pitfall, The Big Clock, Cry of the City,* and *Force of Evil.* It doesn't take much more than the titles to tell these are film noir; but the details of the creative credits for all eight—that is, producer, director, writers, cinematographer, composer, and actors—are what is truly remarkable.

Before anything was recorded on film, eight different scripts were written by fourteen different people and six scripts were adapted from novels or original stories by others. Eight different producers oversaw the development of these screenplays into movies working with eight different directors

180

and eight different cinematographers. This octet of films starred twenty different actors and was scored by eight different composers. Finally, each film was released by a different one of the eight major studios. These are eight ostensibly unrelated motion pictures from completely diverse hands with one cohesive visual style. Such a cohesion is clearly not coincidental. And among the titles that preceded them, *Double Indemnity* more than any other movie was the seed of the noir movement.[68]

In terms of nuanced performances also, *Double Indemnity* brought together prototypes of how any actor should portray the fatal woman, the investigator, and the ill-fated male seduced into crime. Underplaying every scene to the hilt, Fred MacMurray "never dreamed it would be the best picture I ever made."[69] A grumpy, glib perfectionist who cannot keep the ashes off his vest or find his own match inspired his perfect line readings on every take from Edward G. Robinson, who wanted to portray Keyes again. Stanwyck, playing the part of a woman who is playing a part, owning every second of the scheming without tipping it, an enormous challenge for the most skilled of actors—did she not expect that Academy Award nomination?

Anyone who researches the chronology of the film noir movement, of its content and of its defining characteristics, will eventually stumble across those who would deny that film noir exists. It was created they say, after the fact. Yes, those French critics in 1945 saw something; but the people who made the movies did know what kind of movie they were making, of what sort of phenomenon they were a part.

Forget for a moment that movements exist because of their contents, because of the works that define them. We have used the example of French Impressionist painting before and noted how a second-rate playwright and disdainful critic named Louis Leroy coined the term as an insult.[70] Should it not be sufficient by now to say that no amount of either pedantic hogwash or anti-intellectual posturing can convince a sensible moviegoer that the makers of *Double Indemnity* (of any film noir) did not know what they were doing. All right, maybe Ruth and Judd were a tad disorganized, but they weren't out to create art. Cain and Chandler and Wilder and Pereira and Head and Seitz and Harrison and Rózsa—each and every one of them knew

181

what kind of fiction they were crafting. Wilder had his own fairly concise list, which to recap from various comments above, included: *Caligari*, *The Crowd*, German Expressionist painters, *M*, American gangster films, *Oedipus*, and Zola.

Wilder also knew that imposing a style need not be a conscious act. As he told Bob Porfirio about film noir, "I do not imagine Monet painting the landscapes and telling himself, 'Now, wait a minute, I'm an Impressionist. Therefore I must do it this way.' He didn't think. He painted…If you have any kind of style, the discerning ones will detect it."[71] Call it a thriller, call it a psychological or "tough melodrama,"[72] call it crime film, call it film noir—whether or not they had a consensus term for it yet, filmmakers of the classic period knew what it was.

———————◆———————

But her heart belongs to just one;
Her heart belongs to Tangerine.
Johnny Mercer
"Tangerine"[73]

Victor Schertzinger's orchestral arrangement for "Tangerine" is wafting into the Dietrichson living room from some "radio up the street." When Walter Neff decides "I don't like that music anymore," the double meaning is clear. He is no longer dancing to Phyllis' tune and that noise is annoying. Many of the movie's original audience must have known the lyrics and perhaps saw the third meaning: Phyllis only cares for herself. So, it's no surprise that "I never loved you, Walter, not you or anybody else. I'm rotten to the heart, I used you just like you said. That's all you ever meant to me." Nor is it a surprise—a lead slug got into his shoulder somehow—that she shoots him. Once, not twice (Why? Because she really did love him down deep? As she says.). And wordlessly, without the script's whispered "Walter!"

James Maxfield argues that Neff does resemble Cain's Huff in his suicidal behavior at the movie's ending. "Walter consciously aims to kill Phyllis

182

Phyllis waits for Neff to arrive, while "Tangerine" wafts in through the window.

and frame Nino for the crime. Unconsciously he is presenting Phyllis with the opportunity to kill him. Why else would he make it clear that he intended to kill her—and then turn his back on her?"[74] Good question. Janet Bergstrom believes that this "shootout in the near darkness between Neff and the woman he can stop himself from loving, except in that way, feels like a double suicide."[75] That may be, but isn't it Phyllis who is suddenly suicidal when she lets Neff take the revolver from her hand? After deducing that Phyllis wants him dead, does Neff not anticipate? "Like so many noir heroes, Walter foolishly believes that he can absolve himself of his guilt by killing the woman who inspired his murderous fantasy," writes Elisabeth Bronfen. The problem: "because she astutely anticipated that he has come to kill her,"[76] the viewer has seen that her preparations include a pint-sized nickel-plated revolver.

Simply put, bleeding as he dictates, Walter must realize that his "little man" got him shot because it was less astute than Keyes'. Sure, he does shoot her, twice. But all this tough talk and gun blasting belies what Joe

183

Sistrom said at the start of the process that "all characters in B-pictures are too smart."[77] "I thought you were a shade less dumb than the rest of this outfit," Keyes clarifies his process as the fulcrum scene ends. He stands a foot shorter in a medium shot and accepts a match from Neff, who has refused to switch from sales to claims. "Guess I was wrong. You're not smarter. You're just a little taller." One has to ask: would this line have worked if Alan Ladd had accepted the part? Elizabeth Ward believes that "Keyes represents Wilder in the film. Wilder is about the same size as Robinson, and also the type of funny character who would have said things like, 'You're not smarter, you're just a little taller.' "[78]

Being a shade less dumb is what leads Neff to bad choices. Bronfen casually compares Neff to "so many noir heroes." There is no ironic cut back to the wounded Neff in that office possibly thinking about what Keyes said then. "As the noir anti-hero confesses his guilt, the process of self-dissolution leads to the further process of questioning and subverting the triumph of the enterprising individual, here given its darkest, most despairing perspective."[79] Is he film noir's first anti-hero or would that be Bogart as "Mad Dog" Roy Earle in *High Sierra* (1941)? Despite being a career criminal, Earle actually lives by a code. Neff is no career criminal, just a misguided opportunist, or was he looking to score all along, or did fate point the finger? There are no simple answers.

V.F. Perkins asserted that the way any film succeeds is by "making the spectator an accomplice and not merely a witness."[80] Yes, for the PCA's L. Greenhouse, it is clear that for Walter and Phyllis, the "X" mark belongs in the "unsympathetic character" column. Still the audience is an accomplice, wanting the La Salle car to turn over, wanting that outward-opening door to conceal Phyllis in the corridor, perhaps even wanting Neff—because he is tall, an affable guy, even if only just a shade less dumb—to make it to the elevator and on to Mexico. Call him a hero or anti-hero, Perkins' formula works for both, and for films both noirs et blancs.

Call Phyllis an abused spouse or a femme fatale. "Phyllis deftly alters her persona to attract and manipulate men with the goal of one day leading an independent, self-determined life without them," suggests Anne Dennon.

184

Phyllis couldn't pull the trigger a second time and so…

"However, the events she sets in motion quickly escape her control. For the femme fatale, both the performed identity and its consequences are predetermined in a society constructed to first allow for divergence and then cancel its effects."[81]

In the last scene at Jerry's Market, Phyllis plays the part, surveys the items, then peers up at the tall man over a stack of boxed macaroni and calmly reminds Neff. "I loved you, Walter. And I hated him. But I wasn't going to do anything about it, not until I met you. I only wanted him dead."

Walter sputters back, "I was the one who fixed it so he was dead. Is that what you're telling me?" What she's telling him is that now his course is fixed. "And nobody's pulling out." She pointedly removes the sunglasses: "Straight down the line for both of us, remember." This time Wilder does add irony. Before a dissolve back to the confession, the camera dollies to a very tight closeup, as Neff swallows hard and does remember "about that trolley car ride."

Call Keyes a triumphant claims man (who is also "a doctor and a bloodhound and a cop and a judge and jury and a father confessor") or a bereft parent. "I'm a very great man," he announces to Neff, "Papa has it all figured out." The script had a lot more dialogue between Dietrichson and Phyllis in the car before the murder including a jibe about "that rope he hands out for cigars" that could well allude to Keyes' brand of stogie.[82] For all his eccentricities, Keyes does not follow the William Ockham model in this thinking. Rather his "little man" makes him something of an occult teleologist, who can work back from conflicting facts and deduce the details of "as fancy piece of homicide as anybody ever ran into. Smart, tricky. Almost perfect, but…"

Double Indemnity has inspired and, long after this book, will continue to inspire a lot of ink. And a lot of different perspectives. The author of the study *In a Lonely Place* says that he is "driven by a determination to reconcile" opposing camps of "theorists" and "historians."[83] Then as regards *Double Indemnity* he proceeds to rehash the "theorists" (?) who focus on Freudian constructs (with a measure of Metzian and Lacanian overlays) from castration anxiety to superego. A footnote regarding the latter claims to discover the "extent to which Neff has internalized Keyes as superego" in the homonyms "keys" and "Keyes." Cute concept. But more than a bit silly.

It's possible, Chandler and Wilder chuckled to themselves, said "let's foreshadow the claims manager being Neff's Freudian conscience," when they came up with the line, "I always carry my own keys," riffing off the character name that comes from Cain. Or maybe the writers just thought it was the kind of cheap *bon mot* that Neff might throw out when told the liquor cabinet was locked up. Is "Wilder's cinematic schema," as Phillip Sipiora asserts, "integrally related to fundamental principles of phenomenology, the philosophical home of perception and personal relationships for the last century"?[84] Attribution of a "cinematic schema" may be a tad auteurist but, sure, why not? Many interpretations are possible, but remember what Wilder said to Bob Porfirio about happenstance. Of course, Wilder was a raconteur to the end; and four years after he spoke with Bob Porfirio, he told Elizabeth Ward that film noir was not his cup of tea.[85]

That was Wilder's opinion. But in the end, does his opinion matter? Would that film analysis were so simple that it divided into merely two opposing camps. Of course, contexts are worth considering but ultimately the movie is what it is. Was the movie to which Charles Brackett gave mixed reviews in 1943, the same one that Bob Porfirio saw in 1963, Claire Johnston, in 1973, Frank Krutnik, in 1983, James Naremore, in 1993—you get the point, the answer is "Yes." And, except for that superfluous addition of that Universal Pictures logo, it is the same movie as anyone has even seen or will see. So where do all these voices possibly coincide?

Conspiracy and betrayal, love and sex, murder and the perfect crime—all linchpins of noir are integral to *Double Indemnity*. Surely murder for profit or murder for love are conceits much older than the noir cycle; but as a tale of murder that combines the two, *Double Indemnity* is for many the quintessential film noir. Like nature and a vacuum, the noir cycle abhors a perfect crime and seldom paints any picture of perfection. Even for those not familiar with the original novel, the failure of would-be "perfect criminals" Walter Neff and Phyllis Dietrichson was never likely to surprise the viewer. Or as *Double Indemnity*'s heroic/anti-heroic protagonist sarcastically notes when he begins his narration of failure: "Pretty, isn't it?"

Pretty it's not. In fact, the sordidness of *Double Indemnity* is counterbalanced only by the serendipitous elements that came together and permitted it to be made. As we have seen from a true crime, Cain fashioned two stories which were soon optioned by Hollywood. But no one could initially get a script past Joe Breen and the Production Code Administration. A World War and a nuanced (and piecemeal) approach by Paramount finally made it possible.

Even then, *Double Indemnity* might have turned out quite differently had Billy Wilder's regular collaborator, the patrician Mr. Brackett not turned up his nose; had Cain himself not been busy elsewhere under contract to a rival studio; had Joe Sistrom not read some hard-boiled prose by Raymond Chandler, who almost certainly came up with "Pretty, isn't it," since he pointedly used the same phrase early in *The Blue Dahlia* (1946), when Doris Dowling as the wartime grass widow remarks, "A call from the house detective. Pretty, isn't it?" In the end, with homespun Fred MacMurray being cast after Raft, Ladd et al had passed, with Barbara Stanwyck in a hand-me-down blonde wig from Marlene Dietrich, with Edward G. Robinson wishing the canny Keyes had more screen time, Wilder and his collaborators fashioned from an imperfect process applied to a plot about an imperfect crime what might well be the perfect film noir. Beyond the influences of Cain as novelist, Chandler as the co-scenarist, and Billy Wilder, the former Austrian journalist, there is the superb sometimes chiaroscuro (when appropriate) cinematography by John Seitz, the scintillating score by Miklós Rózsa, and, of course, Stanwyck, MacMurray, and Robinson, all cast somewhat against type.

In *Double Indemnity,* the filmmakers did create an ambience and narrative that resonates with multiple antecedents from true crime to hard-boiled fiction, from expressionist lighting to the gangster film's dark and menacing streets. As Wilder wondered, isn't it *Caligari* and *Little Caesar,* Sophocles and Zola, German expressionism and French poetic realism, all "wrapped up in tissue paper with pink ribbons on it"? This early noir construction both colors and restricts whatever trace of romanticism may exist in Neff's character and emphasizes instead the doomed and obsessive qualities of his entanglement with Phyllis, whom few women in film noir could ever rival.

Jane Palmer in *Too Late for Tears* (1949), who kills a corrupt private detective and her own husband (and probably killed her first husband as well); the cool, aristocratic exploiter Lisa Bannister in *The Lady from Shanghai* (1949); the sociopathic Ellen Harland in *Leave Her to Heaven* (1945); even the repeatedly duplicitous Kathie Moffat in *Out of the Past* are all distant seconds. The black widow played by Stanwyck is the archetype of film noir's classic period. In fact, *Double Indemnity* has a panoply of prototypes beyond a perfect plan

188

The old/young attraction of Neff for the nymphet Lola whose visit to the insurance office is another threat to derail the enterprise.

that goes awry and a femme fatale. In terms of content there is the ironic, first-person narration; extensive flashbacks; greed and lust that leads to murder; as forthright a portrayal of adultery as the PCA would permit; several other "pairings" not just the old/young attractions of Neff and Lola and Phyllis and Nino but also Neff and Keyes; intricate detective work; and finally, of course, betrayal and death (actual and implied) for the illicit lovers.

From the first, the tone is far different from Cain, as stylistically *Double Indemnity* also sets several standards. It opens with an unusual title sequence: while Rózsa's minor chords portend some vague doom, the silhouette of a man on crutches moves towards the camera. As the composer explained it, "I wanted to establish the mood of the whole picture, which is murder and horror—actually the fatality of the whole thing. As you must know, in the *Fifth Symphony* of Beethoven, the opening notes are fate knocking on the door. And this was the motif, this is fate: bom-bom-bom."[86]

In the first sequence, a car speeds through a downtown area at night and stops in front of a large office building. There is bizarre comic relief as the elevator operator jokes about his purported heart condition but soon the wounded Neff has the Dictaphone in hand and the first-person flashbacks can begin. Cain reveals the situation more directly and traditionally, with the first hint of something abnormal only coming halfway through the opening chapter: "All of a sudden she looked at me and I felt a chill creep up my back and into the roots of my hair. 'Do you sell accident insurance?'" For all its notoriety, Cain's novel was actually fairly tame. His Walter Huff is described as having a "vividness of speech"; but it consists of some occasional argot and misuse of some third person, plural and singular.

From the earliest images of him, overcoat draped awkwardly over his shoulder and answering the elevator man with a clipped, "Let's ride," the viewer can see that Neff is someone entirely different. Cain's ending in which Huff and "Mrs. Nirdlinger" execute a suicide pact on the high seas is more melodrama than noir. So Wilder and Chandler had to do a lot more than just change their names. Their construction of Neff's narration is repeatedly more chilling than any moment in the book.

Wilder's deft use of selected longer takes and fluid two shots in the scenes between Neff and his mentor Keyes sharply focus that relationship. There is straightforward suspense staging, but there is also the long take when Keyes asks Neff to be his assistant. It runs for over two minutes without a cut. Neff spends the entire first part of the scene in profile or facing Keyes, who paces back and forth, compelling the camera to pan slightly to keep him in the shot. In 1944 (and for the most part, today also) a viewer expected a cut, anticipated close shots of the two men to be inserted. Withholding the cut, irrespective of viewer's awareness, creates a subtle but certain tension. It has taken the audience away from Neff's opening voice-over comments about time passing and no looming opportunity to put the deadly plan into play and into Keyes' forced rhetoric about the excitement of claims management. Then the telephone rings. Keyes grabs it but continues, then finally hands the receiver to Neff with a curt "there's a dame on your phone."

Finally, there is a cut, a momentary release of tension. Now the shot is Phyllis in a phone booth at the market; and when she says, "it's very urgent," the scene and the narrative reset completely. In the cut back to the office, Neff, still perched on the edge of his desk, shifts around awkwardly to fill more of the frame's foreground; and Keyes lurks. Neff shifts the handset to his right ear, but Keyes stays put. Finally, the call ends and a two-shot of the men resumes the scene in the office. Neff gets up and now mostly has his back to camera, as Keyes "confesses" to him. It's another long take, ending

Jealous much? As Keyes pitches Neff about working together, he does not like to be interrupted by a "dame" on the phone.

with a cut back to a wide shot, when Keyes finally leaves and closes the door, the click of knob (and a low musical cue) reset everything again. "Those fates I was talking about had only been stalling me off," realizes a forlorn Neff, who walks to the water cooler in full-figured medium long shot. "Now they had thrown the switch. The gears had meshed."

For Neff much more than for Huff, the desire for a woman and for money are confounded with the desire to beat Keyes, to overcome a powerful father figure. But most significantly, the narration, the performance, plus Wilder's staging and cutting, all underscore the inescapable fatality of the plot. As Neff says in voice-over after everything has gone as planned, "Suddenly it came over me that everything would go wrong. It sounds crazy, Keyes, but it's true so help me: I couldn't hear my own footsteps. It was the walk of a dead man."

The fatalistic tone of *Double Indemnity*, the subtle sense of malaise, is sustained as much by its naturalistic and hard-bitten performances as by its visual style. Certainly, Seitz's work here and with several other Paramount noirs from the earlier *This Gun for Hire,* to the later *The Big Clock* (1948) and *Night Has a Thousand Eyes* (1948), would help define approaches to interior lighting and staging perfected by John Alton later in the decade.

The flashbacks begin with a familiar image of Hollywood from the 1930s or '40s, a Spanish-style house in the Hollywood Hills. Inside the house Neff recounts "sunshine coming in through the Venetian blinds showed up the dust in the air." Outside as he drives away and notices that "smell of honeysuckle all along that street. How could I have known that murder can sometimes smell like honeysuckle?" Although the drive-away is a process shot and the house interior a stage reconstruction, the essentially realistic composite geography of the movie fully underscores the narrative tone. This house and its surroundings are a core metaphor of the film. To Neff it contains all the possibilities of the American dream: wealth, love, and beating the system.

When the blonde-haired Phyllis first appears on the second-floor landing, wrapped in only a towel, Neff is awestruck. When she comes down later to indulge in a bit of classic double entendre, Neff cannot keep his eyes off her dangling foot and its "honey of an anklet." Phyllis embodies not only sexual possibilities to him but also the wealth for which he yearns. On the second visit, denser shadows and shallower light show less dust and become a visual equivalent of the web in which Phyllis is about to enmesh Neff.

It may or may not be true that Neff's apartment, where the turning point in the narrative occurs, was modeled after one of Wilder's living spaces at the Chateau Marmont. In contrast to the Dietrichson home, it's cramped, shadowy, and spare. Does it thus reflect a bitter, world-weary tenant? After the crime, when the couple furtively meets in the aisles of Jerry's Market, the flat lighting and stacks of canned goods visually reinforce the lovers' sense of still being trapped in the mundane and everyday, the very thing they killed to escape. In Keyes' impromptu visit to Neff, who is waiting for Phyllis at his apartment, all the peril of the noir universe is distilled into one sequence. At the same time, as illustrated above, the emotional triangle of the film is restaged and restated.

The final deadly embrace of Neff and Phyllis in the parlor lit only by the thin shafts of light that manage to pierce the closed Venetian blinds is a tour-de-force of noir lighting. Lit otherwise, the scene's impact would surely be altered, but in the final analysis, it is the screen presence of the actors that sells the moment. The perfect crime having eluded them, Neff and Phyllis suffer the fate predicted by his mentor Keyes: "Murder is never perfect. When two people are involved…it's not like taking a trolley ride together where they can get off at different stops. They're stuck with each other and they've got to ride all the way to the end of the line. It's a one-way trip and the last stop is the cemetery."

There are certain characters, like Walter Neff in *Double Indemnity*, whose behavior is more classically existential. In Neff's case this is because he understands from the beginning that he need not have chosen, as is metaphorically explained to him, to get on that trolley that only goes one way. Because he is subsequently entrapped by the undesired aftereffects of his choice, unlike the equally anguished Bradford Galt in *The Dark Corner* (1946), who is "backed up" in the locus of the film's title, Neff has created his own dark corner, from which he can never escape. Still as he sits in his darkened office at the film's conclusion finishing the dictation of his bleak narrative, Neff may begin to perceive that his choice was not so free as it seemed. As so many have pointed out, Neff is a victim of alienation but also the second key emotion in the noir universe: obsession. As Neff winces from the pain of his bullet wound at the conclusion of *Double Indemnity*, and Keyes, the man who represents the system, which Neff tried to defeat, lights a match for him, everything (as Wilder believed) has been said. With that gesture, the subtlest nuance of the noir sensibility is invoked: the greatest failure is not in succumbing to the temptation, in falling prey to illicit attraction or being caught in a double bind. The greatest failure is never accepting the possibility of redemption, however small.

A few last words from various perspectives, essential, phenomenological, and pedagogical, on why *Double Indemnity* deserves a place in the pantheon of film noir:

> By 1944, plenty of movies that would later be recognized as "film noir" had already been produced—but Double Indemnity *was arguably the first to bring together all the major elements of the style. It was so successful that it became an archetype, ushering in many more noirs in the years that followed. It's also a crackling good drama with some of the sharpest dialogue of the era.*[87]

> Double Indemnity *is a groundbreaking cinematic masterpiece exemplifying Wilder's obsessive, probing intellectual curiosity, his insatiable inquiry into the impenetrable inscape of human consciousness, a strikingly aggressive and personalized descent into the subterranean world of noir.*[88]

> In terms of the narrative, which is the aspect of film noir that is readily accessible to most students, Double Indemnity *really packs a wallop: femme fatale (in spades); flashback with first person narration (heavily ironic to boot); ace investigator; more greed than Von Stroheim could throw at you; hetero- and a soupçon of homoeroticism; and, even without the cut scene of Keyes watching Neff entering the gas chamber, some pretty harsh shuffling off this mortal coil by assorted characters.*[89]

194

7.

AFTERMATH AND MOVEMENT: THE RISE OF FILM NOIR

Billy Wilder's nervousness about how *Double Indemnity* would be received was allayed during a sneak preview in Westwood in July 1944. In his monograph Richard Schickel recounts:

In any case, the first preview confirmed the buzz about the film and banished any lingering doubts Wilder may have entertained about it. The preview was in one of the big theaters in Westwood, and that locale assured that a jury of the director's peers were present. They were gripped by what they saw... Walking out of the theater, surrounded by elated co-workers and executives, he spotted Cain, standing quietly, almost hidden by a pillar. He went over to him and was embraced by the writer, who told the director what he later told interviewers that Wilder had greatly improved his original work.[1]

Wilder's version to Moffat was "Cain said that it was the first time that somebody did a good job on any of his stuff, and he kissed me." Wilder continued, "Chandler sneaked out because he did not want to be seen with his wife... she was a grey-haired lady, [so] people would turn to him and say, 'Oh, is this your mother'?"[2] As usual Cain was generous and even sentimental. In fact the author became one of the movie's most enthusiastic cheerleaders. In interviews throughout the years he praised the film. He even went to bat for the film when ultra-patriotic and prudish singer Kate Smith tried to organize a boycott of the movie on its release later that year in New York. Cain wrote an advance review of the movie for the *New York Daily News* defending the film against "this fat girl Kate Smith [who] carried on propaganda asking people to stay away from the picture."[3]

Whether he snuck out or not, whether the experience with Wilder had shortened his life or not, by the time *Double Indemnity* was released Chandler was still "under contract to Paramount [for] several pictures," and between gigs, having finished punching up *And Now Tomorrow* (1944) and not yet called back to work on *The Unseen* (1945) for producer John Houseman. It was years later (1951) when Chandler wrote a surprising letter about "how anyone can survive in Hollywood":

> *I personally had a lot of fun there. You meet a lot of bastards, but usually they have some saving grace...A really creative writer out to become a director, which means that in addition to being creative he must be very tough, physically and morally. Otherwise by the time he has been kicked around enough to write a script that can be shot, that is camera-wise and not just writing, he has probably lost all his bounce.*[4]

Cain and Chandler aside, the film was mostly well-received by the trade papers, newspaper critics, and the world of Wilder's peers. A survey of the contemporary reviews of *Double Indemnity* also evidences its generally positive reception; but the industry writers in April 1944 made some specific points that are still very pertinent. One anonymous staffer gave Wilder the basis for his story about the wig: "MacMurray has seldom given a better performance. It is somewhat different from his usually light roles, but is always plausible and played with considerable restraint. Stanwyck is not as attractive as normally with what is seemingly a blonde wig, but it's probably part of a makeup to emphasize the brassiness of the character."[5]

And did the stringer for *The Hollywood Reporter* foresee the rise of film noir?

196

With his Double Indemnity *for Paramount, Billy Wilder has broken open a door hitherto locked to all those connected with the creation of motion pictures. He has made the hero and heroine of his stark drama a pair of murderers. There is no gloss to their wrong-doing, no sugar frosting to make palatable their misdeeds. It is a drama the like of which no other picture in recent memory brings to mind, more than a little reminiscent of the late lamented, excellent French technique [poetic realism]. To the capital performing of MacMurray and the gorgeously blonde hussy depicted by Miss Stanwyck can be added the name of Edward G. Robinson, who superbly underplays the law and order assignment to give the picture three star performances, any one of which would grace a lesser film.*[6]

"No sugar frosting": the plan comes together after some adulterous canoodling in Neff's dark, cramped apartment.

Put another way, there was no lapel bit. *Film Daily* and the *Motion Picture Herald* continued along the same lines:

Double Indemnity *is one of those unusual productions, a melodrama that succeeds in reaching for quality and intelligence without the slightest sacrifice of audience appeal. It is a distinguished film of its kind without a weakness in any discernible department. It wouldn't be at all surprising when all the chips are in to find it acclaimed as the top melodrama of the year.*[7]

The film should hold an adult audience rooted to their seats for the final frames although the identity of the murderer is announced at the beginning. The characters are allowed neither glamour nor sudden repentance. The screenplay, on which [director] Billy Wilder collaborated with Raymond Chandler, is a gem of tight construction and terse but natural dialogue.[8]

Of course, beyond the highest ratings for script and direction, the trades included multiple "huzzahs" for Seitz's cinematography and Rózsa's score. As the movie made its way around the country (and eventually overseas to England and Australia), many newspaper reviewers were struck by what they saw and, from its first opening in Baltimore, some, like the *Hollywood Reporter* reviewer, caught a glimpse of the beginning of the film noir movement (they just did not have a name for it yet):

This has been a good year for screen murder mysteries. First there was The Lodger, *then* Gaslight, *and now* Double Indemnity, *which is an almost literal translation of James M. Cain's book, even capturing some of that author's gift for being sardonic and objective at the same time. His ending has been altered, radically, in deference to the Hays code and the sensitivity of insurance companies, but the new one will do. In all other respects this is one of the best jobs of the kind ever done in Hollywood.*[9]

In every region, women and men alike came away impressed. Can you tell the gender or geographic location of the writers that found the movie "a powerful, ruthless, and almost cruelly exciting picture"[10] that "never compromises with the realistic...dealing with foul and dirty people and Mr. Wilder keeps them that way to the grimly bitter end."[11] Yes it is "a corking melodrama, a hard-boiled story in murder for cash"[12] that makes for "superb drama— strong meat—one of the best films to come out of Hollywood in this or any other year"[13] because of its "stark realism with no fancy touches"[14] except perhaps when "Stanwyck turns up the heat and goes plumb bad—and is she 'moider'!"[15] Yes, that last review is written by a man, but where's he from? Not Brooklyn. Of course, Kate Cameron, the staff reviewer (not Cain) for the tabloid *New York Daily News*, had to note that:

Stanwyck has never given as subtle and indelible a characterization as the one of Phyllis Dietrichson in Double Indemnity. *Her murderess recalls to mind the story of Ruth Snyder and her lover, who paid the death penalty for bludgeoning her husband to death some years ago.[16]*

While *Time* magazine, in its clipped and clever way, called the movie "the season's nattiest, nastiest, most satisfying melodrama,"[17] there were a few nay-sayers. Bosley Crowther at *The New York Times* was typically less than fully engaged by "a tough melodrama." After his opening bon mots about the theater's cooling system being "supplemented yesterday by a screen attraction designed plainly to freeze the marrow in an audience's bones," he found some fault:

But the very toughness of the picture is also the weakness of its core, and the academic nature of its plotting limits its general appeal. The principal characters—an insurance salesman and a wicked woman, which Mr. MacMurray and Miss Stanwyck play—lack the attractiveness to render their fate of emotional consequences. And the fact that the story is told in flashback disposes its uncertainty.

"Sign here, sucker." Neff calmly makes a deadly sale. It's what he does, "the sensitivity of insurance companies" be damned.

Miss Stanwyck gives a good surface performance of a destructively lurid female, but Mr. MacMurray is a bit too ingenuous as the gent who falls precipitately under her spell. And the ease of his fall is also questionable. One look at the lady's ankles and he's cooked.[18]

James Agee, the critic for *The Nation* was similarly unmoved: "The picture never takes hold of its opportunities, such as they are, perhaps because those opportunities are appreciated chiefly as surfaces and atmospheres and as very tellable trash."[19] Ouch. Surfaces and atmospheres and trash? Apparently *Double Indemnity* was insufficiently high-flown for Mr. Agee.

Agee and Crowther were among the few who were not bowled over. Even that mouthpiece for the Catholic Church (one of the major lobbying forces behind the Production Code Administration), *The Tidings,* liked the movie.[20] Philip K. Scheuer of the *Los Angeles Times* was so taken with *Double Indemnity* that he wrote two pieces about it within a week. His August 6 piece was actually an article about censorship; but his review called it "one of the strongest pictures Paramount (or anyone else) ever made. The so-and-sos have thought of everything. You no sooner wonder, for instance, why a claim hasn't been put in on a certain broken leg than the actors explain. The would-be critic hasn't a leg to stand on, either."[21]

Obviously World War II limited film exports except for parts of the British Commonwealth, which prints reached around the end of the year. "Hollywood has scored many of its greatest successes in films of crime and violence. *Double Indemnity* can stand comparison with the best of them," opined an anonymous reviewer in Australia. "Many will find the atmosphere too sordid, for there is no redeeming feature, no sympathetic touch in the leading characters, unpleasant as only Cain's can be."[22] In the UK, Mary Crozier wrote for *The Guardian* that "it would be accurate to say of this film—as is generally said inaccurately of most crime stories—that it is full of suspense. It is not only full of power to make one feel anxiety about the action, but it has realistic and gloomy suggestions of the shadows of guilt which increases it forcefulness without sentimentality, and without exaggeration."[23] Dilys Powell, the longtime and often dismissive critic for *The Times* of London, had none of the snobbish issues of James Agee or that writer for the imposter *Times* across the pond, except perhaps in singling out an old-school boy (and the scene Wilder insisted would play):

The name of Raymond Chandler, as collaborator with Billy Wilder on the script of Double Indemnity *struck me; pleasantly, for Chandler's writing is at its best sharply visual, getting its effect by observed detail, the small shocking thing seen.* Double Indemnity *is told with much sureness and control: no lingering over the expensive and unnecessary set, no sentimental expansiveness, no*

201

description of trivial actions. In this film when a character tries to start a car, well, that means something, because if the car doesn't start (and it nearly doesn't) the murder planned to look like an accident is going to look like murder.[24]

Buoyed by the movie's worldwide (or as wide as it could be in 1944) success, Wilder first reunited with the man who had gravely doubted that he could "ever bring myself to work with Billy again." Charles Brackett had already significantly revised his opinion of the movie that Wilder made without him, so why not hitch back up to his rising star. For his part, according to Ed Sikov, "knowing how good his new film was, and confident…Billy could afford to pull a few pranks."[25]

David Selznick's latest production, *Since You Went Away*, would become one of the year's most successful movies; and the producer took out trade advertisements claiming his new title's four words were the most important since his 1939 monster hit *Gone with the Wind*. Selznick (and others) also solicited and published endorsements from "community leaders." Wilder was disdainful of such tactics, so as Brackett recalled on May 14:

Billy announced that he would take an advertisement for Double Indemnity *with (still following the Selznick pattern) a letter from Mr. Oblath, the proprietor of the hash-house across the street from Paramount. Since then I had to work with him on the letter, making it semi-factual, and compose the tag-line, "Double Indemnity— the two most important words for the motion picture industry since* Broken Blossoms." *Billy ostensibly (and I think honestly) didn't realize where the thing came from and I felt nothing but amusement until today, when the advertisement appeared and I hear him, very patronizingly, say to congratulatory friends, "Oh, Charlie and I write everything together."*[26]

Brackett does not explain why he would fear Selznick's (or anyone else's) opprobrium over helping with the gag. His next ad substituted "Capital Gains" for *Broken Blossoms*. Apparently, Selznick was not amused and possibly threatened to cut off his spending (which was considerable) with any trade periodicals that kept running those from Wilder that ridiculed him. Wilder finally let up after receiving a telegram from an appreciative Alfred Hitchcock that read: "Since *Double Indemnity* the two most important words in motion pictures are Billy Wilder."[27]

At the same time, publicists at Paramount had their own, relatively standard approach to selling the movie. The fact that the ad art boldly announced, "From the Moment They Met It Was Murder!" or that the trailer left little to the imagination worked as expected. Puff pieces on the stars appeared in the movie magazines before the release. In fact, pre-release publicity had begun building up expectations about this melodrama, thriller, mystery, whatever you might want to call it, in late 1943.

Sikov notes wryly that "this perverse film's marketing provided a few choice ironies" including encouraging insurance companies to arrange attendance by their employees and "planting fake stories in Los Angeles newspapers."[28] At one point, despite all the changes of character names and other fact checks, a woman had contacted the studio to complain that her phone number was the one given out by Neff to Nino Zachette. She was exhausted from answering calls for Lola Dietrichson and wanted compensation. But just as Barton Keyes might have done, Paramount found this claim suspicious. How the woman got a number with the Beverly Hills exchange "Granite" when she lived in West Hollywood is unclear: but a Paramount-All-Risk claims manager discovered she had not requested it until July 1944 or shortly after a sneak preview.

As with Gorlopis, the claim was denied. Perhaps inspired by this "Paramount told the *Los Angeles Examiner* that some of the film's fans dialed the number...and got none other than [Mrs.] Judith Wilder who would ask how they liked the movie."[29] While this was studio mummery, Sikov reports genuine requests for Stanwyck to provide endorsements for cosmetics and jewelry and Robinson's two-for-quarter cigars inspired hype by the Cigar Institute America.

Selznick and stunts like this notwithstanding, Wilder received numerous enthusiastic letters and telegrams from executives at other studios

offering to work with him if he was available, including Jerry Wald at Warners[30] (who would produce Cain's *Mildred Pierce*—in flashbacks, of course—
the next year). And although *Double Indemnity* did not win any Oscars, it
was nominated for seven of them: Best Picture, Best Actress, Best Director, Best Adapted Screenplay, Best Black-and-White Cinematography, Best
Sound Recording, and Best Music.

The story Wilder told repeatedly of almost tripping director Leo McCarey, as he went up to pick up Oscars for writing and directing *Going My Way*
is apocryphal. But the fondness of Academy voters for sentimental pictures
in that era was undeniable (and arguably continues to the present day). It
didn't help that Y. Frank Freeman did not like *Double Indemnity* and supported keying studio promotion to *Going My Way* instead. In fairness, that
family movie was the highest grossing pictures of 1944, outpacing *Double
Indemnity* by a factor of at least more than double. Sources differ considerably on the earnings of the movie. Richard Schickel notes "*Double Indemnity* was not a huge box office success. It appears nowhere on the list
of 1944's top grossers, and although it did not lose money, it did not make
much either."[31] Whatever *Double Indemnity* actually grossed, the fact that it
initially returned 147% of its release costs[32] meant that Wilder would have
no trouble getting a green light from Paramount on future projects (or until
one of them flopped).

One exception to this flood of praise, not written until almost a year after the film's release, was the August 1945 article by Lloyd Shearer for *The
New York Times*. Besides the earliest iteration of the secretary in the ladies'
room story, the title, subtitle, and first lines of the article say it all:

Crime Certainly Pays on the Screen; The growing crop of homicidal films poses questions for psychologists and producers. *Of late
there has been a trend in Hollywood toward the wholesale production of lusty, hard-boiled, gat-and-gore crime stories, all fashioned
on a theme with a combination of plausibly motivated murder and
studded with high-powered Freudian implication... When will the
trend stop? Probably not until the market has been glutted with*

poorly made pictures of the type. So long as producers turn out interesting and entertaining murder pictures, the public will flock to them.[33]

Shearer contacted Cain, who, as a former journalist when asked to comment by a representative of all the news that fits to print, gladly gave him an answer:

The reason Hollywood is making so many of these so-called hardboiled crime pictures is simply that the producers are now belatedly realizing that these stories make good movies. It's got nothing to do with the war or how it's affected the public or any of that bunk. If Billy Wilder, for example, had made Double Indemnity *back in 1935 the picture would have done just as well as it has now. It's just that producers have got hep to the fact that plenty of real crime takes place every day and that it makes a good movie. The public is fed up with the old-fashioned melodramatic type of hokum.*[34]

Next Shearer tracked down Chandler, another former journalist, whom he would praise as "a reserved, quiet writer with an unusual talent for literary imagery":

My own opinion is that the studios have gone in for these pictures because the Hays office has become more liberal, probably because they feel people can take the hard-boiled stuff nowadays. Of course, people have been reading about murderers, cutthroats and thieves in the newspapers for the past hundred years, but only recently has the Hays office permitted the movies to depict life as it really is. The Hays office has lost Warner Brothers and United Artists and may be a little fearful of antagonizing the remaining studios, which support it. Then again it's entirely possible that the studios have become smarter and have submitted story treatments which satisfy the production code. In any event, the public likes well-done crime

205

films for the very same reason they like good detective stories. They're escapist and interesting.[35]

Chandler may have played it close to the vest, since his own exposé of the evils of the industry, "Writers In Hollywood," would not appear in *The Atlantic* until November. Did Shearer ring up Wilder at the Campus? If so, either there was no answer or he did not care for what that former journalist had to say.

Obviously Raymond Chandler's opinion of the movie was inextricably tied to his experience with Wilder, so always somewhat ambiguous. At various times he claimed he was never invited to screenings; but he was. Did he hate Hollywood with every ounce of the bitterness that oozes out of "Writers in Hollywood" or did he "have a lot of fun there"? He certainly made a good deal of money. While biographers agree that his studio earnings and the sales of rights to his books finally permitted him sufficient wealth to decamp from Los Angeles and move 120 miles south to live out his years in La Jolla (with his wife/mother Cissy).

Is it true that Paramount offered Chandler $2,000 per week to write, produce, and direct any project that he wanted? Postwar 1946 dollars were a bit inflated but that would still have been $30,000 every week today. Given that, like *Double Indemnity*, his solo effort writing *The Blue Dahlia* got him a second Academy Award screenplay nomination, Paramount would certainly have sweetened the pot to keep him there. But he left. Maybe that experience on *The Blue Dahlia*, the "Lost Fortnight,"[36] John Houseman's chronicle of how Chandler on a deadline churned out pages on a movie that was already shooting by remaining inebriated the entire time, had been too much for him.

After Chandler finished a bloated first draft of *The Lady in the Lake*— the only time he adapted one of his own novels—for actor/director Robert Montgomery at MGM, he quit that studio, also. Was that because he really was "one of those lying down writers," who could not work at a studio where Louis Mayer's standing policy forbade couches in their office? Was it because he could not convince Montgomery that the way to write a first-person movie was to use the *Double Indemnity* flashback narration method and certainly not a first-person camera where the entire movie was from the lead character's visual point of view (which is what Montgomery did)? Again, whatever the reason, Chandler went south to write his other critique of the institution that enriched him, the Hollywood novel *The Little Sister.*

When *Double Indemnity* was released RKO had already remade *Farewell, My Lovely* as *Murder, My Sweet* with the Marlowe character restored and Warners was shooting *The Big Sleep* (1945-46) starring Bogart and Bacall for which director Howard Hawks had tried to borrow Chandler from Paramount (they said no). As rewritten by Steve Fisher (Chandler wanted credit until he saw the movie), *Lady in the Lake* was released in 1947, the same year as the Fox remake of *High Window, The Brasher Doubloon,* again with Marlowe restored. More Marlowe movies have followed up to and including 2022's *Marlowe* based on a book by a licensed Chandler imitator, on the titles of which the name of Marlowe's creator is not even listed.

In 1947 Chandler did briefly reunite with Joe Sistrom, who got Warners to hire Chandler to write *Playback* for him to produce. When that project died in development, Sistrom suggested to Chandler that it would make a novel, which was the last of Chandler's book-length works to be published in 1958. Chandler's last script job was also for Warners: adapting a Patricia Highsmith novel for the man who sent Wilder a telegram, Alfred Hitchcock.

What the director did not realize when Chandler was engaged was that his writer would refuse to travel from La Jolla to Burbank for meetings about *Strangers on a Train* (1951). That was annoying enough; but when Hitchcock extracted himself from his chauffeured ride after that long trip south and overheard Chandler's smart remark about his weight, the producer/director angrily replaced the mystery writer with Ben Hecht's secretary. He thought sharing the credit would irritate Chandler, who did not care. In the 1950s as the exploits of Chandler's chivalric detective were less timely than the highly sexualized Mike Hammer or the violent criminal world of Jim Thompson, Chandler mostly rested on his laurels. The death of his wife in 1954 aggravated his alcoholic recidivism and pushed him into a deep depression. He died in 1959.

Cain's trajectory was a bit more salutary. His career was given a huge boost by the success of *Double Indemnity*. The Hollywood taboo fell off his books and the studios began to adapt more of his novels: *Mildred Pierce*, *The Postman Always Rings Twice* (1946), and even a PCA-approved (that is, bowdlerized) version of the sexually daring *Serenade* (1956). Cain continued writing noirish novels up to his death in 1977. He also was politically active. In 1946, Cain proposed the creation of an "American Authors' Authority" to hold writer's copyrights and represent writers in contract negotiations and court disputes. Although the plan was denounced as communist by some writers, Cain, with his background as a writer and journalist who focused on proletarian characters, saw it as a way to protect all novelists from both predatory publishers and Hollywood producers.

According to Wilder, his next film, *The Lost Weekend* (1945), was inspired by his experience working with the irascible Chandler, who fell off the wagon during *Double Indemnity*.[37] Is that true? Charles Jackson's novel was still somewhat hot off the press when Brackett and Wilder started work. However they came to the project, *The Lost Weekend* was a total vindication for the reunited partners, each of whom took home a pair of Oscars for writing (Brackett and Wilder), producing (Brackett), and directing (Wilder). Before those awards, Wilder, who had lost his mother and other relatives to the Holocaust, agreed to work on a documentary ominously titled *Death Mills* (1945). Somehow Wilder managed to face down the personal loss and rediscover some of his journalistic detachment while traveling to Germany to edit and supervise the English version of the movie.

In 1950 Wilder (again with Brackett) used cutting wit and heavy irony for his own critique of the Hollywood he knew so well. When it was released that year, the classic period noir, *Sunset Boulevard*, revealed "tinsel town" as an entertainment-industrial complex that promised the dream but most often delivered the nightmare. The ne'er-do-well writer Joe Gillis (William Holden) and the faded silent star Norma (Gloria Swanson) are distorted reflections of show-business dreams, of which co-star Erich von Stroheim knew all too well from his own experience directing Swanson in the silent era (he was fired from *Queen Kelly* by her paramour Joseph Kennedy).

Wilder even convinced Cecil B. DeMille to interact in a cameo. Like Neff in *Double Indemnity* Joe and Norma wanted the money and the woman/man; but they got neither. Norma entered her fantasy world while Gillis found himself dead in the pool of an old Hollywood mansion on Sunset Boulevard.

In his final noir (and after the end of his partnership with Brackett), *Ace in the Hole* (*The Big Carnival*, 1951), Wilder was at his most acerbic, indicting American journalism as a whole with his depiction of a ruthless reporter who turns a mischance into a literal circus, a media-gone-wild which creates a tragic death where none was in the offing. Wilder continued to be one of the most important American directors in the 1950s with hits like *Stalag 17* (1953) and *Sabrina* (1954). In 1959 he scored another critical and financial success with his paean to the gender-bending decadence of the Weimar scene (which he was part of) and the 1930s American gangster film (including the presence of gangster icon George Raft): *Some Like It Hot*. The film was so far ahead of its time in its sympathetic queer content that it was recently turned into a Tony-winning Broadway musical with non-binary actors in several of the main parts. Wilder would have been proud, and almost certainly ready with a quip or even an apocryphal story for any interviewer.

There was no one to trip at the postwar, 1946 Academy Awards ceremony, where Wilder apparently made his way up to the front of Grauman's Chinese theater to accept his awards for *The Lost Weekend* without stumbling. He bested Leo McCarey for director and over the years was nominated in that category six more times. He won again for *The Apartment* (1960). The were dozens more awards from AMPAS and other organizations, lifetime achievements from the Writers, Directors, and Producers Guilds and the American Film Institure. Nor did Wilder stumble the last time he grasped an Oscar in front of a microphone. When he accepted the Thalberg award in 1989, he thanked the customs official in Mexicali who let him re-enter the United States in 1934. He still had projects in development when he died in 2002.

Despite her original reservations Barbara Stanwyck realized the importance of her participation in the movie and came to "love" the role of Phyllis. In a note to James Cain who had recently listened to her reprise the role on the radio in 1950, she wrote, "Dear Jim, Thanks so much for your letter regarding our 'Indemnity' broadcast. Believe me, it's my favorite and always a joy for me to do…" Stanwyck wanted Cain to write her another part like the "wicked Phyllis" (her words).[38]

Stanwyck had always played strong controversial parts from the first years of her career. Two of her earliest films, *Baby Face* and *The Bitter Tea of General Yen,* both in 1933, were considered downright scandalous because of the female protagonist's sexual daring as well as her forthrightness. In 1941 she even played a stripper in *Ball of Fire.* After *Double Indemnity,* Stanwyck became a mainstay of noir films: *The Strange Love of Martha Ivers* (1945), *The Two Mrs. Carrolls* (1947), *Sorry, Wrong Number* (1948), *No Man of Her Own, The Furies, The File on Thelma Jordon* (all 1950), *Clash by Night* (1952), *Witness to Murder* (1954), and *Crime of Passion* (1957). While never reprising Phyllis, she was a superb femme fatale as both Martha Ivers and Thelma Jordon, and almost always played strong-willed women, especially in Westerns such as *The Furies, Cattle Queen of Montana* (1954), or *Forty Guns* (1957), and ended her career in that sort of part as the ultimate television matriarch in the long-running *The Big Valley* (1965-69).

By the time he portrayed Keyes Edward G. Robinson was already an icon. Not only for his proto-noir gangster roles at Warner Bros. but also for mainstream dramas like the biographical *Dr. Ehrlich's Magic Bullet* (1940) and Jack London's *The Sea Wolf* (1941). He was considered the ultimate professional and amazed his fellow actors with his ability to memorize and deliver long dialogue scenes, like his explanation of various types of suicide and poisons in *Double Indemnity.* Robinson admired the character of Keyes and like Stanwyck asked Cain to write him another work with that character as the centerpiece. This time Cain obliged with his novel *Nevada Moon.* Robinson rejected it because Cain changed Keyes' character too radically (it was later published in 1950 as *Jealous Woman*).[39]

However, Robinson soon found himself working on two classic Fritz Lang film noirs: *Scarlet Street* and *The Woman in the Window* (both 1944), opposite fatal woman Joan Bennett. He also received much praise for his performance in Arthur Miller's *All My Sons* (1948) as the corrupt capitalist father. (One of the sons was played by a young Burt Lancaster, who that

210

same year played Neff in an excellent radio adaptation of *Double Indemnity.*)
And in 1948 Robinson gave an emotional performance as an aging gangster
in John Huston's *Key Largo.*

In 1951 Robinson, who had been a progressive activist and anti-fascist,
like so many of his compatriots, was called before HUAC to testify about
his supposed involvement with the Communist Party. Because he named
names (mainly people who had already been jailed for contempt of Congress
like Edward Dmytryk and Albert Maltz) he was dismissed. Unfortunately,
he could not avoid being graylisted, which kept him idle for months then
made it difficult to secure roles in major films. Ironically it was one of the
most reactionary directors in Hollwood, Cecil B. DeMille, who definitively
broke the graylist for Robinson by hiring him to portray the idol worshipper
Dathan in his epic remake of *The Ten Commandments* (1956).

Fred MacMurray's trepidation and Wilder's persistence were frequently
recalled by both men. MacMurray did return to roles as a breezy, handsome,
serio-comic lead that, while not putting him at the top of the list like Stanwyck, had by 1943 made him one of the highest paid actors in Hollywood.
His earnings that year were just under $500,000—not much today, at the
equivalent of $8.5 million but a colossal sum in the era of contract actors.[40]

Of course once MacMurrary saw *Double Indemnity,* all reservations
about possible negative impact on his career vanished. On February 4,
1944, James Cain sent a letter to MacMurray praising his performance,
"Your portrayal of that character is simply terrific, and the way in which
you found tragedy in this shallow, commonplace, smart-cracking soul will
remain with me a long time, and, indeed, reinforce an aesthetic viewpoint
that many quarrel with; for if I have any gift, it is to take such people to
show that they can suffer too as profoundly as anyone else…"[41] MacMurray
responded on February 9 with his usual self-deprecating humor, "As you've
probably been told, it took a lot of persuading by a number of people to get
me to tackle the part. I was crazy about the story but having never done anything like it, I was afraid to take a crack at it. Even after seeing the finished
picture, I was sure I'd given an Academy performance—in underacting! But
if you, the author, liked it—that's good enuff for me!"[42]

211

Although MacMurray fell back into familiar roles after *Double Indemnity*, he did step out a few times to recapture the psychological darkness of Neff. In 1954 he was a corrupt detective in *Pushover*. Plotting with a femme fatale (this time a real blonde—Kim Novak) that he and his partner have under surveillance, this character also does not survive. That same year he was the opinionated, cynical, and cowardly lieutenant who urges the title action in *The Caine Mutiny*. In 1960 Wilder cast him again as a morally bereft character, Sheldrake, the venal, exploitative corporate executive in *The Apartment*.

In his other noir, *Borderline* (1950, a B-budget independent), MacMurray and co-star Claire Trevor both had badges behind their lapels. Like Stanwyck he also did a few Westerns in the 1950s. By the end of the decade, as a successful real estate investor, MacMurray took work that permitted him to spend the most time away from Los Angeles. The production method for *My Three Sons* (1960-72) in which all his scenes for the entire season were shot first was adopted by other older stars transitioning from movies to television. The same formula was used in his work for Disney: *The Shaggy Dog* (1959), *The Absent-Minded Professor* (1961), and *Son of Flubber* (which had no father, 1962). MacMurray retired for good in 1978.

Already one of the most experienced and prestigious cinematographers in Hollywood in 1943, John F. Seitz had been one of the architects of "Rembrandt" lighting, a key motif of film noir. Seitz developed the style over decades beginning in the 1920s working with Rex Ingram. He had already shot the early noir *Fly by Night* and *This Gun for Hire* (both 1942), before his first work for Wilder on *Five Graves to Cairo*. Four of his seven Academy Award nominations were his movies with Wilder that immediately continued with *The Lost Weekend* and ended on *Sunset Boulevard*. Seitz was equally at home on Preston Sturges comedies, but continued applying a low-key style at Paramount on *The Unseen, Chicago Deadline* (1949), *Appointment with Danger* (1950), and for John Farrow on *Calcutta* (1947), *The Big Clock, Night Has a Thousand Eyes* (1948).

Composer Miklós Rózsa was yet another émigré moving west to escape the rise of fascism in Europe. Rózsa had worked extensively in England

212

during the 1930s, and his transition to Hollywood came after global conflict had begun. His second score for Wilder was his first noir film. Before 1944 was over, he had two more noir credits: *Dark Waters* and *Ministry of Fear* for Fritz Lang. In 1945, besides his third score for Wilder (*Lost Weekend*) came, he contributed *Spellbound, The Man in Half Moon Street, Lady on a Train*, and *Blood on the Sun*. By the time he did *Double Indemnity*, Rózsa had already been nominated for an Oscar five times. To win on *Spellbound*, Rózsa had to beat himself (twice), as he was also nominated that year for *The Lost Weekend* and *A Song to Remember.*

More noir films followed in 1946, *The Strange Love of Martha Ivers* and *The Killer* (for director Robert Siodmak including the theme that Universal re-used for *The Dragnet* series). Even more in 1947, *Brute Force, The Red House, Desert Fury, A Double Life*, and *Secret Beyond the Door* (again for Lang). Before the decade ended, *A Woman's Vengeance, The Naked City* (both 1948), and arguable his best score since *Double Indemnity, Criss Cross* (again for Siodmak, 1949). The following year, *Crisis* and *The Asphalt Jungle*, Rózsa blended his predilection for avant-garde music in the style of Schoenberg and Honegger (many of his classical music compositions are in this style) with the Romanticism of movie composers like Erich Korngold. Even today, while more soundtrack listeners may know his epic scores for *Ben Hur* (1959) or *El Cid* (1962), his themes for *Double Indemnity, The Killers*, and *Criss Cross* stack up against any other composers' scores in discussion of the finest of the classic period. He parodied this work in his last full score, the film noir spoof *Dead Men Don't Wear Plaid* (1982).

Doane Harrison, who edited *Double Indemnity*, had been an editor or editorial supervisor since the silent period, working on a number of actor-director Richard Talmadge's movies. In the 1930s he secured a contract at Paramount where he worked with Mitchell Leisen (*Easy Living*, 1937, *Midnight*, and *Hold Back the Dawn*), which led to helping Wilder on *The Major and the Minor*. Wilder would continue to rely heavily on Harrison for the next several decades (for twenty features in all): "I worked with a very good cutter, Doane Harrison, from whom I learned a great deal. He was much more of a help to me than the cameraman. When I became a

213

director from a writer my technical knowledge was very meagre"[43] and Harrison was there every day. His work with Wilder garnered three Academy Award nominations.

For persons whose work in the industry concluded before the website came into existence, the Internet Movie Database uses an algorithm to display the four best-known titles when a researcher types in someone's name. For Stanwyck, MacMurray, Edward G. Robinson, John F. Seitz, and Raymond Chandler, the first movie selected by that algorithm is *Double Indemnity*. It's the third listed for Rózsa (from among 234 feature credits, preceded only by *Ben-Hur* and *Spellbound* on a list rounded out by *The Lost Weekend*). Wilder's later movies won both acclaim and awards. So for him, ironically, *The Apartment* is first, and *Double Indemnity* does not even make the cut.

For Joseph Sistrom, the intellectual crime novel enthusiast, who brought *Double Indemnity* to Wilder and refused an "Associate Producer" credit, there is no record of whether he ever regretted that decision. After he also was denied an on-screen listing as producer on *Wake Island*, he did accept "Associate Producer" on director John Farrow's *The Hitler Gang* (1944). Being the son of a proficient, silent era producer, William Sistrom, had gotten him a start as a production assistant, and Sistrom understood how policy at all studios was to restrict formal producer credits, no matter how involved the contract employee had been in the development of a project.

Sistrom finally became an official producer at Paramount on the Betty Hutton comedy *Incendiary Blonde* (1945), a title somewhat less prominent in film history than *Double Indemnity*. For Sistrom, IMDb lists Paramount's 1952 B-budget crime picture *Atomic City* most prominently along with another John Farrow movie *Botany Bay* (1952). Sistrom was also a dedicated anti-fascist. He was among the distinguished Hollywood delegation (headed by Humphrey Bogart and Lauren Bacall) that went to Washington D.C. to protest the toxic HUAC hearings. Sistrom transitioned to television work in the late 1950s. His last feature credit was for Frank Capra, for whom he had been an assistant on *Mr. Smith Goes to Washington* (1939): he was Associate Producer on *Pocketful of Miracles* (1961).

Hal Pereira worked his way up the art director ladder to become head of the art department at Paramount in 1950 after Hans Dreier retired. He was nominated for 23 Oscars in his long career, winning for *The Rose Tattoo* (1955). His last credit on a Wilder movie was *Sabrina*. He became Alfred Hitchcock's favorite art director throughout his time at Paramount in the 1950s and worked as designer on such legendary titles as *To Catch a Thief* (1955) and *Vertigo* (1958). In the 1960s he worked on features for Howard Hawks.

Edith Head was one of the best-known costume designers in the industry. She began at Paramount in the 1920s and lasted amazingly until the 1960s. She dressed many of the most important actresses of the classic period, including Grace Kelly, Bette Davis, Audrey Hepburn, and of course Barbara Stanwyck. She worked repeatedly with a wide range of directors from Alfred Hitchcock to Jerry Lewis. She won eight Oscars, one of which was for Wilder's *Sabrina*. Like Miklós Rózsa, after scores of film noir credits, one of Head's last jobs as costume designer was on *Dead Men Don't Wear Plaid*, which is also dedicated to her.

Official and Unofficial Remakes
Apology for Murder (1945)

Hollywood, with its penchant for imitations of success, waited only a few months before starting to copy elements of *Double Indemnity*. Only a Poverty-Row studio like Producers Releasing Corporation (PRC) would have the temerity to shoot the same story with but a few minor changes. Director Edgar G. Ulmer in an interview with Peter Bogdanovich admitted that he had written the first draft of the script and it was called *Single Indemnity* (possibly a working-title joke?).[44] It was ultimately directed by the prolific low-budget director Sam Newfield. When Paramount got wind of the movie, their lawyers obtained an injunction that barred the film's original release. PRC changed the title to *Apology for Murder* but did little else to hide their "homage" to the greater work.

This is not to say that *Apology* lacks virtues or is a photocopy of *Double Indemnity*. In fact it has a few significant differences. Anne Savage (most famous for her role in Ulmer's 1945 PRC noir classic *Detour*) plays Toni, the Phyllis equivalent, but more brazen and much tawdrier. Yes, she still seduces the hapless chump (here a reporter named Blake, played by Hugh Beaumont, who soon after this movie worked for Paramount in the Chandler scripted *The Blue Dahlia*); but she has little of the "sex kitten" persona that Phyllis projects at times—a quality more obvious in Cain's original novel. Although she can use her shapely "gams" and come-hither looks to significant advantage, just like Phyllis does, she does raise her skirt a bit higher to give Blake a better look (and we don't mean at her anklet). Once the job is done and Blake is superfluous, Toni flaunts her new lover, the lawyer she hires to contest her husband's will. Subtlety is not her forte, very much like her portrayal of the sardonic Vera in *Detour*.

Beaumont's Blake also has a vaguely homoerotic, oedipal relationship with his boss and ultimate pursuer, McKee, played by Charles D. Brown. The lighting of the other man's tobacco is still there. But while Neff wants both the money and the woman (in that order), Blake shows little interest in the cash; and he says as much to Toni several times. This fatal woman,

Femmes fatales on the phone. Anne Savage in *Apology for Murder* and the call from Phyllis in the drug store that resets the plan of the fates.

216

of course, only cares about a payday. In the murderous climax of the movie Blake seems more in a jealous rage than Neff ever was. Of course this emotion is enhanced by the fact that he finds Toni with her new lover-lawyer. He shoots the lawyer dead and then, as in the original film, the ex-lovers shoot each other. But before he limps back to his office to write his confession, he leans down over Toni's body and says plaintively, "Wait for me, baby. I won't be long," something one cannot imagine coming from the mouth of the more jaded Neff.

In 1954 Lux Video Theatre adapted the screenplay of *Double Indemnity* into a 60-minute television episode directed by staff director Buzz Kulik (who would produce and direct *Warning Shot* at the margin of the classic period in 1966) with Laraine Day as Phyllis, character actor Ray Collins as Keyes, and sometime film noir tough guy Frank Lovejoy (Bogart's cop friend in the 1950 *In a Lonely Place*) projecting no trace of homoeroticism as Walter Neff.

In 1960 Granada Television in Britain adapted the novel for the ITV network's series *Play of the Week*. The episodes were 90 minutes (originally broadcast live then videotaped). *Double Indemnity* was scripted by Gerald Savory (a playwright and prolific writer for television) and featured Donald Pleasance as Keyes, Madeleine Sherwood as Phyllis, and William Sylvester as Walter, who next starred in director Cliff Owen's UK noir *Offbeat* (1961).

Double Indemnity (1973)

In 1973 Universal Television (which now purchased the bulk of the Paramount feature library in 1958) opted to remake *Double Indemnity*, based on the script by Wilder and Chandler. Universal is said to have showed the final script of the remake to Wilder and he approved it. That was not his reaction when he watched the first airing of it in October of 1973. He immediately called up Barbara Stanwyck who was watching it simultaneously and said, "Missy, they just didn't get it right" and hung up the phone.[45] That was quite

217

an understatement, particularly from a man known for more colorful and witty critiques.

Universal brought on two talents who they believed could update the story for a modern 1970s TV audience raised on TV crime mysteries like *Ironside* (1967-75), *Columbo* (1971-78), and *McMillan and Wife* (1971-77). The writer was Steven Bochco (who would create the award-winning *Hill Street Blues* in the 1980s), and the director was the prolific Jack Smight. Bochco had written for both *McMillan and Wife* and *Columbo* while Smight had worked on *Columbo* as well as numerous crime drama series dating back to early 1950s television.

To make the Wilder/Chandler script into a television movie, the creators first stripped the movie of any remnant of Seitz's photographic style and replaced it for the most part with a high key look. The director of photography segued from *Bonanza*, and the composer came off a soap opera. As was common in TV product of that period, zoom-ins replaced tracking shots and cutting favored masters and singles with merely occasional over-the-shoulder shots. The movie is a paean to affluent and sunny Southern California (think *Charlie's Angels* with an actual femme fatale). Locations were moved from the core and east side of Los Angeles in the original film (Downtown, Los Feliz, Glendale-Burbank, Hollywood) to the newer and more affluent Westside (Century City, Marina Del Rey, Westwood, Beverly Hills).

Even though the plot points of the movie and almost all of the dialogue remain the same, the sense of doom and menace created by the camerawork and music in the original is almost totally gone. One of the few scenes that manages to maintain the mood is the final shootout in Phyllis' house and the closing scene between Keyes and the wounded Neff, as he finishes his confession and tries to make it to the elevator with a bullet in his chest. For those scenes alone the director shifted to a darker lighting style but much too late to establish any of the original's sense of fatality and mischance.

There is effective use of the classic noir location, the city's 1939 Union Station—used frequently in both the classic period of noir and many neo-noirs—when Phyllis and Neff as Dietrichson board the train. There is an effective if brief juxtaposition of the sleek Amtrak trains, which had only been running there for a few years, and the interiors of the pre-World War 2 building and platforms.

Richard Crenna portrays Neff in this version. Although Crenna had played serious dramatic characters before this, as in *Slattery's People* (1964-65) in the 1960s, he was best known to most viewers for his comic roles, the juvenile Walter (last name Benton) in *Our Miss Brooks* (1952-58) and the befuddled son of a cackling Walter Brennan in *The Real McCoys* (1957-63, an informal prequel to the *Beverly Hillbillies*). This is not to say that Crenna's on-screen persona, the roles in which audiences expected to see him, was that different from Fred MacMurray's thirty years earlier; but Crenna either was not asked or opted not to exploit the casting against type, so the performance does little to erase the imprint of earlier roles. British actor Samantha Eggar, best known as the kidnapped and imprisoned art student in the 1965 feature adaptation of John Fowles' *The Collector* (directed by William Wyler), had just arrived in Los Angeles before being cast as Phyllis. Eggar received an Academy-Award nomination for a daring performance in *The Collector* but had been working mostly in less weighty fare in Europe in subsequent years starting with *Doctor Dolittle* (1967). Eggar might have found in the scheming Phyllis a way back to the darkly emotional performance she gave for Wyler; but ultimately she is as uninspired as Crenna. Robert Webber's cameo also transforms Norton from a stuffed shirt to another unctuous swinger, clad in a high-collared snap front, pastel jacket with layered cut, blow-dryed hair. This is not a man, who would say "uncomfortably warm day"; but he does.

There is neither need nor time to see Neff's Mercedes convertible careening down Wilshire (these filmmakers have barely 70 minutes to get it all done). Instead main titles are superimposed—in a bright lemon yellow font, oversized for television screens—as the camera follows Neff past the glass façade of his insurance company's Century City headquarters. His overcoat is buttoned up over one of his modish polyester suits of the era. It could be a cool night, as this version takes place in December, but under that overcoat there is very little sense of the character's serious gunshot wound, that he may be bleeding to death. Somehow a bullet in the shoulder has given him

219

a slight limp; but he is otherwise quite spry and voluble. Once seated comfortably in his own office, he dictates with ease into a cassette recorder. Only later does some bright blood, that seems to have been over-applied by the makeup person, stain his shirt, which undercuts his unaffected behavior.

After this invocation of an idyllic Southern California—barely post-hippie, en route to yuppie—the insouciance carries over into the flashbacks. There are no glimpses of the anxiety that was visible in MacMurray's eyes. This Neff is a 1970s swinging bachelor with a sunny, Marina Del Rey swinging-bachelor pad that is nothing like the 1938's dark and cramped Hollywood apartment. Whereas that era's Neff, after he realizes he has to think of Phyllis dead, was sardonic and unrelenting in his showdown with Phyllis (suggestions by some commentators that he was suicidal notwithstanding), 1973's pursuer of money and the woman displays neither determination nor vacillation, scant emotion at all, when he dispatches Phyllis, who has become simply an encumbrance to his lifestyle and threat to his well-being.

None of the particular changes add anything; instead they mostly diminish. The walk of a dead man is not down a dark street but out of a parking garage. There is no hiding behind a door in the corridor. No speeding car down a dark street to open the narrative. It is a "big supermarket" lacking in claustrophobically narrow aisles. The policy payout has increased fourfold but the cut in salary is still $50, a third of what it was in 1938 money. Los Angeles has no more trolley lines, so the murderers ride a bus to the end of the line; but the last stop is still the cemetery. Keyes lights his own cigars until near the end when Neff flicks a Bic for him. With a relatively lower budget, it's understandable that many physical details look cheap or slipshod, like a shadow cast on the trans-screen view outside Neff's office or the glint (from some unseen light) off the metal crutches on the observation platform. Dumping the body ends with Neff brushing away footprints, so presumably the engine in the Dietrichson family station wagon starts right up. There is finally a dolly move around to Phyllis when she can't shoot again into a profile two-shot, so that only half the actors' faces are visible for their last few words. To say this version lacks suspense approaches understatement. It would have taken more than a little rum to get it up on its feet. Maybe it could have benefitted from a gas chamber scene, except, of course, there was a moratorium on executions in 1973, so that line has be changed to "so I can walk under my own power into a cell in San Quentin?" Not quite the same impact.

The first movie meeting between Neff and Phyllis is renowned for how MacMurray and Stanwyck handle the sharp dialogue and sexual undertone, how Phyllis "shoots down" Neff without diminishing his interest. All the same repartee is there, but without nuance, and not just because the speed limit is now 65 mph and 90 is well below the top notch on the gauge of 1973 models. The delivery is flat, and no glimpse of Phyllis' long leg can substitute for a simple honey of an anklet, for the chemistry created by the dialogue and the looks between MacMurray and Stanwyck. Why did they change that "honey of an anklet" to a bracelet? Was the TV network's Codes of Practices coming down on them? Because it was just a little too kinky for 1973?

The one performance that does capture some of the brilliance of what Wilder and Chandler wrote and Edward G. Robinson delivered is Lee J. Cobb as Keyes. Of course Lee J. Cobb had a long-established gravitas beyond that of his co-stars, going back to his 1949 star turn as Willy Loman, the title figure in Arthur Miller's *Death of a Salesman* on Broadway. In film, his gruff, hard-bitten acting style earned him accolades for *On the Waterfront* (1954) and *12 Angry Men* (1957). In the classic period, his roles ranged from the conniving concessionaire Mike Figlia in *Thieves' Highway* to the sympathetic cop who crosses the line for a woman in *The Man Who Cheated Himself* (1950). The 61-year-old Cobb does not try to mimic Edward G. Robinson (who was under 50 in 1943) but brings his own toughness and fatigue to the character. The movie maintains the "I love you too" line, which establish the father-son relationship although it only has impact in the final scene in the office as Keyes does thumb-flick (a 70s safety match?) to light Neff's cigarette.

If nothing else, this remake is a great argument for the auteur theory and/or the production values of old-school Hollywood. How exactly does one start with a script that has been extolled by more than one commentator as one of the finest every written and produce a mediocre result? One does have to acknowledge that this TV version of *Double Indemnity* is on the crest of a new wave of movies and television shows now called "neo-noir" and starting roughly around the time that Don Siegel (one of the few directors to start in the classic period and move on to neo-noir) directed a remake of *The Killers* (1964). It was originally intended to be one of the first movies-of-the-week but was too violent for then-network standards and re-leased theatrically. Siegel's *The Hanged Man* (also 1964), a remake of *Ride the Pink Horse*, however, was suitable for broadcast. By 1973 restrictions in both features released and network television were loosening. But neo-noir really did not begin to flourish until the advent of movies made for pay cable and direct to videocassette over a decade later.

As with the original *Double Indemnity* the producers cast a number of recognizable names (in this case from TV), character actors sometimes best known from comedy. As the man from Medford, Oregon, Wilder used Paramount stock actor Porter Hall, who was a fixture in several of comedy director Preston Sturges' movies from *Sullivan's Travels* (1941) to the *The Miracle of Morgan's Creek* (1943). In the remake that part is played by John Fiedler, who was a comic fixture in TV and movies from the late 1940s. He was typecast as a weaselly character whose high-pitched voice and small stature were perfect for that stereotype (from which Fiedler rarely escaped, as he did opposite Cobb and Henry Fonda in *12 Angry Men*). Another tele-vision mainstay Arch Johnson plays the hapless Dietrichson. As with Tom Powers in the original movie, Johnson tended to specialize in overbearing characters that were tough-guy poseurs. Their names appear in the same yellow, superimposed over Keyes and Neff in the doorway, as they wait for the cops to show up and the credits to end.

Body Heat (1981)

As was obvious to its first viewings, *Body Heat* is writer/director's Lawrence Kasdan unmistakable riff on *Double Indemnity* well into the post-Code era, a conspicuous reworking of the Cain novel as adapted by Chandler and Wilder without being an official remake or even acknowledging its sources. While

Kasdan's screenplay alters quite a few details, the Florida setting is another sunny clime (where murder can still smell like honeysuckle), his attorney protagonist Ned Racine (William Hurt) is another semi-sleazy hustler, more intent on ambulance chasing than criminal law, just as Neff was more about a "finger on a doorbell" than actuarial tables. The Barton Keyes part is split between the two acquaintances, a canny detective and an even sharper assistant district attorney, both of whom the protagonist knows must be deceived when he concocts a murder scheme for love and money.

In fairness while Neff is a top agent ("two years running") with Pacific All Risk, Ned Racine is a low-rent mouthpiece, who, as a judge remarks, is sorely in need of a better class of client. While the plot to kill the husband of Matty Walker (Kathleen Turner) involves a will rather than an insurance policy, the most important twist—and subsequently most imitated in neo-noir—is that the murdering couple does not ride the trolley to the end of the line together. Instead the femme fatale gets away with it by finding a corpse to "take that ride for me."

Body Heat also offers the neo-noir viewer what a 1944 audience could only imagine. When Walter Neff dug his fingers into Phyllis Dietrichson's sweater and said, "I'm crazy about you, baby," the scene ended. Whether by cut, dissolve, or fade out, sex between the murderous couple in *Double Indemnity* was the unseen event, in a Production Code-mandated ellipsis. *Body Heat* opens with a naked, sexually sated Racine staring out a window at a distant fire, wondering if a client of his is responsible for it.

One quickly loses count of the subsequent sex scenes, not to mention the variety of props and positions, between Racine and Matty, which certainly contributed to both the notoriety and the popularity of the film (which grossed domestically the equivalent of $80 million today—that's about twice as much as *Double Indemnity* but so was its effective budget). Matty tells Ned, in one of the many bits of dialogue that mirror the more oblique double entendres in *Double Indemnity,* that her "engine runs a little hotter than normal" and then proves it to him (and the viewer): she leads him to her home, provokes a 1940s style metaphor for sex by having him break a glass door to get in, and finally surrenders to him on the carpet with unabashed concupiscence.

223

Cinematographer John Seitz employs his "Rembrandt" lighting style from the first meeting in the Dietrichson house on Stages 8/9. A less stylized look in and around practical locations is employed by Richard Kline in *Body Heat*.

As it was with Neff and Dietrichson, the characters' reckless passion for each other makes it difficult for them to stay apart after the murder of her husband Edmund (portrayed, in a remarkable coincidence by the 1973 vintage Neff, Richard Crenna). But unlike the 1944 vintage Neff, who realizes the mistake of permitting Phyllis to meet at his apartment and insists again on the local market, and despite the fact that Edmund's niece is staying in the Walker house, Ned rushes over in the throes of uncontainable lust for Matty to fellate him—all this as if to demonstrate the truth of Matty's early remarks: "You're not too smart, are you? I like that in a man."

The particular complications which ensue continue to mirror *Double Indemnity*: like Neff, Racine suspects that Matty may be setting him up. Certainly, when the investigators become suspicious of the accidental nature of Walker's death, they focus on the wife; but Racine still never manages to use the inside information of their process to his advantage. The final mirror between the adulterous killers in both movies is their last fateful and fatal meeting.

By the boat house, Matty again confesses her love for Racine, even though she no longer thinks he believes her. Although she lured Neff into her darkened parlor, Phyllis' inability to shoot again and finish him off unexpectedly confirms her mixed emotions, some actual possible attachment to him. Matty is a blacker widow. While Neff can look back, accept that he killed for money and a woman, and ruefully conclude the ugliness of getting neither, the imprisoned Racine continues to delude himself that his purposes were somehow purer than Matty's, that she was and is a woman "who could do what was necessary. Whatever was necessary."

The coda that reveals Matty on the beach, as a young stud serves her drinks, evidences a new third-wave feminist point of view on the part of the filmmakers. In classic-period noir, a female criminal, no matter how appealing or wronged, like Debby March in Fritz Lang's *The Big Heat*, had to suffer and die for her mistakes. In neo-noir, a criminal woman's sheer force of will may permit her survival, her triumph over the conventions of society. But there is a caveat. As Matty stares out at the beach before her, she looks genuinely melancholy, even wistful. Is it possible that, like Phyllis, Matty had mixed emotions, that using Ned Racine for murder and sex resulted in some semblance of love?

225

Is this really the implication in Kathleen Turner's performance—or just a desperate patriarchal grasp for a morsel of residual potency?

Body Heat remains the earliest and perhaps best example of neo-noir films that directly confront the love/sex, honor/money dichotomies. Certainly Kasdan's script has as many twists and turns as the most complicated classic-period narrative, but his male protagonist is emotionally closer to Steve Thompson in *Criss Cross* than to Walter Huff in Cain's novel or Neff in the movie. That leaves him vulnerable to the ultimate double-cross by an 80s-style femme fatale not only more cunning than Phyllis Dietrichson but more ruthless than just about any of her antecedents or her successors.

Double Indemnity on the Air

Double Indemnity had a significant afterlife on the second most popular medium of the 1940s, radio. Radio was to the American public what television, cable, and streaming services are today, a major source of entertainment in the home as opposed to the movies which required audiences to venture out into the streets to find a movie theater. But radio had another advantage. It required visual imagination. Movies then television bathed the viewer in a barrage of image and sound, making them passive receivers, while radio required a bit more participation in the dramatic process. Through the use of dialogue, music, and sound effects radio allowed the listener to envision the settings, the characters' faces, and the core sense of a piece. Each listener in their own peculiar and individualistic way had an interactive relationship with radio drama. *Double Indemnity* was adapted for radio four times: in 1945, again in 1948, and finally twice in 1950.

Lady Esther Screen Guild Theater

The Screen Guild radio program began as a way to raise money for the Motion Picture Relief Fund. The Motion Picture Relief Fund was founded by the motion picture industry to take care of its members who had fallen on hard times, particularly during the Great Depression (and was largely responsible for building and maintaining the industry retirement home in Woodland Hills, California).

On March 5,1945, *The Lady Esther Screen Guild Theater* presented a thirty-minute version of *Double Indemnity* with Barbara Stanwyck and Fred MacMurray reprising Phyllis and Walter. Because of contractual obligations Edward G. Robinson was not able to reprise his role as Keyes. He was replaced by the veteran stage and screen actor Walter Abel—who had made his theatrical mark in the 1930s in such productions as Eugene O'Neill's *Desire under the Elms* and *Mourning Becomes Electra*. He transitioned into movies by the 1930s, appearing in landmark films like Fritz Lang's proto-noir *Fury* (1936) and *The Three Musketeers* (1935). In this half-hour version the Keyes part is heavily truncated and the whole father-son rivalry is missing. Except for a brief moment at the end of the show when Keyes calls for an ambulance to take the wounded Neff away and refers to Neff as his "friend," the emotional, even homoerotic overlay which the movie treats the audience to is missing.

The *Screen Guild* version does make great use of sound effects and an omniscient narrator to help the listener visualize the scenes, as they presumably sit in their dimly lit living rooms (or maybe their cars). The narrator describes the bloodstains on Neff's shirt as he returns to his insurance offices to record this confession. Except in this case it is not a verbal confession via Dictaphone but a more sound-effects friendly typewriter. By having Neff hit the keys of the typewriter vigorously the listener is urged to visualize the wounded protagonist bent over his manual typewriter while bleeding to death.

The staff writers for the *Screen Guild* show had the same job each week: cut two-thirds of the content out of full-length movies but capture their essence. They had to compress but not alter the plot, deliver original dialogue without significant change, and still create the mood, themes, and drama of the original. In this case most of the dialogue in this version is from the script, including the repartee between Neff and Phyllis when they first meet

227

and the ominous verbal leitmotif of phrases like "straight down the line" (which in this instance gets its own ominous chord of music).

To adhere to a thirty-minute time frame, the murder of Dietrichson and the disposition of his body on the railroad tracks is covered by very few narrative words, words which are not terribly descriptive or graphic (which would likely please Joseph Breen). Lola and boyfriend Nino are almost non-existent, so that sub-plot had little impact. But the murderous climax when Phyllis tells Neff she knew she loved him when she could not shoot him a second time is intact. There is no mention of the writers Cain or Chandler or even the writer-director Billy Wilder or anyone else for that matter at the end of the show except Lady Esther.

Ford Theater, October 15, 1948

Ford Theater (sponsored as might be expected by Ford Motor Company) was an anthology series which began in New York in 1947. It was modeled after the long-running series *Lux Radio Theatre*, that also featured adaptations of successful movies. However this New York version of radio renditions of famous films was not as initially successful largely because they tried to cut corners on production. In addition their pool of actors were theater performers who lacked the nationwide name appeal of Hollywood stars. The producers of the show took the hint and moved the series to Hollywood. Consequently their second season garnered a wide audience. With the rise of television, the sponsor and producers decided that this new medium might be more lucrative, so they burned down the radio show that phoenix-like became *The Ford Television Theatre* (which ran from 1948 to 1957).

Of the *Double Indemnity* radio adaptations this one is arguably the most interesting in that the cast is entirely new and features actors who bring a different interpretation to the text. Particularly memorable is Burt Lancaster as Neff. By 1948 Lancaster was a seasoned film noir protagonist, specializing in ostensibly macho but emotionally vulnerable protagonists, whose Achilles' heel is, of course, a femme fatale. Before being the ill-fated "chump" in *Criss Cross,* Lancaster had already projected a mixture of tough cynicism with a sense of fatalism in *The Killers, Brute Force,* and *I Walk Alone* (1947).

In the first two titles, as it would be in *Criss Cross,* Lancaster's characters end up dead. These qualities are of course perfect for the protagonist of *Double Indemnity,* particularly Cain's version. While Fred MacMurray underplays to the point of seeming semi-detached in Wilder's film, Lancaster brings more of the nervous vulnerability of the novel's protagonist to the fore. Listening to his take on Neff, one has to wonder what impact Lancaster would have had on screen; he could never have been on Wilder's list, as Lancaster was in General Mark Clark's Fifth Army marching up the boot of Italy and pushing back the Nazi Wehrmacht.

Joan Bennett also has strong noir credentials. She was after all the star of two of Fritz Lang's most daring, in terms of PCA restrictions, films: *The Woman in the Window* and *Scarlet Street* in which she twice entangled and used Edward G. Robinson's characters as submissive puppets. Her performance as Phyllis is a little more detached but effective nonetheless.

Myron McCormick does a great imitation of Robinson as Keyes. Of course McCormick was a respected character actor who appeared in numerous plays, movies, and radio shows and already possessed a gruff voice, which allowed him to mimic Robinson. Lola was voiced by Mercedes McCambridge, whom Orson Welles had dubbed "the world's greatest living radio actress."[46] Although Welles like Wilder was often prone to hyperbole, this bit of praise was not exaggerated. McCambridge could alter her voice to play a variety of characters. And in her thirties she convincingly inhabits the voice of a teenage Lola.

The director-producer of the show was Fletcher Markle, at one time the husband of Mercedes McCambridge. Markle had a prolific career in radio and television. He was uncredited but (according to IMDb) purportedly contributed to the script of the Welles' noir classic *The Lady from Shanghai.* He also directed two notable noir films himself: *Jigsaw* (1949) and *The Man with a Cloak* (1951). On both radio and television he acted as a producer-writer-director on anthology series such as *Ford Television Theatre* (1952-57) and

229

Boris Karloff's *Thriller* (1960-62). Howard Rodman adapted the Chandler-Wilder script for the show. Rodman wrote extensively for radio and then television. In the 1970s Rodman created the noir TV series *Harry-O* (1973-76) around David Janssen's private detective figure. Rodman hews closely to the original screenplay, including the conflicted father-son relationship between Keyes and Neff and the "love you too" bit.

Rodman wrote a perspicacious intro to the show, putting the emphasis on Cain's influence. It was spoken by the director Markle: "We are about to step into the brassy, yellow afternoon and nervous nights of summertime Los Angeles to enact for you one of James Cain's Californian thrillers. *Double Indemnity* is a curious blend of passion, violence, and justice, the kind of story that rings the bell even more times than Mr. Cain's renowned *Postman*."

The Screen Guild Theater, February 2, 1950

Barbara Stanwyck switched partners briefly in 1950 and reprised her role opposite her then husband Robert Taylor. The production and the script were straightforward; but Taylor's performance lacked the cynical bite of MacMurray's. Within a few months Stanwyck was back "in the arms" of MacMurray for the *Lux Radio Theater*.

Lux Radio Theater, October 30, 1950

Lux Radio Theater was a landmark broadcast. It lasted over two decades from 1934 to 1955 and was most often on the list of top-rated shows, particularly after its move in 1936 from New York to Hollywood where it also could access the wider array of stars the local industry had to offer. Unique among these radio anthologies, *Lux Radio Theater* allowed for significant rehearsal time, sometimes over a week, for the stars that appeared. Their fee was also usually heftier and when Cecil B. DeMille took over as host and director, the stars were in the hands of one of Hollywood's most legendary producer/directors.

DeMille left in 1945 because of a dispute with the American Federation of Radio Artists, which had negotiated a closed shop deal with the networks which required DeMille to pay dues. A staunch conservative and vocal anti-unionist, DeMille refused. He was replaced by director William Keighley. After the gradual demise of radio drama in the 1950s, like many of its kin on the air, *Lux Radio Theater* moved to the world of television, where it had a short-lived run.

The adaptor of the Wilder-Chandler screenplay was Sanford Barnett. He had done dozens of similar projects over the years and was an expert at tailoring the script to the needs of the audio-only medium. He kept much of the dialogue and only excised, as had other radio adaptors before him, most of the Lola-Nino scenes and some of the interplay between Keyes and Neff in the offices. Barnett worked in TV in the 1960s and 1970s including the Western series *Bat Masterson* (1958-61) and the Jack Webb police show *Adam-12* (1968-75).

After DeMille quit, Keighley was no match for his predecessor in terms of prestige; but he was certainly more familiar with the noir movement and its radio genre than C.B. Among his credits were *Each Dawn I Die* (1939) with James Cagney, *The Man Who Came to Dinner* (1942), and the classic-period noir *The Street with No Name* (1948). Keighley was also no Billy Wilder but still managed to elicit compelling performances from MacMurray and Stanwyck, even underscoring elements in their characters at which the film only hinted. There is also a compelling variation at the end of Act Two. When Keyes shows up at Neff's apartment while Phyllis is en route, Keighley adds suspense by the sound of the doorbell that puts the audience and Neff into a panic, expecting that it is Phyllis. The invisible curtain for Act Two comes down. Will Phyllis be there waiting at the door or will she have heard them talking and hidden down the hall?

Fred MacMurray's performance, always on point and professional, reveals in this first-person narration more of the nervousness of Cain's original

231

protagonist. Although his Neff is still a smart aleck, particularly towards the beginning as he projects that salesman superficiality and glibness, in this iteration the murderous insurance man seems more genuinely unsettled by both Keyes' circling in on him and by Phyllis' cold-bloodedness.

Barbara Stanwyck also varies from the film: her voice had become huskier and smokier as she moved into middle age. There was even less of the "sex kitten" from the book. Instead Phyllis is forceful and domineering. This change in her persona is likely colored by some of her post-1943 roles, such as *Sorry, Wrong Number, File on Thelma Jordon*, or *The Furies*. There is also added in the post-performance dialogue a slightly strange comic repartee between MacMurray and Stanwyck where he calls her "a witch"—either an awkward allusion to Halloween on the next day or a confusion of "w" with "b." Maybe MacMurray caught a tinge of something new in her performance. If the always confident Stanwyck had a comeback, it was not recorded in the final show.

William Conrad was a mainstay of radio as well as movies and television. His voice was immediately recognizable on the air, where he was Marshal Matt Dillon in the pre-television *Gunsmoke* (1952-1961) series for almost a decade. Too portly to be a standard Hollywood hero, he is best remembered as one of the title characters in *The Killers*. On television he was a constant presence and finally took the lead role in two successful series in the 1980s: *Nero Wolfe* and *Jake and the Fatman*. As Keyes, Conrad does not imitate Edward G. Robinson but opts for a sinister, even threatening, quality which is typical of his many noir performances.

The Rise of Film Noir, 1944-1955

We cannot overstate the influence of *Double Indemnity* on the film noir movement. Before 1944 there was a trickle of titles. After there was a flood. Between 1944 and 1955 (often marked as the year when tide of noir films began to ebb), film noir dominated the slates of both low-budget production companies studios PRC or Republic and major studios Paramount and 20th Century-Fox. And starting with the faithful adaption of *Farewell, My*

Lovely as *Murder, My Sweet* in 1944, the filmmakers at RKO—right next to Paramount and a couple of hundred yards from its writers campus—fully embraced the classic period's style and substance. How extensive was this movement of roughly 25 years? Even the selective criteria used in the 4th Edition of our *Film Noir The Encyclopedia* resulted in over 400 titles. Given their freer application of the term there are one or two hundred more in the lists of the Internet Movie Database and Wikipedia. Obviously the themes, motifs, and characters so vividly realized in *Double Indemnity* influence not just the films that follow but scores more.

Another doomed criminal couple: Yvonne De Carlo and Burt Lancaster as Anna and Steve Thompson, facing the business end of a .45 in *Criss Cross*.

233

Perhaps the fastest way to exemplify the rise of film noir is through its key creators, its directors who repeatedly embraced the movement's dark vision. One them worked with Wilder on *Menschen am Sontag*, Siodmak, another refugee from Germany, who was in fact criticized in the press for his 1933 film *The Burning Secret* by none other than Minister of Propaganda Goebbels for its "decadence." After that none too subtle hint, like Wilder, Siodmak hit the road.

It is easy to make a case for Siodmak as one of the most important of the noir directors. Just *Phantom Lady*, *The Suspect*, *Christmas Holiday* (both 1944), *The Strange Affair of Uncle Harry* (1945), *The Killers*, *The Spiral Staircase*, *The Dark Mirror* (last three all in 1946), *Cry of the City* (1948), *Criss Cross*, and *The File on Thelma Jordon*—these more than double Wilder's noir output. His work with the noir icon Burt Lancaster was particularly fertile. In *The Killers* and *Criss Cross* Siodmak remolds Lancaster's sometimes sneering façade to reflect an inner vulnerability. Obsessed with a femme fatale in both movies, these sympathetic, only slightly anti-heroes end up riding the same trolley as Neff.

Edward Dmytryk, another victim of the Hollywood Blacklist (at least until he caved in and named names), made three landmark film noirs: *Murder, My Sweet, Cornered* (1945), and *Crossfire* (1947). As noted, with the remake of Chandler's novel, as with *Double Indemnity*, a non-hard-boiled star, Dick Powell, changed his career by giving him heft as the detective Marlowe. And in *Crossfire*, Dmytryk rubbed America's anti-semitism in its face and received an Academy Award nomination for it. Shortly thereafter a subpoena to appear before HUAC arrived. He became one of the infamous/famous Hollywood Ten.

Another victim of HUAC and the Hollywood Blacklist, director Joseph Losey went to Europe instead of jail. In 1951 while Losey was pondering his future overseas as a put-out-of-work exile, three of his most important noir films were released: *M, The Prowler*, and *The Big Night*. His remake of Fritz Lang's German film with the same single letter for a title casts the ultra-normal David Wayne instead of a bug-eyed Peter Lorre as the child predator. Losey's *M* moves the same general plot line around the city of Los Angeles, making the city a character as he shoots on actual locations of the downtown core: Bunker Hill, Angels Flight, and a final chase in the art deco Bradbury Building (where *Double Indemnity* did not shoot).

The *Prowler*, written by blacklisted Dalton Trumbo, takes on the notoriously corrupt LAPD by centering on a murderous and obsessed cop played by Van Heflin. Losey went on to have a fruitful career in Europe, receiving accolades for "art" movies like *Eva* with Jeanne Moreau (1962), Harold Pinter's *The Servant* (1963) with Dirk Bogarde, and his underappreciated master turn with performances from Richard Burton and Alain Delon, *The Assassination of Trotsky* (1972).

After languishing at MGM for several years, Jules Dassin found a niche in film noir with the help of producer Mark Hellinger. *Brute Force* with Burt Lancaster is a brutal critique of the prison system with Hume Cronyn as the sadistic captain of the guards. Art Smith (another future blacklistee) acts as the film's progressive chorus, Dr. Walters, who seems to see the holocaust to come as the desperate inmates attempt to escape. Dassin's *The Naked City* (1948) was a tremendous success financially and critically and set the standard for the police procedural, a genre which became very popular in 1950s noir movies and early cop shows such as *Dragnet* (starting 1951 and through several revivals, most recently in 2003).

Equally remarkable was the 1949 *Thieves' Highway* adaptation of the proletarian novel by A.I. Bezzerides (who adapted his own work) with noir regular Richard Conte as a truck driver determined to break through the exploitation of truckers by produce brokers and an exotic Valentina Cortese as a prostitute who refuses to be fatal. When the shadow of HUAC fell on Dassin, Fox chief Darryl Zanuck sent him to London for his final pure noir, the original *Night and the City* (1950). Like director Joseph Losey, Dassin managed to transform himself into a successful European director, particularly after wedding his career to that of Greek actor/politician/activist Melina Mercouri. *Never on Sunday* and *Topkapi*, 1960 and 1964, secured his international reputation. He also came back to the United States in 1968 to

235

bring a noir ambience to his collaboration with Black activists/artists Ruby Dee and Julian Mayfield in *Uptight*, one of the first films of the Black cinematic renaissance in the late 1960s through the 1970s.

Actor Robert Montgomery cut his directing teeth in 1944, replacing the injured John Ford on the war film *They Were Expendable*. Following that experience and as one of MGM's biggest box office stars, Montgomery directed two of the most important noir films of the 1940s: *The Lady in the Lake* based on the Chandler novel at MGM and then *Ride the Pink Horse*, based on the novel by one of the best noir novelists of that period, Dorothy B. Hughes (*The Fallen Sparrow, In a Lonely Place*).

The Lady in the Lake is particularly innovative as Montgomery, refusing to see it Chandler's way, used a subjective camera for most of the film to reify the novel's first-person POV. MGM did not want Montgomery to be a voice only throughout the movie, so he appears in a prologue speaking directly to the audience and in selected reflections while speaking to other characters. With *Ride the Pink Horse,* Montgomery was on-screen protagonist Lucky Gagin, spitting out dialogue honed by one-time Snyder-Gray commentator Ben Hecht and Charles Lederer. This was the sixth noir title for Joan Harrison (no relation to Doane), one of the noir movement's only female producers, who had come to the United States with Hitchcock and had already worked extensively with Robert Siodmak. Her last noirs, before rejoining Hitchcock on his television series, were again with Montgomery on *Eye Witness* (1950) and another émigré Jacques Tourneur on *Circle of Danger* (1951).

Nicholas Ray began his long and creative directorial career in the world of film noir. He came to Paramount from a varied background, working for the Federal Theater Project in the 1930s, then in radio for the United States Office of War Information, and finally a brief stint as a feature film dialogue director, to be producer John Houseman's assistant and, like John Berry on *Double Indemnity,* learn to direct. As it happens, Houseman could not launch Ray as a director until they both left Paramount. It probably was not because Ray had a brief liaison with Wilder's ex-girlfriend Doris Dowling (before her post-break-up appearance for Wilder in *Lost Weekend* and as Alan Ladd's femme fatale wife in the Houseman/Chandler *The Blue Dahlia*).

236

Eminent film noir producer Joan Harrison with émigré director Robert Siodmak (left) and actor Franchot Tone on the set of *Phantom Lady*.

Ray would direct three key film noirs: *They Live by Night* (1948), *In a Lonely Place*, and *On Dangerous Ground* (1951). *They Live by Night* is one of the earliest examples of the "fugitive couple" trope, a very youthful one in this early example, which became so popular in not only the classic noir period but also in the neo-noir period, as in the adaptations of Jim Thompson's *The Getaway* in 1972 and 1994 or Terence Malick's revisitation of the "teen" couple in *Badlands* (1973).[47]

In a Lonely Place was Ray's second project with Humphrey Bogart's Santana Productions (after the socially conscious *Knock on Any Door* in

1949) and another adaptation of a Dorothy B. Hughes work. The movie and book are among the most incisive dissections of toxic masculinity (it oozes out of the character's very name) with Bogart as the violent, alienated screenwriter Dixon Steele. Ray developed that theme even further in his next noir, *On Dangerous Ground*, adapted by Ray with A.I. Bezzerides. Early in the film Robert Ryan, a burned-out cop who roughs up suspects, promises a call girl (portrayed by the low-budget femme fatale Cleo Moore) more abuse if she does not give up her criminal boyfriend.

Robert Wise was steeped in noir as he worked as an editor for Orson Welles then broke in as a director for the noir horror producer Val Lewton (*The Curse of the Cat People* in 1944 and *The Body Snatcher* in 1945). He tested the noir waters with *Criminal Court* (1946), with the criminal couple (Claire Trevor and Lawrence Tierney) who are *Born to Kill* (1947), and the sci-fi, literal alien protagonist in *The Day the Earth Stood Still* (1951). His two seminal film noirs, a decade apart, are *The Set-Up* (1949) and *Odds against Tomorrow* (1959).

The Set-Up stars another of the male icons of film noir (along with Bogart, Lancaster, and Robert Mitchum): Robert Ryan. Ryan is a boxer on his last legs, who is also involved with gangsters. The final scene where Ryan's hand is crushed by mobsters because he refused to take a dive during a fight throws a violent and emotional punch, particularly when his wife celebrates the end of his career with the line: "We both won tonight."

Odds Against Tomorrow (1959) was written by blacklisted noir writer-director Abraham Polonsky (also scenarist on *Body and Soul*, 1947, and *Force of Evil*, 1948) using a front. It is a caper film with a subtext focused on racism in America. As he had in *Crossfire*, Ryan plays a white supremacist while Harry Belafonte (who was also an uncredited producer on the film) is a jazz musician trying to make a life (make that stay alive) in Ryan's America. The next year Wise left the world of noir or, maybe more appropriately, the movement disappeared from under him, and he remains best known for *West Side Story* (1961) and *The Sound of Music* (1965).[48]

Jacques Tourneur was the son of the silent-era French director Maurice Tourneur who was an eminent part of early Hollywood as an émigré. The younger Tourneur was, like Wise, a graduate of Val Lewton's noir horror

238

school at RKO. His most notable noirs are *Out of the Past* (1947) and *Nightfall* (1957). *Out of the Past* is considered by many critics, along with *Double Indemnity*, one of the best noir films ever made. Critic Roger Ebert writes in his 2004 re-evaluation of the movie:

> Out of the Past *is one of the greatest of all film noirs, the story of a man who tries to break with his past and his weakness and start over again in a town, with a new job and a new girl. The film stars Robert Mitchum [as fugitive private detective Jeff Bailey], whose weary eyes and laconic voice, whose very presence as a violent man wrapped in indifference, made him an archetypal noir actor. The story opens before we've even seen him, as trouble comes to town looking for him. A man from his past has seen him pumping gas, and now his old life reaches out and pulls him back...* [49]

Another fatal woman in a fur, not behind bars but in a phone booth: Jane Greer as Kathie Moffat makes the call to seal Jeff Bailey's fate, while Paul Valentine as gunsel Joe Stephanos looks on in *Out of the Past*.

239

Although not as notable, *Nightfall* (1956) is also a fine noir based on a novel by the prolific noir novelist David Goodis (*Dark Passage, Down There,* adapted by Francois Truffaut as *Shoot the Piano Player*—1960). Made near the end of the cycle, the dilemma of *Nightfall's* protagonist is archetypically noir. A victim of several mischances, the paranoia of tough-guy James Vanning (Aldo Ray) compounds these problems significantly while Tourneur's editing scheme relegates these causal incidents to a flashback halfway through the film while allowing them to be distorted by Vanning's point-of-view. Vanning is basically innocent of any wrongdoing as Jeff Bailey clearly was not, so the trap into which this protagonist has fallen can and must be interpreted as impersonal or deterministic, not retributive. In the climactic sequence, the snowplow lumbering after him like a gigantic beast becomes the concluding metaphor for the larger-than-life menace that can at any time emerge from the noir underworld.

The award-winning and wildly independent Otto Preminger was an established actor/producer/director by the time he took on his first noir, the landmark *Laura* (1944), based on the Vera Caspary novel. Preminger made some of the most important noirs of the period: *Fallen Angel* (1945), *Whirlpool* (1950), *Where the Sidewalk Ends* (1950), *Angel Face* (1951). What makes classic-period Preminger movie particularly noir is a sense of ironic distance and an attraction to strong female characters who are, with the notable exception of the psychotic Diane in *Angel Face*, not really femmes fatales.

Even when handed a star like the exotic Gene Tierney who had cut her teeth on femme fatale roles like Poppy in Josef von Sternberg's *The Shanghai Gesture* (1941) and as the bandit Belle Starr in the film of the same name (also 1941), Preminger refused to submit to typecasting. The character Laura, as in the novel, is an ambitious career woman who happened to be the "obscure object of desire" of three unstable male figures: a detective, a radio personality, and a fickle fiancé. In *Where the Sidewalk Ends* Tierney also incarnates a well-balanced, forthright character who helps redeem a violent and emotionally unstable cop. Preminger's sympathy for strong female characters carried over into his non-noir films like *Saint Joan* (1957) and *Bonjour Tristesse* (1958).[50]

240

Two men compete for the love of a dead woman: Clifton Webb as the effete Waldo Lydecker and Dana Andrews as Det. Mark McPherson in *Laura*.

Purportedly, Wilder resented how easily director Fritz Lang became a top-notch director in Hollywood after emigrating from Europe in 1935. But one has to remember that Lang was a star at the German Expressionist factory UFA. Films like *Metropolis*, the *Dr. Mabuse* series (1922), the two *Die Nibelungen* (1924) movies were worldwide hits. So it is not hard to understand why the major studios immediately offered him proto-noir projects like *Fury* (1936) and *You Only Live Once* (1937), while Wilder was relegated to the 1940s equivalent of the writer's room.

But by the time of *Double Indemnity*'s release Lang's career had begun to falter. Not that his films were any less creative and hard-hitting but his

241

budgets became more constricted as he segued to an independent company, partnered with Joan Bennett and her then husband Walter Wanger in Diana Productions, for both *The Woman in the Window* and *Scarlet Street* and later *The Secret Beyond the Door* (1947). His next independents *Clash by Night* (1952) and *The Blue Gardenia* (1953), which made extensive use of new technology for location shooting, had female stars Stanwyck and Anne Baxter but limited releases. From there Lang moved to the second tier of major studios like Columbia and RKO for *The Big Heat* and *Human Desire* (1954, like *Scarlet Street* another American version of a naturalistic Jean Renoir movie). At Columbia Lang films began to lose style, both the expressionist approach he had helped to develop in the 1920s and the docu-noir look of *Blue Gardenia*. As with many classic period titles after the 1950s, noir became harsher in its high key, flatter look, more in a way like television, already drawing large chunks of audience away from the feature-film industry's product. Lang's last noirs in 1956 had a semi-documentary approach for the story of journalists seeking a serial-killer in *While the City Sleeps* and the elaborately-planned-perfect-crime-with-a-fatal-error in *Beyond a Reasonable Doubt*.[51]

John Farrow, Australian by birth, is among the most ignored of noir directors. But between 1948 and 1950 he made four of the most important film noirs: *The Big Clock* and *Night Has a Thousand Eyes* (from the novel by one of the best of contemporary melodramatic novelists Cornell Woolrich aka Willliam Irish), both in 1948 and both photographed by John F. Seitz. In 1950 he made the masterful *Where Danger Lives*, that even the erratic Howard Hughes could not diminish, especially given that it was impossible to cut down the remarkable series of long takes that Farrow created at the end of the movie.[52] These takes focus the remarkable performance that Farrow obtained from Robert Mitchum and Hughes' protégé Faith Domergue as the deeply disturbed and conflicted femme fatale Margo. Farrow's consistent use of the long take, which he had perfected in his earlier noirs with Seitz, is particularly tension-inducing. In 1951 he followed *Where Danger Lives* with another Hughes project, *His Kind of Woman*, lighter fare but starring

Mitchum once again with yet another Hughes protégé, Jane Russell. Iron-ically Hughes had lured Farrow away from Paramount with a promise of greater artistic control, on which he completely reneged with his extensive reshooting and recutting of *His Kind of Woman*.[53]

As the classic period began to implode around 1955, the movie which most critics use as a demarcation line is Robert Aldrich's brilliant *Kiss Me Deadly* (which appropriately ends with its own implosion—a nuclear one on a beach in Malibu). Aldrich began his career in the movies as an assistant director to a number of the most important noir writer-directors: Abraham Polonsky, Joseph Losey, etc. He also made a few of his own before *Kiss Me Deadly*: most notably, working in the television series *China Smith* and its feature spin-off *World for Ransom* (1954).

1955, the end of an epoch. Film noir has fulfilled its role by creating a particular disquiet and providing a vehicle for social criticism in the United States. Robert Aldrich gives this happening a fascinat-ing and shadowy conclusion, Kiss Me Deadly. *It is the despairing opposite of the film which, fourteen years earlier, opened the noir cycle,* The Maltese Falcon. *A savage lyricism hurls us into a world in full decomposition, ruled by the dissolute and the cruel, to these wild and corrupted intrigues, Aldrich brings the most radical of solutions: nuclear apocalypse.*[54]

Kiss Me Deadly was unique in many ways. Aldrich and screenwriter A.I. Bez-zerides (who had, as noted, adapted his novel *Thieves' Highway* for Jules Dassin) set out to deconstruct Mickey Spillane's politics and ethos, as well as his macho detective Mike Hammer and in so doing expose the dark side of the zeitgeist in 1950s America. What Aldrich saw, as a committed progres-sive (who worked with many blacklistees),[55] was an America becoming more and more frightened and repressive (witness the Hollywood Blacklist, the Red Scare, nuclear war anxiety, and thoughtless jingoism). And Spillane was one of the more popular cultural exponents of this mentality. So Bezzerides

Gaby Rodgers as Lily Carver opens the box that triggers the atomic explosion at the end of *Kiss Me Deadly*.

and Aldrich turned the Spillane novel upside down and created a meta film noir, which returns the movement to its political and cultural roots, to the trenchant social critique of the American Dream seen so clearly in movies like *Double Indemnity*. Or as Wilder himself put it:

> *The main characters in* Double Indemnity *have a problem... They aren't living the American dream and they hope to correct that.* [56]

244

FILMOGRAPHY AND SYNOPSIS

DOUBLE INDEMNITY

A Paramount Picture.

Directed by: Billy Wilder.

Screenplay by: Billy Wilder and Raymond Chandler, from the novel by James M. Cain.

Producer: [uncredited] Joseph Sistrom.

Executive Producer: [uncredited] Buddy DeSylva.

Music: Miklós Rózsa [as Miklos Rozsa].

Director of Photography: John [F.] Seitz, ASC.

Editorial Supervision: Doane Harrison.

Art Direction: Hans Dreier (studio department head) and Hal Pereira.

Process Photography: Farciot Edouart. ASC.

Costumes by: Edith Head.

Make-up Artist: Wally Westmore.

Sound Recording by: Stan Cooley and Walter Oberst.

Set Decoration: Bertram [C.] Granger.

Cast: Fred MacMurray (Walter Neff).
Barbara Stanwyck (Phyllis Dietrichson).
Edward G. Robinson (Barton Keyes).
Porter Hall (Mr. Jackson).
Jean Heather (Lola Dietrichson).
Tom Powers (Mr. Dietrichson).
Byron Barr (Nino Zachette).

Richard Gaines (Edward S. Norton, Jr.).
Fortunio Bonanova (Sam Gorlopis).
John Philliber (Pacific-All-Risk janitor/Joe Pete).

[Uncredited]

Source Music: excerpts from *Symphony in D Minor* by César Franck and "Tangerine" written by Johnny Mercer (lyrics) and Victor Schertzinger (music).

Art Direction: David S. Hall.

Special Effects Photography: Gordon Jennings. ASC.

Make-up Artists: Robert Ewing, Charles Gemora.

Hair Stylist: Hollis Barnes.

Sound Department: Loren L. Ryder.

Casting: Harvey Clermont.

Paramount Production Supervisor: George Bertholon.

Unit Production Manager: Hugh Brown.

Assistant Production Manager: Al Trosin.

Assistant Directors: Charles C. "Buddy" Coleman (First Assistant Director), Bill Sheehan (Second Assistant Director).

Script Clerk: Nancy Lee.

Dialogue Director: Jack Gage.

Props: Jim Cottrell, Jack Golconda.

Jewelry Design: Eugene Joseff.

Set Costumers: Neva Bourne, Bill Rabb.

Still Photographer: Ed Henderson.

Camera Assistants: Otto Pierce (operator), Harlow Stengel.

Set Sound Assistants: Bill Pillar (boom), Jack Duffy.

Grips: Walter McLeod (key), Paul Tranz (dolly).

Electricians: Chet Stafford (key).

Location Manager: Norman Lacey.

Stand-in: Dorothy Staton (for Stanwyck).

Assistant Editor: Lee Hall.

Publicist: John R. Wolfenden.

Uncredited Cast, Day Players (in order of appearance): Betty Farrington (Nettie the Dietrichson maid), Miriam Nelson aka Marion Franklin (Keyes' secretary), George Magrill (colleague who greets Neff), Constance Purdy (shopper with a child in market), Sam McDaniel (Charlie, garage attendant), Howard Mitchell, Harold Garrison (train conductors), Oscar Smith (redcap), Kernan Cripps, Floyd Shackelford (Pullman porters), Edmund Cobb (other conductor), Dick Rush, James Adamson (other Pullman porters), Bess Flowers (Norton's secretary), Judith Gibson aka Teala Loring (Pacific-All-Risk telephone operator), Douglas Spencer (Lou Schwartz).

Cameos/Bits: Raymond Chandler (man reading magazine outside Keyes' office), Eddie Hall (man in store), Florence Wix (train passenger), John Berry (young man leaving elevator), Clarence Muse (Pacific-All-Risk janitor).*

Gas Chamber Sequence: George Anderson (warden), Edward Hearn (warden's secretary), Boyd Irwin, George Melford ($1^{st}/2^{nd}$ doctors), William O'Leary (chaplain), Lee Shumway (door guard), Allan Bridge (chamber guard).†

Completed: November 24, 1943.

Released: Paramount, September 7, 1944.‡

Running time: 107 minutes.§

Notes:

*After Mona Freeman was replaced in the part of Lola, there is no evidence to indicate that she appeared anywhere in the movie. Normally an actor who has been replaced for any reason would no longer be given access to the set (or even the studio lot). The woman who tells Neff that Keyes would like to see him in the first flashback to the insurance offices is Miriam Nelson (aka Marion Franklin) not Mona Freeman. It is unlikely that she appears with any background performers in any scene.

†Sequence "E," Scenes E-1 through E-12 were shot in a replica of the San Quentin gas chamber and a prison corridor on November 17 and November 19, 1943 (Days 44 and 46), but were never included in the final cut.

‡There are different accepted ways of determining the release date for American films. These are sometimes complicated by the ongoing distribution tactic of a short, one week run in Los Angeles or New York to qualify for Academy Award consideration before the end of the year. Accordingly, some movies have a December limited release date and a general release (in theaters or nowadays to streaming platforms) months later in the following year. This was not the case with *Double Indemnity.*

Trade reviews of *Double Indemnity* did appear in late April 1944 (April 26 for *Variety* and April 24 for the *Hollywood Reporter*). However, these reviews were written after a preview of the movie, not an actual release or even a one-week run. The first advertised release theatrically was on the east coast: a special engagement in a single Baltimore theater began July 3 and a wider release on July 6. Generally this would be the consensus initial release date. However, contrary to what you may have read this was not (could not be) a nationwide release. Film prints being expensive and raw stock being in limited supply during wartime, instead of an actual nationwide release Paramount (and most studios) would roll out their new movies city-by-city/region-by-region. So July 6 was Baltimore, Washington, D.C., Miami, and possibly a few other locations between those of Baltimore and D.C. The next week, July 13, was Philadelphia and Pittsburgh. Los Angeles and Dallas were not until August 10; Boston, August 24; New York, September 6; and Chicago was likely last on Nov. 1.

A final way of determining release date for movies of the 1940s would refer to a standard form that all production companies filed with the Academy for award consideration. This information sheet, or Academy record, contains "official" information such as main cast, crew, technical specs, and release date. When Elizabeth Ward and Alain Silver were compiling credits for the first edition of *Film Noir The Encyclopedia*, they reviewed hundreds of these records in the AMPAS Library clipping files. The date stipulated by Paramount on that sheet was September 7, 1944.

§The running time from Paramount logos and music cues at beginning and end is 1:47:06. On current copies with the Universal logo added the running time is 1:47:28.

Synopsis:

A dark coupe drives towards men doing repairs for the Los Angeles Railway Corp. and veers around a welder. As a traffic semaphore switches from "Go" to "Stop," the car continues through an intersection where it almost hits a newspaper truck. Finally, it pulls up in front of a building on Olive Street in downtown Los Angeles.

A hatted figure with an overcoat draped over his shoulders emerges from the passenger side and approaches the locked lobby doors of the building. A night watchman opens the door and greets him as, "Mister Neff." [No time is specified but it may be past midnight.]

The same watchman operates the elevator and stops on a floor with glass doors marked as the entrance to the "Pacific All Risk Insurance Co. Founded 1906." The camera dollies forward behind Neff as he exits the elevator and passes through the doors then continues past the figure to reveal janitors cleaning up around a large array of desks on the floor below. Neff strides slowly along a railed upper platform to an office. Inside he removes the coat, crosses to a desk, and turns on a lamp. As he sits and loosens his ties, a dark circle is visible in the left shoulder of his jacket. Painfully he takes a pack of cigarettes from an inside pocket. On the second try he ignites a match with his thumbnail and lights one of the smokes. Then he rolls the chair to the right and uncovers a Dictaphone machine on a typing table. He inserts a disk and starts to record: "Office Memorandum. Walter Neff to Barton Keyes, claims manager. Los Angeles, July 16, 1938 [which was a Saturday]. Dear Keyes, I suppose you'll call this a confession when you hear it. I don't like the word 'confession.'" Neff introduces the subject: a murder...for money...and a woman. After two minutes he sets a start date—"Around the end of May, it was"—and a flashback begins.

The same two-door coupe drives up a narrow hillside roadway with a view of the city below, past some children playing baseball, and pulls up in front of a double garage with two arched doors. Neff's narration continues, as he goes up six steps and a walkway to the front door of a two-story house. At the front door he asks to see Mr. Dietrichson; but a short woman with an apron and feather duster resists his entering. Discussion continues as he pushes past her. Another woman appears on a landing at the top of a semicircular staircase to the upper story. She is wrapped in a patterned towel, which Neff takes in as he explains the reason for his visit: two unrenewed policies on the family vehicles that has left them pointedly "not fully covered." Mrs. Dietrichson instructs Nettie, her housekeeper, to "show Mr. Neff into the living room," while she gets dressed. As he waits the narration recounts Neff's impression of the Dietrichson living room, "still stuffy from last night's cigars." He checks out family photos and even feeds the goldfish but mainly is "thinking about that dame upstairs and the way she had looked at me...I wanted to see her again, close."

She comes down the stairs buttoning a white dress with a frilly bodice. When she sits opposite him, and Neff notices "a honey of an anklet" below her stockinged

249

left calf, she demurely uncrosses her legs. Then she paces in front of the fireplace, as Neff touts his policies. Finally she sits and crosses her legs again before asking if he also sells "accident insurance?" Neff wants to know what's engraved on the anklet. "Phyllis." Ultimately an appointment to see her husband is made for the next evening. Neff flirts more explicitly on the way out, but gets cold water from Phyllis.

When Neff visits the office to check his mail, a blonde woman tells him "Mr. Keyes has been yelling for you all afternoon." Inside the office marked with his name and title of "claims manager" is Barton Keyes in the midst of excoriating Sam Gorlopis, whose truck has burned. After Keyes explains that it was arson and threatens to have him arrested for fraud, Gorlopis signs a waiver on the payment of $2,600 "a lot of money where I live" [which would be $45,000 converted from 1943 dollars, or $56,000 from 1938]. Because he had clipped a note to the policy he sold Gorlopis, Neff refuses to accept recrimination from Keyes. After more banter, as he threatens to "throw his desk" at Neff, Keyes searches in his vest pocket. He lights a match, hands it to Keyes for his cigar, and adds with a chuckle, "I love you, too."

In his own office, Neff finds a message from Phyllis asking to change the meeting to Thursday afternoon. [Later interaction reveals that present time would be a Tuesday, probably May 31, 1938.] A dolly shot moves in close as Neff's narration and smile indicate he is looking forward to the next meeting with Phyllis and her anklet.

Neff arrives to discover that Mr. Dietrichson is not home, despite his wife expecting him to be. Also Phyllis has forgotten that this is Nettie's day off. Consequently they are alone, as Phyllis again banters with Neff and pointedly returns to the question: "Could I get an accident policy for him without bothering him at all?" Neff's expression changes, as he understands her intent. Before he leaves he says bluntly, "Look, baby, you can't get away with it." He takes Phyllis' suggestion and gets out of there "but quick."

That night Phyllis shows up at his apartment. Even before she arrives Neff's narration reveals that he "hadn't walked out on anything at all. That the hook was too strong. That this wasn't the end between her and me." The reason for her visit is clearly not to return his hat (she does not have it); and they dance around the issue of sexual attraction for a while then finally kiss. After that, while he pours glasses of bourbon for them in the kitchen, Neff gives her several examples of murder-for-insurance plans gone awry, that for one woman it meant "a stretch in Tehachapi." Phyllis notes, "Perhaps it was worth it to her." Back in the living room, she explains that "He never lets me go anywhere, he keeps me shut up. He's always been mean to me...He gets drunk and slaps my face." It's Neff who moves closer to her on the sofa and returns to the idea of turning the husband she hates "into some cold hard cash." After reiterating that "if there's a death mixed up in it, you haven't got a prayer," he pulls her into an embrace. "Maybe she had stopped thinking about it, but I hadn't." The camera dollies to a wider shot, and there is a dissolve back to Neff's office.

Another dolly shot moves in on the dictating Neff. The blood stain on his shoulder has grown. He admits: "It was all tied up with something I had been thinking about for years, long before I ever ran into Phylllis Dietrichson…" Neff confesses that he had thought about how "to crook the house," but he needed "a shill to put down the bet. Suddenly the doorbell rings and the whole setup is right there in the room with you."

Back in the apartment, as Phyllis fixes her make-up and gets her coat, Neff is stretched on the sofa. Whether it was there or in the bedroom, it's clearly [or as clear as it could be in 1943] après sex. When Phyllis tears up, Neff announces that he will help her do it. After she leaves, as he crosses back to open the window, Neff uses his toe to straighten a kink in the rug [a Lubitsch touch, not in the script?].

Back in his office for a third time, Neff continues the story. A side angle reveals the spinning cylinder in the Dictaphone, as Neff recalls the particulars of his plan.

As Neff describes Phyllis playing Chinese checkers with Lola Dietrichson, there is a dissolve back to that action in the living room. The camera pulls back to reveal Dietrichson reclining on a sofa, while Neff does a hard sell on an accident policy. As expected, Dietrichson won't got for it. Neff and Phyllis exchange knowing glances, as the husband signs a "duplicate" auto application. Outside in the doorway, Neff announces that he must take the train at the end of the month to attend that Stanford reunion he mentioned, because if he dies on a public carrier, the double indemnity payout will be not 50 but $100,000 [which is $2.1 million converted from 1938 dollars].

When he reaches his car, Neff discovers that Lola is inside waiting. She wants a ride to meet Nino Zachette, the boyfriend of whom her father and Phyllis strongly disapprove. Neff obliges. After dropping her off to meet the quarrelsome Zachette, Neff drives away and ponders about Lola's father being "a dead pigeon."

Neff and Phyllis meet at a local market, where she reveals that the Stanford trip is off because her husband has broken his leg. She becomes emotional at the prospect of waiting indefinitely for a safe opportunity; but Neff is adamant. Her expression as Neff leaves suggests something more than merely pining after her new lover.

A week later (the 15th of June), Neff is opening mail in his office and musing about the vagaries of fate, when Keyes enters and proposes that Walter take a pay cut to become his assistant and join him in sorting out "twisted hopes and crooked dreams." While Neff is expressing genuine disinterest, the phone rings. Keyes picks it up then hands it to Neff while noting it's a "dame on your phone." Phyllis is calling to say her husband has decided to leave for Stanford by train that very night. Keyes waits while Neff obliquely confirms the details on the plan to kill him. As he accepts a light for his cigar, a disappointed Keyes lectures Neff about his short-sightedness in not taking the claims job. Alone Neff steels himself to the prospect of what he is about to do.

Neff then narrates his final preparations—which include leaving his car with the garage attendant, by whom he wants to be seen, and what he does secretly, including indicators of whether someone has called him or come by his apartment—all to make certain his alibi is established.

251

He is hiding in the back of the car when Phyllis comes down from the house with her husband, whom she is driving to the station. At the dark street they agreed upon, Phyllis turns off and signals with the horn. Off-screen Neff breaks Dietrichson's neck.

Dressed in the same color suit and with his foot wrapped to simulate a cast, Phyllis escorts Neff to the train, which he boards as Dietrichson. Neff makes his way to the observation platform at the rear of the last car and discovers that another passenger, Mr. Jackson, is already seated there. On the pretext of having forgotten his cigar case, Neff cajoles the man into fetching it for him. Once alone, Neff tosses the crutches on the tracks then goes over the guardrail and slips off the train.

Phyllis is close by at the prearranged spot and flashes the car headlights. Neff hurries to reach her. While she fetches the crutches, Neff drags Dietrichson's body to the tracks. Back in the car, Phyllis cannot get the engine to turn over. After repeated attempts, Neff slides over, works the starter himself, and succeeds.

As Phyllis drives back to his apartment, Neff notes that Phyllis was "perfect. No nerves, not a tear, not even a blink of the eyes." As Phyllis and he exchange professions of love, it's Neff who is rattled. After verifying that no one has seen him go out or called in his absence, Neff reestablishes his presence with the garage attendant and walks towards an all night diner. "Nothing had been overlooked. And yet, Keyes, suddenly it came over me that everything would go wrong. I couldn't hear my own footsteps. It was the walk of a dead man."

A fade out/in returns to Neff's office (for a fourth time), where he elaborates on how he "could feel my nerves pulling me to pieces."

Two days later, Keyes intercepts Neff by the main doors. As they walk together to confer with Norton, "the big boss," Keyes updates him on the autopsy report and inquest: "Verdict...accidental death." Inside Norton wonders if Keyes has "one of those interesting little hunches of yours." To the surprise of Keyes and Neff, Norton first announces that he rejects the finding that it was an accident then, after a second surprise of Phyllis arriving at his request, he asserts that it was suicide. When Norton proposes a settlement, Phyllis gets to her feet saying that she was not even aware of the policy but now, "You want to bargain with me at a time like this." Denouncing Norton's insinuations and methods, she storms out. At that point, Keyes lectures Norton on his foolhardiness and details the history of suicides concluding "of all the cases on record, there is not one single case of suicide by leap from the rear end of a moving train... No soap, Mr. Norton. We're sunk, and we'll have to pay through the nose." Then Keyes storms out. In the outer office, a grinning Neff hands Keyes a match.

At his apartment that evening, Phyllis calls. Neff okays a visit with the admonition of not letting anyone see her. Then the doorbell rings. It's Keyes. His "little man is acting up again." He knows "something has been worked on us" but cannot determine exactly how. In the corridor Phyllis arrives, reaches Neff's door, and hears the discussion. She waits then hides behind it when Keyes leaves. Realizing she is there, Neff holds the door then leaves it to her when to grab the nob when he steps forward to provide Keyes a match.

Inside Neff confirms that Keyes doesn't know what happened; but "it's those stinking hunches of his." Now Keyes will be watching, so they cannot "see each other for a while…until this dies down." When Neff asks, "You afraid, baby?" Phyllis expresses concern that "it's pulling us apart, isn't it, Walter?" She turns around and forces him to face her and kiss her.

The next morning, Lola Dietrichson comes to Neff's office. She is convinced that her stepmother Phyllis is behind her father's death. Lola's mother also died under suspicious circumstances, while Phyllis was her nurse. Lola saw Phyllis trying on a hat with a black veil before the fact. Realizing Phyllis has killed before, Walter takes Lola to dinner, then on Sunday to the beach, to distract her from going to the police with her suspicions. Monday morning when a note from Keyes is on his desk, Neff wonders if he has been seen with Lola. Instead Keyes has brought Mr. Jackson down from Medford, Oregon. Neff is relieved not to be recognized. But Keyes has divined the actual plan of killing Dietrichson beforehand and dumping his body on the tracks. He just doesn't know who impersonated him on the train. But for the murderers "it's not like taking a trolley ride together where they can get off at different stops. They're stuck with each other…to the end of the line, and the last stop is the cemetery." Keyes has the claim and plans to throw it back in her face.

From a phone booth, Neff summons Phyllis to the market to update her and warn that pursuing the insurance claim in court is too risky. Phyllis refuses to withdraw it. "Nobody's pulling out. We went into this together and we're coming out at the end together…straight down the line for both of us, remember?"

In the office (for the fifth time), as he continues his dictation, the blood stain is larger. Neff confesses that he started thinking differently about Phyllis: "How would it be if she were dead?"

Neff continues to meet Lola. As they sit in the hills above the Hollywood Bowl, Lola tells Neff that she has discovered that boyfriend Nino has been visiting Phyllis behind her back: "They killed my father together, he and Phyllis. He helped her do it. I know he did."

"The real brain-twister" for Neff comes "the next day. You sprang it on me, Keyes, after office hours in the lobby." At the tobacco counter, Keyes fills Neff in: "the guy has been spotted." Keyes has pegged Nino Zachette as "that somebody else." After giving Keyes the usual match for his cigar, Neff goes back upstairs and listens to the latest dictation on Keyes' machine. He reports checking Neff's whereabouts on the murder night and clearing him; after all he has "known Neff intimately for eleven years and personally vouches for him without hesitation." But Zachette has visited the Dietrichson house (where Lola no longer lives) "on the nights of July 9th, 10th, 11th, 12th, and 13th." Keyes thinks it's time for the cops and the District Attorney. Neff calls Phyllis from Keyes' office. He must see her and tells her "not to worry about Keyes."

Neff imagines how Phyllis prepared for his arrival. Lights are dimmed. A revolver is hidden under a chair cushion. She is smoking a cigarette and seated in that chair when Neff arrives to confront her. He knows about her and Zachette. He guesses she is planning for Zachette to kill both Lola and him but affirms that he "is getting off the trolley car right at this corner...two people are going to ride to the end all right...but I've got another guy to finish my ride for me." He will kill her and frame Zachette. "That's just what's going to happen, baby." Phyllis calmly counters, "Maybe I don't go for the idea." She claims she was working on Zachette to make him jealous enough to kill Lola. Neff half believes her because "it's just rotten enough." Neff accepts that they are "both rotten"; but she is a bit more so. When he moves to close the window, she retrieves the gun and shoots him. Somehow she falters. Instead of firing again, she lets Neff take the gun. While she wonders aloud about her own feelings, Neff shoots her twice. Then outside he waits for Zachette and warns him not to enter the house. Instead he offers him a nickel with which to call Granite 0386, Lola's new number.

The sun is rising as Neff ends his dictation and realizes that Keyes has arrived, summoned by the night crew. Neff questions why a doctor should be called to patch him up, just so that he can "walk into that gas chamber up in San Quentin on my own power." Keyes lets him try to get to the elevator, but Neff collapses in the front doorway. After calling for an ambulance, Keyes arrives, finds a match, and lights Neff's cigarette.

PROTO-NOIR

I n a memo where James Cain suggested to director-writer Billy Wilder some changes that might get around the PCA's objections to his novel *Double Indemnity*, most of which were not used, Cain makes an off-handed but perspicacious observation about a change he noticed in some recent movies: "It could make, I think, a fine picture of the psychological disintegration kind that has been popular lately."[1] Those movies of "psychological disintegration" which Cain and others began to see as the world moved closer to war were in fact the earliest examples of film noir.

Of course, as we have discussed no one used a term that had not yet been coined. It took the astute critical eye of the French (who had saved American authors like Edgar Allan Poe from obscurity) to notice the shift and categorize it after the end of the World War II. Not that the phenomenon was hard to miss. With the cessation of blockades by the occupying Nazis at the end of the war, American releases, not seen in continental Europe since late 1941, arrived in a flood.

The critic and screenwriter Nino Frank in his 1946 article "A New Kind of Police Drama: the Criminal Adventure" made this observation:

Seven new American films are particularly masterful: Citizen Kane, The Little Foxes, How Green Was My Valley, *plus* Double Indemnity, Laura, *and, to a certain extent,* The Maltese Falcon *and* Murder, My Sweet... these "noir" films no longer have any common ground with run-of-the-mill police dramas. Markedly psychological plots, violent or emotional action, have less impact than facial expressions, gestures, utterances, rendering the truth of the characters...[2]

Frank identified not only the emotionalism and violence of the burgeoning film noir movement but also the realism of the characters and their dialogue, the psychological depth of the films or, as Cain put it, the "psychological disintegration."

Frank introduced the term "film noir" based it on the *serie noire*, a French publishing imprint, founded in 1945 by Marcel Duhamel. The company released collections of crime fiction in the hard-boiled style (most notably Dashiell Hammett, Raymond Chandler, James Cain, and Chester Himes). However it was not until the movement was waning in the conformist 1950s that *the* seminal book on the subject of film noir appeared, in French (the complete volume was not translated and published in English until 2002). That was Raymond Borde and Étienne Chaumeton's *Panorama du Film Noir Américain* (1955), which included a preface by Duhamel and effectively defined the film noir movement as American. The authors focused in many of the movement's key elements: the moody photography, the existential fatalism, the leftist political critique, the power of the femme fatale, the flawed male protagonist, etc., with studies of key representatives of the movement like *Double Indemnity*.

Given that film noir did not emerge full-blown from the head of Billy Wilder (and his collaborators) what were its sources? How did it become such a powerful influence in American cinema even to this day through the genre neo-noir? We have commented on its origins in the literary world of crime fiction in the chapters on Cain and Chandler. But what about its filmic ancestors? What about what is now called Proto-noir?

German Expressionism

German expressionism in film was an outgrowth of the artistic explosion of the Weimar Republic in post-World War I Germany. In spite of the devastation of "the great war" or maybe because of it, Germany developed a vibrant and inclusive art scene, which included painters like Ernst Kirchner, Käthe Kollwitz, and George Grosz, bisexual cabaret-movie performers like Marlene Dietrich and Anita Berber and directors like Fritz Lang and F.W. Murnau. Also present in Weimar for a few years was an Austrian journalist named Billy Wilder. Feeling the effect throughout the 1920s by a burdensome debt imposed by the triumphant Allies and then the rise of the Nazi party, the artists still managed to create a movement that shook the world of art and drama *and* film.

Chiaroscuro Effects

Many of the eleven theaters that Max Reinhardt oversaw in 1930 Berlin used expressionist set design and lighting following a trend that antedated the war. Reinhardt had been producing and directing stage plays since 1901 and was interested in cinema; but the limitations of film production proved frustrating. By the end of the war, the combination of sensitive film stock and bright arc lights could produce startling chiaroscuro (shadowy) effects that typified the expressionist cycle on stage. In terms of both lighting and production design, that is evident in the most frequently cited examples from that era, *Das Cabinet des Dr. Caligari* (1920) and F. W. Murnau's *Nosferatu* (1922). From the late silent era through the mid-1930s many of the UFA productions that Wilder admired continued in this style. When these effects were assimilated by American proto-noir films, the use of panchromatic film stock (that replaced the red-sensitive/blue-insensitive orthochromatic negative starting in the mid-1920s), incandescent lighting, and the general constraints of the "studio look" subdued the harsh contrasts into what might best be described as a "balanced" low key, somewhat shadowy style.

However, during the classic noir period (1940-1955), the harsher lighting contrasts of the expressionist cycle began to reappear, though modified at times by the use of higher-speed film stock and the confines of low budgets. Some of these contrasts are in evidence of Fritz Lang's mid-1940s noir films *Scarlet Street* and *The Woman in the Window* and in John F. Seitz's lighting for *Double Indemnity*. As briefly noted before John F. Seitz was a master of what he liked to call "Rembrandt lighting." Developing his style in the 1920s while collaborating with the brilliant silent director Rex Ingram (*The Four*

Horsemen of the Apocalypse and *Conquering Power*, both 1921; *The Magician*, 1926), Seitz gave *Double Indemnity* its shadowy, stylized patina.

Mood and the Femme Fatale

A dark, mysterious mood seemed to fit best the needs of the expressionists who wished to express the inner vibrations of the soul, a goal that was partly psychological, partly metaphysical. Lighting and set design evoke a mysterious almost sinister mood in films like *Alraune* (1928) or Lang's *Metropolis*. This emphasis translated easily into the tonalities of the American film noir: most often seen in wet city streets, blinking lights, and shafts of light from window blinds, etc., as exemplified in *Double Indemnity*.

In addition, *Alraune*, based on the novel by Hanns Heinz Ewers, foregrounded the mystical, powerful femme fatale, embodied by the Teutonic beauty of Brigitte Helm. Helm also used her beauty to taunt her geneticist "father/creator" in much the same way in Fritz Lang's earlier dystopian science fiction classic *Metropolis*. She also incites a worker rebellion in the form of the cyborg Maria. Her influence along with icons like Marlene Dietrich (particularly in her series of films directed by fellow émigré, Austrian Josef von Sternberg, from *The Blue Angel*, 1930, to *The Devil Is a Woman*, 1935) can be felt all the way down the cinematic timeline to Phyllis Dietrichson in *Double Indemnity*.

Set Design and Visual Motifs

Joyless Street (1925, directed by G. W. Pabst) is one of the best of a subset of German expressionism called the "street film." It depicts the breakdown of the middle class world. Unlike later instances of this genre, *Joyless Street* was studio bound and demonstrates the strong, lingering influence of earlier expressionist stagecraft. In several scenes the manner in which the diffused light emanates from half-closed blinds evokes the atmospheric remoteness of the chiaroscuro style.

Such Venetian blind "effects," heightened still further, would become a veritable trademark of the American film noir. Siodmak's *Criss Cross* lacks the traditional Venetian blinds yet creates the same mood quite efficiently with the play of lights in several scenes shot in the dilapidated apartments on Bunker Hill. where the duped protagonist lives. In addition, the inclusion of the elevated streetcar "outside" the window adds even more mood to the dark urban setting so endemic to film noir.

The scenario (by proletarian writer Dan Fuchs from the novel by Don Tracy), by centering attention on the chaotic lives of the money-hungry petty bourgeoisie who dwell in the vicinity of Los Angeles' Bunker Hill district, immediately echoes the "street films." And like many of the earlier "street films," *Criss Cross* shrewdly blends location exteriors with a majority of studio interiors. While markedly different from his *Menschen am Sonntag* it is rather appropriate that this American noir/"street film" was directed by Robert Siodmak and photographed by Franz Planer, also both refugees from the soon-to-be Nazified German film industry. Of course, *Double Indemnity* makes particularly effective use of these same motifs of Rembrandt lighting and precise, character-driven set design, whether it's the bourgeois Spanish stucco Dietrichson abode or Neff's dingy apartment in Hollywood.

The Corrupt Capitalist

The expressionistic cycle's preoccupation with the corrupt capitalist class, epitomized by figures like Fritz Lang's Dr. Mabuse in his *Dr. Mabuse* series (*Dr. Mabuse the Gambler* 1922; *The Testament of Dr. Mabuse*, 1933, particularly) carried over to the film noir movement in spades. One can see this clearly in the noir films of Orson Welles.

In her controversial essay, "Raising Kane," Pauline Kael asserts that a good deal of what Orson Welles imparted to his first noir, *Citizen Kane* (1941), was drawn from the American film *Mad Love* (1935), directed by German film industry emigre Karl Freund and adapted from the earlier German horror classic *The Hands of Orlac* (1924). Her assertion rests primarily on

Welles' stylized performance and makeup as the elder Kane, and the associations she makes with *Mad Love*. Kael's hypothesis becomes quite revelatory if one views Welles' treatment of Charles Foster Kane as simply the start of a series of corrupt capitalists influenced by Lang's *Mabuse* films—Col. Haki in *Journey into Fear* (1943); Franz Kindler in *The Stranger* (1946); Harry Lime in *The Third Man* (1949); Gregory Arkadin in *Mr. Arkadin* (1955); Hank Quinlan in *Touch of Evil* (1958)—"where a stylized performance and mannered visuals heighten ambiguity and suggest a debt to German expressionism that goes back at least to Welles' exposure to the German classics at the Museum of Modern Art just prior to his work on *Citizen Kane*."[3]

Film noir's politics, however, never needed inspiration from German expressionism. Many of the creatives involved in film noir were leftist/progressives (Edward Dmytryk, John Garfield, Dalton Trumbo, Joe Losey, Jules Dassin, etc.) whose noir and non-noir films brought down the ire of the right-wing HUAC in 1947 and resulted in long periods of exile from Hollywood for scores of actors, writers, and directors.

The Universal Horror Film

Universal's horror series of the 1930s has often been cited as a source of film noir, particularly in its visual style. Under the influence of German expressionism, émigré filmmakers like Karl Freund (cinematographer on Fritz Lang's *Metropolis*), Edgar G. Ulmer (who worked with German expressionist director F.W. Murnau), and the British James Whale (who created *Frankenstein*, 1931, and *Bride of Frankenstein*, 1935) transplanted the extravagances of expressionism in the more "realistic" soil of Hollywood. Stretching from *Dracula* in 1931 (which Freund photographed), through *Frankenstein* and *Bride of Frankenstein*, *The Mummy* (Freund) in 1932, and *The Black Cat* (Ulmer) in 1934, the early Universal horror series combined chiaroscuro lighting and expressionistic set design with alienated anti-heroes and obsessive love, essential elements of the classic period of film noir and intrinsic to the greatness of *Double Indemnity*.

260

Perhaps the best examples of incorporating elements from German ex-pressionism are *The Black Cat* and *The Mummy*. While the *Frankenstein* and *Dracula* films are more "fantastic" in setting and characterization, both Ulmer and Freund attempted to create a "believable" milieu for their fantas-tic stories. Ulmer, who had studied architecture, based the main setting of his film, an art-deco mansion, on the designs of the Bauhaus school of mod-ernist architecture and the California houses of Frank Lloyd Wright. Freund for his part was intent on recreating the settings of ancient Egypt, the Cairo Museum, and the mansions of the wealthy with an attention to detail within the confines of the studio back lots.

The American Gangster Film

The style and substance of the American gangster film in the late 1920s and 1930s are essential parts of the cinematic line that leads to the classic period of film noir. In transforming genres of fiction into a movement, icons and char-acters mutate.[4] Instead of tommy-guns blazing out of car windows, discrete gats are concealed under double-breasted suits. Molls wearing diamonds and furs to the speakeasy are succeeded by femmes fatales crooning love songs in smoky nightclubs or seducing insurance agents with a "honey of an anklet."

But the male protagonists of the pre-noir gangster film and many of those in the noir movement have the same character cores: men driven to achieve success and capable of extortion, larceny, or even murder to achieve it. The classic period of noir is rife with explicit gangster figures, mostly as antagonists to the alienated detectives or federal agents in pictures such as *T-Men* (1948), *The Big Heat*, or *The Big Combo* (1955). Frequently, the gang-ster himself, from small time gambler to cheap grifter, from hit man to syn-dicate mouthpiece is the principal of the noir narrative: *This Gun for Hire*, *Nobody Lives Forever* (1946), *The Gangster* (1947), *Force of Evil*, *White Heat* (1949), *Kiss Tomorrow Goodbye* (1950), *Night and the City*.

If one defines gangsters simply as criminals allied with others of like mind and intention, as opposed to the more complex structure of a mafia or tong, then a movement as rife with criminal enterprise as film noir must also be full of them. In noir, however, many if not most of the gangs are ad hoc: small, one-project entities put together with a mind to the requirements of the enterprise at hand. Films like *The Asphalt Jungle* or *The Killing* (1956) are typical. Many writers, producers, directors, cinematographers, and actors who began their association with criminal narratives in the gangster genre continued to work in that vein making film noir.

Purely in terms of style, the influence of the gangster on the noir movement is even more striking. In the transition from the silent era, traditional film history asserts that visual options were severely restricted by the physical requirements of early sound recording, that the lighting and staging in pictures such as von Sternberg's *Underworld* (1927), *Thunderbolt* (1929), and *Docks of New York* (1928) became more difficult if not impossible to achieve. In fact, while some early talkies did spend much of their screen time on sound stages, *Little Caesar*, *The Public Enemy* (1931), and *Scarface* went outside, with many sequences shot on the streets and alleys of a back-lot or on actual locations away from the studio, often at night as when Rico in *Little Caesar* and Tony Camonte in *Scarface* meet their makers. Frequently effects are added, as in the nocturnal rainstorm in which Cagney as the title figure in *The Public Enemy* dies while proclaiming not, "Top of the World, Ma" but, "I ain't so tough."

Whether day or night, whether actual locations or the wet-down pavement of Warners' New York Street, the perilous urban landscape of film noir is fully anticipated. Although noir may be a movement and not a genre, icons and themes help define its style and tone also. The movement's dark view of the world embraces a wide range of plots and cuts across studios, budgets, and creative personnel in the manner we detailed on pages 180-181, to create consistencies of both style and narrative. Like their gangster antecedent, classic-period protagonists are threatened or caught in a bind. While the problem may not be of their making, because they are falsely accused or entrapped by an obsession, alienated from normal society; but they're infrequently thugs or megalomaniacs, just "ordinary joes" who find themselves thrust deeply in the noir underworld.

The most coincident concept between the gangster and noir cycles is this underworld. In both genre and movement an essential presumption is that such an underworld exists, a parallel society outside of the normality, in which the people who go to the movies live. The depth and breadth with which these worlds are evoked can entail the use of characters inspired by actual criminals, whether the mafioso who perpetrated the violence that made for newspaper headlines in the 1920s or the Snyder-Gray trial. Captivated readers of gangster chronicles who became enthralled film audiences lay the foundation for the viewers of film noir. For the viewers who watched town cars spraying bullets and careening across movie screens in the 1930s, the subtler but no less deadly dangers of film noir in the following decades were easy to accept.

Motifs

Most if not all of the typical motifs of film noir first appear in the early gangster talkies, in both the movies and the ad art.[5] The simple use of shadows on walls as in the opening of *Scarface*, in *The Public Enemy*, *Little Caesar*, or the end of *Angels with Dirty Faces* (1938) is a typical noir motif as in *The Killers*. While the figures in *The Public Enemy* and *Little Caesar* become anonymous during flight, the menace in *The Killers* is focused on the identifiable protagonist—the "Swede." In *Little Caesar* Rico's shadow leads him towards death and low light exaggerates the dark shapes on the wall in *Angels with Dirty Faces*. Fourteen years after *Scarface*, director Howard Hawks creates a more complex motif in *The Big Sleep* by placing the shadow at the center of a noir triptych.

The car, a key motif, is at once a refuge and an escape but only when it starts, as Rico's hapless minion in *Little Caesar* discovers. For Neff and Phyllis in *Double Indemnity* the starter motor grinds and grinds and finally catches.

When Camonte in *Scarface* uses the phone in a store after he wrecks his car escaping an ambush, the extreme backlight is typical of noir cinematography. The phone booth in film noir often suggests vulnerability as in

Out of the Past or in *Double Indemnity*, where it symbolizes the clandestine affair between the two lovers. In their own need for secrecy both Neff and Phyllis use pay phones.

The mirror motif, which is part of a moment of comic relief in *Little Caesar*, evolved into a more somber suggestion of doppelgangers and the perils of the parallel underworld in many noir films, including another starring Edward G. Robinson, John Farrow's adaptation of Cornell Woolrich's *Night Has a Thousand Eyes*. In noir, the mirror often permits interposing closer shots of antagonists in a single frame, as in the meeting of the conspirators in *The Killers* or the detective and a prime suspect in *Laura*. In *Scarface* the mirror easily permits the ironic revelation of a character's expression and the figure that motivates it, as in *The Thief* (1952) and *Kiss Me Deadly*.

What is so remarkable about *Double Indemnity*, of course, is how neatly it combines so many of the motifs and visual stylings of the proto-noirs, whether it be from German expressionism or the gangster film. The movie's syncretism makes the film a touchstone for the entire noir period to follow it.

The guns, the dames, the grim expressions, all in full color, are all part of the advertising-art come-on for *Little Caesar*, *The Public Enemy*, and *Scarface*. Such elements are replicated scores of times in the poster art for noir films, which topped them off with taglines. Some subtly alluded to that noir underworld *The Ashphalt Jungle* revealed "The City Under the City!" 1957's *The Burglar* followed "a trail or perfume and violence!" Some incorporated the title, "Once I trusted a dame...now I Walk Alone!" or "Thrill Crazy, Kill Crazy, Gun Crazy." But none said it better than "From the Moment They Met It Was Murder!"

BIBLIOGRAPHY

Prologue: Moonlight and Roses

Elliott, Robert Greene with Albert R. Beatty. *Agent of Death: The Memoirs of an Executioner*. New York: E.P. Dutton, 1940.

Morris, James M. *The Rose Man of Sing Sing: A True Tale of Life, Murder, and Redemption in the Age of Yellow Journalism*. New York: Fordham University Press, 2005.

1. True Crime

Adams, Jad. *Double Indemnity: Murder for Insurance*. North Pomfret, VT: Trafalgar Square, 1995.

Black, J. Anderson. "Snyder & Grey [sic] Momsie and Loverboy" in *Crimes and Victims*. Edited by Frank Smyth. London: Bookmart, 1992.

Dickson, Grierson. "Ruth Snyder: The Iron Widow" in *The Mammoth Book of Women Who Kill*. New York: Carroll & Graf, 2002, 382-91.

Gado, Mark. "A Morality Play: Ruth Snyder and Judd Gray," in *Death Row Women*. Westport, CT: Praeger, 2008, 7-40.

Gray, Henry Judd. *Doomed Ship: The Autobiography of Judd Gray*. Edited by Margaret Gray. New York: Horace Livewright, 1928.

Jones, Ann. "She Had to Die!" *American Heritage*, October–November, 1980, 3-6.

Knowlton, Steven K., and Bill Reader. "Ruth Snyder: Still Dead but Now Her Picture Is Mainstream" in *Moral Reasoning for Journalists*. New York: Praeger, 2008, 184-187.

Kobler, John, editor. *The Trial of Ruth Snyder & Judd Gray*. New York: Doubleday, Doran, & Company, 1938.

MacKellar, Landis. *The Double Indemnity Murder: Ruth Snyder, Judd Gray, and New York's Crime of the Century*. New York: Syracuse University Press, 2006.

Margolin, Leslie. *Murderess!* New York: Pinnacle Books, 1999.

New York Court of Appeals. *The People of the State of New York, Plaintiff-Respondent, Against Ruth Snyder and Henry Judd Gray, Defendants-Appellants*. Volume 1, pages 1-500; Volume 2, pages 501-1000; Volume 3, pages, 1001-1500; Volume 4, pages 1501-2000; Volume 5, pages 2001-2500; Volume 6, pages 2501-2850. London: Forgotten Books, 2017-18.

"Text of Confession Mrs. Snyder Made." *New York Times*, April 27, 1927, 16.

Pelizzon, V. Penelope, and Nancy Martha West. "Multiple Indemnity: Film Noir, James M. Cain, and Adaptations of a Tabloid Case." *Narrative* 13, no. 3 (October, 2005), 211-37.

———. *Tabloid, Inc.: Crimes, Newspapers, Narrative*. Columbus, OH: Ohio State University Press, 2010, 117-45.

Ramey, Jessie. "The Bloody Blonde and the Marble Woman: Gender and Power in the Case of Ruth Snyder." *Journal of Social History* 37, no. 3 (March 1, 2004), 625-50.

Robbins, Trina. "Dubious Distinctions" in *Tender Murderers: Women Who Kill*. Newburyport, MA: Conari Press, 2003, 56-62.

Schweizer, Karl W. *Seeds of Evil: the Gray/Snyder Murder Case*. Bloomington, IN: 1st Books, 2001.

Snyder, Ruth Brown. *Ruth Snyder's My Own True Story, So Help Me God!* New York: King Features Syndicate, 1927.

Styron, William and John Phillips. "Dead! A Screenplay." *Esquire*, December 1, 1973, 161-8.

Treadwell, Sophie. *Machinal*. London: Nick Hearn Books, 1993.

2. Human Interest [James M. Cain]

Original US Editions of Novels by Cain:

The Postman Always Rings Twice. New York: Alfred A. Knopf, 1934.

Serenade. New York: Alfred A. Knopf, 1937.

Mildred Pierce. New York: Alfred A. Knopf, 1941.

Love's Lovely Counterfeit. New York: Alfred A. Knopf, 1942.

Three of a Kind. New York: Alfred A. Knopf, 1943.

Career in C Major in *Three of a Kind*. New York: Alfred A. Knopf, 1943.

The Embezzler in *Three of a Kind*. New York: Alfred A. Knopf, 1943.

Double Indemnity in *Three of a Kind*. New York: Alfred A. Knopf, 1943.

Past All Dishonor. New York: Alfred A. Knopf, 1946.

The Butterfly. New York: Alfred A. Knopf, 1947.

Sinful Woman. New York: Avon, 1947.

The Moth. New York: Alfred A. Knopf, 1948.

Jealous Woman. New York: Avon, 1950.

The Root of His Evil (original title: *A Modern Cinderella*). New York: Avon, 1951.

Galatea. New York: Avon, 1953.

Mignon. New York: Dial Press, 1962.

The Magician's Wife. New York: Dial Press, 1965.

Rainbow's End. New York: Mason/Charter, 1975.

The Institute. New York: Mason/Charter, 1976.

Cloud Nine. New York: Mysterious Press, 1984.

The Enchanted Isle. New York: Mysterious Press, 1985.

The Cocktail Waitress. New York: Hard Case Crime Press, 2012.

Abbott, Megan E. *The Street Was Mine: White Masculinity in Hardboiled Fiction and Film Noir*. London: Palgrave Macmillan, 2002.

Cain, James M. "Preface" in *Three of a Kind*. New York: Knopf, 1943.

Hoopes, Roy. *The Biography of James M. Cain*. Carbondale and Edwardsville, IL: Southern Illinois University Press, 1982.

Leonard, John. "James M. Cain, the Author of *Postman Always Rings Twice*." Obituaries. *New York Times*, October 29, 1977.

MacShane, Frank. *The Life of Raymond Chandler*. New York: E.P. Dutton, 1976.

Madden, David. *James M. Cain*. New York: Twayne Publishers, 1970.

——. *The Voice of James M. Cain: A Biography*. Lanham, Maryland: Lyons Press, 2020.

Madden, David and Kristopher Mecholsky. *James M. Cain: Hard-boiled Mythmaker*. Toronto: The Scarecrow Press, 2011. Kindle.

Oates, Joyce Carol. "Man under Sentence of Death: The Novels of James M. Cain" in *Tough Guy Writers of the Thirties*. Carbondale: Southern Illinois University Press, 1968.

Pengelly, Martin. "Lost Story by the 'Poet of the Tabloid Murder' James M. Cain Discovered in the Library of Congress." *The Guardian*, May 26, 2023.

Shearer, Lloyd. "Crime Certainly Pays on the Screen" in *Film Noir Reader 2*. New York: Limelight Editions, 1999.

Wilson, Edmund. "The Boys in the Back Room" in *Literary Essays and Reviews of the 1930s and 1940s*. New York: The Library of America, 2007.

3. The Mystery Writer [Raymond Chandler]

From 1933 to 1959, Raymond Chandler published seven novels and twenty-three short stories. These stories and all seven novels are still in print. Other stories, the unfinished novel, *Poodle Springs Story*, a novella *English Summer*, and two other screenplays, "The Blue Dahlia" and "Playback," have been published posthumously. The most extensive collection of Chandler's work, including numerous out-of-print editions and original manuscripts available to the public, is housed in the Special Collections Division of the UCLA Research Library.

Original US Editions of Novels by Chandler:

The Big Sleep. New York: Alfred A. Knopf, 1939.

Farewell, My Lovely. New York: Alfred A. Knopf, 1940.

The High Window. New York: Alfred A. Knopf, 1942.

The Lady in the Lake. New York: Alfred A. Knopf, 1943.

The Little Sister. Boston: Houghton, Mifflin, 1949.

The Long Goodbye. Boston: Houghton, Mifflin, 1954.

Playback. Boston: Houghton, Mifflin, 1958.

Brackett, Leigh. "From 'The Big Sleep' to 'The Long Goodbye' and More or Less How We Got There." *Take One* 4, no. 1 (September–October, 1972), 26-8.

Bruccoli, Matthew J., editor. *Chandler Before Marlowe: Early Prose and Poetry, 1908-1912*. Columbia, SC: University of South Carolina Press, 1973.

———. *The Blue Dahlia*. Carbondale, IL: Southern Illinois University Press, 1976.

———. *Raymond Chandler: A Descriptive Bibliography*. Pittsburgh: University of Pittsburgh Press, 1979.

Clark, Al. *Raymond Chandler in Hollywood*, 2nd ed. Los Angeles: Silman-James Press, 1986.

Day, Barry, editor. *The World of Raymond Chandler in His Own Words*. New York: Alfred A. Knopf, 2014.

Durham, Philip. *Down These Mean Streets a Man Must Go*. Chapel Hill, NC: University of North Carolina Press, 1963.

Gardiner, Dorothy and Katherine Sorley Walker, editors. *Raymond Chandler Speaking*. Boston: Houghton, Mifflin, 1962. [*Raymond Chandler Speaking* includes a reprint of Chandler's 1945 essay for the *Atlantic Monthly*, "Writers in Hollywood."]

Gross, Miriam, editor. *The World of Raymond Chandler*. New York: A & W Publishers, 1977. [*The World of Raymond Chandler* includes a reprint of the 1965 *Harper's Magazine* article, "Lost Fortnight," by producer John Houseman.]

Haycraft, Howard, editor. *The Art of the Mystery Story*. New York: Simon & Schuster, 1946. [*The Art of the Mystery Story* includes a reprint of Chandler's 1944 essay for the *Atlantic Monthly*, "The Simple Art of Murder."]

Hiney, Tom. *Raymond Chandler: A Biography*. New York: Grove Press, 1997.

Hiney, Tom and Frank MacShane, editors. *The Raymond Chandler Papers: Selected Letters and Non-fiction 1909-1959*. New York: Grove Press, 2002. [Originally published in a slightly different form: revised edition of MacShane's 1981 *Selected Letters of Raymond Chandler*.]

Luhr, William. *Raymond Chandler and Film*. New York: Frederick Ungar, 1982.

MacShane, Frank. "He Was a Dead Shot with a Wisecrack." *TV Guide,* April 16, 1983, 40-2.

MacShane, Frank, editor. *The Notebooks of Raymond Chandler and English Summer: A Gothic Romance.* New York: Ecco Press, 1976.

Marling, William H. *Raymond Chandler.* Boston: G.K. Hall, 1986.

Osterwalder, Sonja. "'Alcohol Is Like Love'. Chandler, Marlowe und *The Long Goodbye*" in *Trunkenheit: Kulturen des Rausches.* Amsterdam: Brill, 2008.

Parker, Robert. *Raymond Chandler's Unknown Thriller: The Screenplay of "Playback."* New York: Mysterious Press, 1985.

Pendo, Stephen. *Raymond Chandler, His Novels into Film.* Metuchen, NJ: Scarecrow Press, 1976.

Reck, Tom S. "Raymond Chandler's Los Angeles." *The Nation*, December 20, 1975, 661-2.

Sorel, Edward. "When Raymond Chandler Went To Work for Billy Wilder." *New York Times*, August 20, 2021.

Speir, Jerry. *Raymond Chandler.* New York: Frederick Ungar, 1981.

Stasio, Marilyn. "Off-Broadway Review: Hollywood Comedy 'Billy and Ray.'" *Variety*, October 20, 2014.

Ward, Elizabeth, and Alain Silver. *Raymond Chandler's Los Angeles.* Woodstock, NY: Overlook–Viking, 1987.

Williams, Tom. *A Mysterious Something in the Light: Raymond Chandler: A Life.* London: Aurum, 2012.

Wolfe, Peter. *Something More Than Night: The Case of Raymond Chandler.* Bowling Green, OH: Bowling Green State University Press, 1985.

Zolotow, Maurice. "How Raymond Chandler Screwed Hollywood." *California Living*, July 20, 1980, 12-15 and reprinted in *Action*, January–February, 1978, pages 52-7.

4. The Austrian Journalist [Billy Wilder]

Chandler, Charlotte. *Nobody's Perfect: Billy Wilder, a Personal Biography.* Milwaukee: Applause, 2004.

Crowe, Cameron. *Conversations with Wilder.* New York: Knopf, 1999.

Horton, Robert, editor. *Billy Wilder: Interviews.* Jackson, MS: University Press of Mississippi, 2001.

Lally, Kevin. *Wilder Times: The Life of Billy Wilder.* New York: Henry Holt and Co., 1996.

McBride, Joseph. *Billy Wilder: Dancing on the Edge*. New York: Columbia University Press, 2021.

Phillips, Gene D. *Some Like It Wilder: The Life and Controversial Films of Billy Wilder.* Lexington, Kentucky: University Press of Kentucky, 2010.

Porfirio, Robert, Alain Silver, and James Ursini, editors. *Film Noir Reader 3: Interviews with Filmmakers of the Classic Period*. New York: Limelight, 2001.

Rózsa, Miklós. *Double Life*. Tunbridge Wells: Baton Press, 1982.

Sikov, Ed. *On Sunset Boulevard: The Life and Times of Billy Wilder*. New York: Hyperion, 1998.

Staggs, Sam. *Close-Up on Sunset Boulevard: Billy Wilder, Norma Desmond and the Dark Hollywood Dream*. New York: Macmillan, 2003.

Stevens Jr., George. *Conversations with the Great Moviemakers of Hollywood's Golden Age at the American Film Institute*. New York: Vintage Press–Knopf, 2007.

Wilder, Billy. "Billy Wilder, the Art of Screenwriting No. 1." Interview by James Linville. *The Paris Review* 138, Spring, 1996.

Wilder, Billy, and Noah Isenberg, editor. *Billy Wilder on Assignment: Dispatches from Weimar Berlin and Interwar Vienna*. Princeton: Princeton University Press, 2021.

Zolotow, Maurice. *Billy Wilder in Hollywood*. New York: Putnam, 1977.

5. The Movie: A Fancy Piece of Homicide

Brackett, Charles. *"It's the Pictures That Got Small": Charles Brackett on Billy Wilder and Hollywood's Golden Age*. Edited by Anthony Slide. New York: Columbia University Press, 2014.

Friedrich, Otto. *City of Nets: A Portrait of Hollywood in the 1940's*. New York: Harper & Row, 1986.

Gassner, John, and Dudley Nichols, editors. *Best Filmplays of 1945*. New York: Crown, 1946.

Head, Edith, and Paddy Calistro. *Edith Head's Hollywood*. Los Angeles: Angel City Press, 2008.

Robinson, Edward G., and Leonard S. Robinson. *All My Yesterdays*. New York: Hawthorn Books, 1973.

Schickel, Richard. *Double Indemnity*. London: BFI Publishing, 1992.

Tranberg, Charles. *Fred MacMurray: A Biography*. Orlando, FL: BearManor Media, 2014.

Truhler, Kimberly. *Film Noir Style: The Killer 1940s*. Pittsburgh: GoodKnight Books, 2020.

Wayne, Jane Ellen. *The Life and Loves of Barbara Stanwyck*. London: JR Books, 2009.

6. The Movie: The Top Shelf

Allyn, John. "*Double Indemnity*: A Policy That Paid Off." *Literature/Film Quarterly* 6, no. 2 (Spring, 1978).

Arnold, Jeremy. *The Essentials: 52 Must-See Movies and Why They Matter*. Philadelphia: Running Press, 2016.

Atkinson, Michael. "*Double Indemnity* Returns to the Big Screen at Film Forum." *The Village Voice*, July 30, 2014.

Bastien, Angelica Jade. "The Black Heart of *Double Indemnity*." *Criteron Channel Online*, May 31, 2022.

Biesen, Sheri Chinen. *Blackout: World War II and the Origins of Film Noir*. Baltimore: John Hopkins University Press, 2005.

———. "*Double Indemnity*: A Shadowy Exemplar of Film Noir Visual Style," in *Film Noir Light and Shadow*. Edited by Alain Silver and James Ursini. Milwaukee: Applause, 2017, 210-17.

Borde, Raymond and Chaumeton, Etienne. *A Panorama of Film Noir (1941-1953)*. San Francisco: City Lights Publishing, 2002. Citations refer to the English edition.

Bronfen, Elizabeth. "Gender and Noir," in *Film Noir*. Edited by Homer Pettey and R. Barton Palmer. Edinburgh: Edinburgh University Press, 2014.

Conrad, Mark T., editor. *The Philosophy of Film Noir*. Lexington, Kentucky: University Press of Kentucky, 2007.

Copjec, Joan, editor. *Shades of Noir*. New York: Verso Publishing, 1993.

Dennon, Anne. "Emergence of the Feminist Fatale in American Film Noir." Master's Thesis. Central Washington University, 2017.

Dickos, Andrew. *Street with No Name*. Lexington, KY: University Press of Kentucky, 2002.

Durgnat, Raymond. "Paint It Black: The Family Tree of Film Noir" in *Film Noir Reader*. Edited by Alain Silver and James Ursini. New Jersey: Limelight, 1996.

Ebert, Roger. "*Double Indemnity*." *Chicago Sun-Times*, December 20, 1998.

Flinn, Tom. "Three Faces of Film Noir," in *Film Noir Compendium*. Milwaukee: Applause, 2016.

Frank, Nino. "A New Kind of Police Drama: The Criminal Adventure" in *Film Noir Compendium*.

Gemunden, Gerd. *A Foreign Affair: Billy Wilder's American Films*. New York and Oxford: Berghahn Books, 2008.

Grossman, Julie. *The Femme Fatale: Quick Takes, Movies and Popular Culture*. New Jersey: Rutgers University Press, 2020.

Hansberry, Karen Burroughs. *Femme Noir: Bad Girls of Film*. Jefferson, NC: McFarland, 2012.

Hibbs, Thomas S. *Arts of Darkness: American Noir and the Quest for Redemption*. Dallas: Spence Publishing, 2008.

Higham, Charles, and Joel Greenberg. *Hollywood in the 1940s*. New York: A.S. Barnes and Co., 1968.

Hirsch, Foster. *The Dark Side of the Screen: Film Noir*. Boston: Da Capo Press, 2008.

Kaplan, E. Ann, editor. *Women in Film Noir*. London: British Film Institute, 1998.

Krutnik, Frank. *In a Lonely Place: Film Noir, Genre, Masculinity*. London: Routledge, 1998.

Lamparski, Richard. *Lamparski's Hidden Hollywood*. New York: Simon & Schuster, 1981.

Lyons, Arthur. *Death on the Cheap: The Lost B Movies of Film Noir*. Boston: Da Capo Press, 2000.

Maxfield, James. *The Fatal Woman: Sources of Male Anxiety in American Film Noir, 1941-1991*. Teaneck, NJ: Fairleigh Dickinson University Press, 1996.

Miklitsch, Robert, editor. *Kiss the Blood Off My Hands*. Chicago: University of Illinois Press, 2014.

———. *The Red and the Black: American Film Noir in the 1950s*. Chicago: University of Illinois Press, 2017.

Muller, Eddie. *Dark City: The Lost World of Film Noir*. Philadelphia: Running Press, 2021.

———. *Dark City Dames: The Wicked Women of Film Noir*. New York: ReganBooks, 2001.

Naremore, James. *More Than Night: Film Noir in Its Contexts*. Berkeley: University of California Press, 2008.

Newman, Kim. "*Double Indemnity*." *Empire*, January 1, 2000.

Oliver, Kelly. *Noir Anxiety*. Minneapolis, MN: University of Minnesota Press, 2002.

Park, William. *What Is Film Noir?* Lanham, MD: Bucknell University Press, 2011.

Perkins, V.F. *Film as Film: Understanding and Judging Movies*. New York: Da Capo Press, 1993.

Place, Janey, and Lowell Peterson. "Some Visual Motifs of Film Noir" in *Film Noir Reader*. Edited by Alain Silver and James Ursini. New York: Limelight, 1996.

Porfirio, Robert, Alain Silver, and James Ursini, editors. *Film Noir Reader 3*. New York: Limelight, 2002.

Rivers, Marc. "*Double Indemnity* Is 75, But Anklets (And Film Noir) Are Forever." *NPR*, July 31, 2019. https://www.npr.org/2019/07/31/746391982/double-indemnity-is-75-but-anklets-and-film-noir-are-forever

Robertson, William Preston. *The Big Lebowski: The Making of a Coen Brothers Film*. New York: W.W. Norton, 1998.

Schlotterbeck, Jesse. "The Dynamism of Violent Death: Lighting, Censorship, and Violence in Film Noir," in *Film Noir Light and Shadow*. Edited by Alain Silver and James Ursini. Milwaukee: Applause, 2017, 308-15.

———. "The 'House of Death' in Print and On-screen: Double Indemnity as Journalism, Fiction, and Film" in *Film Noir Prototypes: Origins of the Movement*. Edited by Alain Silver and James Ursini. Milwaukee: Applause, 2018, 320-335.

Schrader, Paul. "Notes on Film Noir" in *Film Noir Reader*. Edited by Alain Silver and James Ursini. New York: Limelight Editions, 1996, 53–63.

Server, Lee, Martin Greenberg, and Ed Gorman. *The Big Book of Noir*. New York: Carroll and Graf, 1998.

Silver, Alain, Elizabeth Ward, Robert Porfirio, James Ursini, and Carl Macek. *Film Noir The Encyclopedia*, 4th ed. New York: Overlook–Abrams, 2010.

Silver, Alain, and James Ursini. *The Noir Style*. New York: Overlook/Viking, 1999.

———. *The Zombie Film: From White Zombie to World War Z*. Milwaukee: Applause, 2014.

———. *Film Noir Fatal Women*. Los Angeles: Silman-James Press, 2022.

———, editors. *Film Noir Reader*. New York: Limelight, 1996.

———. *Film Noir Reader 2*. New York: Limelight, 1999.

———. *Film Noir Compendium*. Milwaukee: Applause, 2016.

Sipiora, Phillip. "Phenomenological Masking: Complications of Identity in *Double Indemnity*," in *Billy Wilder, Movie-Maker: Critical Essays on the Films*. Edited by Karen McNally. Jefferson, NC: McFarland, 2010.

Smith, Imogen Sara. *In Lonely Places: Film Noir Beyond the City*. Jefferson, NC: McFarland, 2014.

Sobchack, Vivian. "Lounge Time: Postwar Crises and the Chronotope of Film Noir," in *Film Noir Compendium*. Milwaukee, WI: Applause, 219.

Spicer, Andrew. *Film Noir*. Harlow, UK: Longman, 2002.

Telotte, J. P. *Voices in the Dark: The Narrative Patterns of Film Noir.* Urbana, IL: University of Illinois Press, 1989.

Vieira, Mark. *Into the Dark: The Hidden World of Film Noir, 1941-1950.* Philadelphia: Running Press, 2016.

7. Aftermath and Movement: The Rise of Film Noir

Adams, Marjorie. "*Double Indemnity.*" *Boston Globe*, August 25, 1944.

Agee, James. "*Double Indemnity.*" *The Nation*, October 14, 1944.

"Mercedes McCambridge, 87, Actress Known for Strong Roles." *New York Times*, March 18, 2004.

Barnes, Howard. "*Double Indemnity.*" *New York Tribune*, September 7, 1944.

Cain, James M. "*Double Indemnity.*" *New York Daily News*, August 14, 1944.

———. "James M. Cain, The Art of Fiction No. 69." Interview by David Zinsser *The Paris Review* 73 (Spring-Summer 1978).

Cameron, Kate. "*Double Indemnity:* A Tense Melodrama." *New York Daily News*, September 7, 1944.

Clute, Shannon Scott and Richard L. Edwards. *The Maltese Touch of Evil: Film Noir and Potential Criticism.* Hanover, NH: Dartmouth College Press, 2011.

Cook, Alton. "*Double Indemnity* Excels as the Perfect Movie." *New York Telegram*, September 7, 1944.

Creelman, Eileen. "*Double Indemnity.*" *New York Sun*, September 7, 1944.

Crowther, Bosley. "*Double Indemnity:* A Tough Melodrama." *New York Times*, September 7, 1944.

Crozier, Mary. "*Double Indemnity.*" *Guardian.* December 12, 1944.

Ebert, Roger. "*Out of the Past.*" *Chicago Sun-Times*, July 18, 2004.

Flint, Peter B. "Fred MacMurray Is Dead at 83." *New York Times*, November 6, 1991.

Goldberg, Albert. "Movie *Double Indemnity* Is Superb Drama." *Chicago Daily Tribune*, November 3, 1944.

Grant, John. *A Comprehensive Encyclopedia of Film Noir.* Milwaukee: Applause Books, 2013.

Hicks, Ida Belle. "Put *Double Indemnity* on Your 'Must' List If You Enjoy Lusty Crime Movies." *Fort Worth Star-Telegram*, August 11, 1944.

"*Double Indemnity.*" *Hollywood Reporter*, April 24, 1944.

Hunt, Mary. " *Double Indemnity:* This is a New Line in Murder." *London Evening Standard*, Sept. 16 1944.

Kahn. "*Double Indemnity*." *Variety*, April 26, 1944.

Lerner, Max. "Cain in the Movies." *PM*, September 21, 1944.

Leyendecker. "*Double Indemnity*." *Film Bulletin*, May,1944.

Mainon, Dominique and James Ursini. *Femme Fatale: Cinema's Most Unforgettable Lethal Ladies.* New York: Limelight, 2009.

Martin, Mildred. "*Double Indemnity* at Fox; A Study in Murder." *The Philadelphia Enquirer*, July 15, 1944.

"*Double Indemnity*." *Motion Picture Daily,* April, 1944.

Scheuer, Philip K. "Film History Made by *Double Indemnity*." *Los Angeles Times*, August 6. 1944.

———. "*Double Indemnity*: Study of Murder without Bunk." *Los Angeles Times*, August 11, 1944.

Silver, Alain and James Ursini. *What Ever Happened to Robert Aldrich? His Life and His Films.* New York: Limelight, 1995.

———. *Film Noir.* Cologne, Germany: Taschen, 2004.

———. *American Neo-Noir.* Milwaukee: Applause, 2015

———, editors. *Film Noir the Directors.* Milwaukee: Applause, 2012.

———. *Film Noir: Light and Shadow.* Milwaukee: Applause, 2017.

"*Double Indemnity*." *Tidings*, August 14, 1944.

"*Double Indemnity*." *Time*, July 10, 1944.

Bogdanovich, Peter. *Who the Devil Made It, Conversations with Legendary Film Directors.* New York: Ballantine Books, 1998.

Wright, Virginia. "*Double Indemnity*." *New York Daily News*, August 14, 1944.

Proto-Noir

Baker, J.I., et al. "Film Noir: 75 Years of the Greatest Crime Films." *Life* special issue, August 19, 2016.

Clarens, Carlos. *An Illustrated History of the Horror Film.* New York: Putnam, 1967.

Eisner, Lotte. *The Haunted Screen.* Berkeley: University of California Press, 1990.

Gordon, Mel. *Voluptuous Panic: The Erotic World of Weimar Berlin.* Port Townsend, WA: Feral House, 2008.

Grant, Kevin. *Roots of Film Noir: Precursors from the Silent Period to the 1940s.* Jefferson, North Carolina: McFarland, 2022.

Kael, Pauline. "Raising Kane." *The New Yorker*, February 20, 1971.

Karydes, Karen. *Hard-Boiled Anxiety: The Freudian Desires of Dashiell Hammett, Raymond Chandler, Ross Macdonald, and Their Detectives.* Salisbury, MD: Secant Publishing, 2016.

Kracauer, Siegfried. *From Caligari to Hitler: A Psychological History of the German Film.* Princeton: Princeton University Press, 2004.

Silver, Alain and James Ursini. *Film Noir Graphics Where Danger Lives.* Santa Monica, CA: Pendragon Books, 2012.

——, editors. *Horror Film Reader.* New York: Limelight, 2004.

——. *Film Noir Prototypes: Origins of the Movement.* Milwaukee: Applause, 2018.

Warshow, Robert. "The Gangster as Tragic Hero" in *Gangster Film Reader.* New York: Limelight, 2007.

NOTES

Prologue

1. Per his autobiography Robert G. Elliott actually did smoke a pipe but not wear a mask; and his identity was eventually outed by an enterprising reporter who followed him home. Having been doxed, Elliott's porch was blown up by a protestor after one of the earliest of his 387 executions: another double-header, Nicola Sacco and Bartolomeo Vanzetti, in Charlestown Prison outside Boston in summer, 1927. He also flipped the switch on "blonde bandit" Irene Schroeder and purported Lindbergh baby kidnapper Bruno Hauptmann, most using his "patented" method of "humane" electrocution, in which a three-second, 2000-volt charge rendered the victim unconscious then a couple of minutes at a mere 500 volts boiled rather than roasted their bodies to death. Elliott (and many members of the reading public) shared the indignation of prison officials over the *Daily News* picture as an invasion of Ruth Snyder's privacy. Maybe that's why he felt his frequently sleepless nights were most haunted by her. Shortly after his death, his life story was published, *Agent of Death*, in which Elliott stated, "The happiest day I'll ever experience will be the day that capital punishment is wiped from the statute books, leaving me a man without a job."

Unlike Cain or Elliott, Thomas Howard never wrote a book, perhaps because the rest of his career as a newspaper photographer, ending with the *Chicago Sun-Times,* was entirely uneventful. After the *Daily News* flaunted its successful subterfuge in an illustrated article, the state of New York explored criminal charges against him and the newspaper but never followed through. His camera is on exhibit at the Smithsonian where the curious—possibly including his notable descendants, the comedic actors George Wendt and Jason Sudeikis—can see it on display.

1. True Crime

1. Gray, Judd, *Doomed Ship: The Autobiography of Judd Gray (Prepared for Publication by his Sister Margaret Gray).* New York: Horace Liverwright, 1928, pages 201-02. Gray, *Doomed Ship,* 201-2.

2. Perriton Maxwell, "The Editor Goes to the Play," *Theatre Magazine,* November, 1928, 46.

3. J. Brooks Atkinson, "The Play—A Tragedy of Submission," *New York Times,* September 8, 1928, 10.

4. Charles Brackett, "Order, Please," The Theatre, *The New Yorker,* September 15, 1928, 4.

5. New York Court of Appeals. The People of the State of New York, Plaintiff-Respondent, Against Ruth Snyder and Henry Judd Gray, Defendants-Appellants, trial transcript Volume 4, page 1965. Also quoted with an emphasis on the argot in Landis MacKellar, *The Double Indemnity Murder: Ruth Snyder, Judd Gray, and New York's Crime of the Century.* New York: Syracuse University Press, 2006, 72.

6. New York Court of Appeals. Trial transcript Volume 3, page 1203. Per various chroniclers of the Snyder-Gray affair, Ruth wanted $50,000 with a kicker to $100,000 for death by misadventure. What she and Ashfield got Albert Snyder to sign was an application for a second $1,000 policy; but such policies automatically included a disability provision, "which provides that in case of total and permanent disability there is to be a monthly income of $10 per month for each one thousand" [Transcript Volume 5, page 2112]. When Prudential's underwriting department notified Ashfield that the projected $500 stipend was slightly larger than Snyder's income would warrant, he forged his signature on a rider to create a $45,000 double indemnity policy and a $5,000 straight life. That $90,000 plus $5,000 plus two $1,000 policies

added up the "97,000" in the *Chicago Tribune* illustration on pages 28-29. [See also MacKellar, page 43.]

7. Damon Runyon, "Murder in the Worst Degree," *International Press Syndicate*, April 19, 1927, reprinted in Snyder, Louis L. and Richard B. Morris, eds., *A Treasury Of Great Reporting: "Literature under Pressure" from the Sixteenth Century to Our Own Time*, New York: Simon and Schuster, 1949, 441.

8. Ibid. Runyon noted about the testimony that, "Mrs. Snyder and Gray have been 'hollering copper' on each other lately, as the boys say. Gray's defense goes back to old Mr. Adam, that the woman beguiled him, while Mrs. Snyder says he is a 'jackal,' and a lot of other things besides that, and claims that he is hiding behind her skirts. She 'belabored him,' Gray's confession reads, and I half expected her to belabor Gray. Her thin lips curled to a distinct snarl at some passages in the statement. I thought of a wildcat and a female cat, at that, on a leash. Once or twice she smiled, but it was a smile of insensate rage, not amusement." [pages 442-43]

9. "Snyder's $95,000 Insurance Voided by Court, Ruling Slain Man's Daughter Can't Collect," *New York Times*, November 10, 1928, 19. However, "Granny" Brown, who brought the suit on Lorraine's behalf, did get the $1,562 refund of premiums that Ruth had refused to accept after her conviction the prior June.

10. "Gray Swears Mrs. Snyder Broached Murder Plot; Her Story Wavers at End," *New York Times*, May 4, 1927, 17.

11. "Widow on Stand Swears Gray Alone Killed Snyder as She Tried to Save Him," *New York Times*, April 30, 1927, 17 and *New York Times*, May 3, 1921.

12. Belasco's comment is replicated in *Ruth Snyder's My Own True Story, So Help Me God!* New York: King Features Syndicate, 1927.

13. Ben Hecht, "Reporter at Large," *New Yorker*, April 30, 1927, 36.

14. H.L. Mencken, "A Good Man Gone Wrong" in *A Mencken Chrestomathy*. New York: Vintage Books, 1982, 278. Mencken's last thoughts are frequently quoted regarding the nature of sin: "It seems to me that his story is a human document of immense interest and value, and that it deserves a great deal more serious study than it will probably get. Its moral is plain. Sin is a dangerous toy in the hands of the virtuous. It should be left to the congenitally sinful, who know when to play with it and when to let it alone. Run a boy through a Presbyterian Sunday-school and you must police him carefully all the rest of his life, for once he slips he is ready for anything." [page 281]

15. Various sources including an Associated Press report in *The Chenango Tele-graph* (Norwich, New York), May 17, 1927 and "Snyder Slayers Go to Sing Sing Today," *New York Times*, May 16, 1927, where extended sub-headlines noted "Both Prisoners Attend Chapel," "Seven Motorcycle Policemen to clear way as Pair speed up Broadway," and "Heavy Traffic cause motor crashes." "They will travel in separate high-power automobiles, shackled to deputy sheriffs or detectives," the article continues effusively then adds details of how, "Mrs. Snyder saw an automobile at Twelfth Street and Jackson Avenue, in which five people were injured." The final note: "A clerk at Sing Sing spent part of yesterday sorting the mail that has already begun to pile up for the prisoners. Much of it is of the 'crank' variety including letters from religious fanatics, proposals of marriage and wild schemes for escaping the death penalty. Only such letters as are considered sane and cheering will be permitted to reach their addressees."

16. Although he really was not quite right in the head, unlike Lizzie Halliday (see next note), Thaw was a model patient at Matteawan Asylum, until a third jury decided he was still crazy. So he escaped to Canada. He was extradited and reconfined but then a fourth jury declared him sane. Amazingly, in less than a year he was arrested for kidnapping and assaulting of a young man he was grooming. When the family money failed to purchase his victim's favorable testimony (as it had with Nesbit), he was sent to another asylum. He was freed from there after eight years and wrote his own book-length version of events entitled *The Traitor* (1926), modestly subtitled "A Crime of Passion without parallel in American history." Then Thaw decided to become, of all things, a movie producer. Unable to get a script that met his exacting standards written about fake spiritualists, Thaw pondered making a movie about his own life. Nothing was ever green-lit, and he died, still a millionaire, in 1947. Not to be outdone (and likely having gone through the $25,000 she was said to have received for testifying in support of her estranged husband) Evelyn Nesbit Thaw wrote two books: *The Story of My Life* (1914) and *Prodigal Days* (1934).

17. Maria Barbella was the second woman given a date with New York state's "old sparky." Irish-born serial killer Lizzie Halliday was the first, but her indisputable sociopathy got her sentence commuted to life in the asylum. Before she died there, she killed one of her nurses. The first woman actually to fry (after three men, number one of the eight women out of 614 total persons executed) was Martha Place on May 20, 1899. She took an ax to her husband after she had burned out her teenage step-daughter's eyes. Many in the public promoted her as a candidate to join Lizzie Halliday but Gov. Teddy Roosevelt refused. Martha's executioners were the first to devise a method for attaching electrodes to a female body that was not indelicate. Ruth was the fourth woman sentenced to death.

280

18. Dubois, Brittany and Gina Tron, "4 Of The Most Bizarre Motives For Murder," *Oxygen,* August 20, 2019. https://www.oxygen.com/killer-motive/crime-time /five-bizarre-motives-murder-greed-love-lust-watkins-angelo-reeves. In Tampa, Florida in 2014, retired cop Curtis Reeves shot Chad Oulson, who irritated his fellow theater-goer by texting during the coming attractions. By claiming he was "standing his ground" after the victim threw popcorn at him, Reeves delayed his trial until 2022, when he was acquitted. Also in Jacksonville, Florida, young mother Alexandra Tobias' son would not stop crying while she played FarmVille. She got 50 years for shaking the infant to death.

For context it was actually in 1986 St. Louis that Nathan Hicks shot his younger brother for using 6 rolls of toilet paper in 2 days. Two decades later in 21st-century Ocala, Florida, Franking Paul Crow took a sledge-hammer to his roommate (who had to be identified by his fingerprints) for using up all the TP. Neither should be confused with Scott Greenberg, who killed a fellow inmate with toilet paper (stuffed down his throat) while awaiting trial in Clearwater, Florida in 2013. In St. Louis (Missouri not Florida), David L. Scott stabbed Roger Wilkes on Sept 4, 2012 over a bag of Cheetos. Sources did not indicate if there were classic, Flamin' Hot or another flavor. He got 23 years.

19. Pelizzon and West, "Multiple Indemnity," 213.

20. Roughead, William, *Nothing But Murder*, New York: Sheridan House, 1946. According to Joyce Carol Oates "Roughead's influence was enormous, and since his time 'true crime' has become a crowded, flourishing field....Much admired by Henry James, [with] a flair for old-fashioned storytelling, his accounts of murder cases and trials have the advantage of being concise and pointed" [*The New York Review of Books,* June 24, 1999].

21. Mabbott, Thomas Olive, *The Collected Works of Edgar Allan Poe, Volume I: Poems*, Cambridge, MA: Belknap Press, 1969, 242. As detailed by Poe editor, Thomas Mabbott, "Sharp, a politician, seduced a girl of good family, Ann Cook or Cooke [it was Cooke]. Their child died, and Sharp refused to marry his inamorata...Beauchamp, though much younger than she, became romantically interested in her. She asked him to avenge her; and Beauchamp tried to challenge Sharp to a duel. The latter refused to fight because he was in the wrong. The lady now got what Beauchamp called a 'true womanish whim' to be her own avenger, and practiced pistol shooting; [but] they married and decided to let the husband do the killing." The assassin himself continues the story in his *The Confession of Jereboam Beauchamp (written by himself) who was executed at Frankfort, Ky., for the murder of Col. Solomon P. Sharp, a member of the legislature, and late attorney-general of Ky. To which is added some poetical pieces written by Mrs. Ann Beauchamp, who voluntarily put a period to her existence on the day of the execution of her husband, and was buried in the*

same grave with him, on page 35: "Col Sharp exclaimed in the deepest tone of astonishment, dismay, and horror and despair, I ever heard 'Great God!! It's him!!!' And as he said that he fell on his knees...I let go his wrist and grasped him by the throat and dashing him against the facing of the door...muttered in his face, 'die you villain.' And as I said that I plunged the dagger to his heart. He sprang up from his knees and endeavored to throw his arms around my neck, but I struck him in the face and dashed off." The madly-in-love couple were permitted to meet in the condemned man's cell, where Ann Cooke Beauchamp tried to kill herself with laudanum (twice!!) but failed and finally smuggled in a dagger so that they could stab each other. She bled out, but he did not, so weary jailers had to carry him to the gallows. If you want more astonishment, dismay, horror, and despair with up to three exclamation points, you can read the entire first-person account online at Cornell Library (http://reader.library.cornell.edu /docviewer/digital?id=sat1109#mode/1up).

Alternately you can track down other fictions such as the novels (1) *Greyslaer: A Romance of the Mohawk* (1840) by ex-journalist Charles Fenno Hoffman; (2) the more aptly titled (with curiously the "e" added rather than removed) *Beauchamp or, the Kentucky Tragedy, or A Tale of Passion* or (!?) *A Sequel to Charlemont* (1842) by the pro-slaver William Gilmore Simms (whom Poe considered America's best novelist); or (3) *World Enough and Time: A Romantic Novel* (1950) by Robert Penn Warren.

22. See Joseph McNamara. *The Justice Story: True Tales of Murder, Mystery, Mayhem*. Champaign, IL: Sports Publishing, 2000 and Dwight Thomas and David K. Jackson, *The Poe Log: A Documentary Life of Edgar Allan Poe 1809–1849*, New York: G. K. Hall, 1987. Mary Rogers aka the "beautiful cigar girl" was an attractive young clerk at a Manhattan tobacconist frequented by noted authors of the period. Her first disappearance in 1838 was quickly debunked by the local press. After she went missing a second time in late July, 1841, her body was found floating in the Hudson River. After a lengthy investigation and inquest failed to resolve the cause of death (failed abortion, gang violence or something else), a series of exposés called for reforms and put pressure on New York police agencies for speedy resolution of such cases that affected all New York's future crimes of the century (including the head-spinning pace of Snyder-Gray) and persists to this day.

23. Hart, Pearl, "An Arizona Episode," *The Cosmopolitan*, October, 1899, 673-7. The editor's introduction continued: "There have been many female stage robbers in books and stories, but only one in the flesh. Viewed psychologically the statement of such a woman is curious." Ruth Snyder testified that her first secretarial job was with *Cosmopolitan Magazine* for "about a year and a half or two years" [New York Court of Appeal, People of the State of New York Vol. 3, 1771].

24. Montague, G.H., "Two American Disciples of Zola," March-July, 1901, 204. Compare the excerpts by an anonymous reporter for the *San Francisco Call* and from *McTeague*: "Collins is unquestionably one of the most brutal-looking men ever brought into the City Prison. His face is of the bulldog character, flat nose, thick lips, heavy jaws and small, fierce-looking eye. He is a strong, muscular-looking man." "McTeague was a young giant...immense limbs, heavy with ropes of muscle. His hands were enormous, hard as wooden mallets, strong as vises. His head was square cut, angular; the jaw silent, like that of the carnivore. Altogether he suggested the draught horse, immensely strong, stupid..." *The Harvard Monthly* cited the prose of its alumnus Norris as an extension of "the exaggerated and explicated realism which distinguished Rougon-Marquart" series by Zola.

25. Not to be outdone by Thaw's autobiographical work, the tagline of Samuels' non-fiction was "The playboy, the beauty, the artist and the murder that shocked the world." When he portrayed Thaw in this movie Farley Granger added a second criminal of the century to his credits, following Richard Loeb/Phillip Morgan in *Rope*. For director Richard Fleischer this was the first of two crime-of-the-century movies. In declining to participate in *Double Indemnity* (*Bluebeard's Eighth Wife* not being what its title might suggest), writer/producer Charles Brackett lost the opportunity to join that club.

26. *Out of the Blue* (written and directed by Neil LaBute) clearly remakes Kasdan's riff on *Double Indemnity* without formal attribution of any of its sources but *with* an obvious homage to James Cain: a copy of *The Postman Always Rings Twice* is stolen from a lending library.

27. New York Court of Appeal, People of the State of New York Vol. 3, 1112-13.

28. New York Court of Appeal, People of the State of New York Vol. 3, 1097-8. Before the names are listed, day five of the trial transcript reports: "After the examination of 394 talesmen [juror candidates], over a period of five days, to wit from Monday, April 18th to Friday April 22, 1927, inclusive, during which the People exercised 17 peremptorily challenges; the defendant Ruth Snyder exercised 20 peremptory challenges; and the defendant Henry Judd Gray exercised 20 peremptory challenges; 337 talesmen were excused by the Court by consent, the following jury was duly empaneled and sworn."

29. New York Court of Appeal, People of the State of New York Vol. 3, 1112-13. The tabloid also asserted that Mrs. Young had been told that she resembled Ruth Snyder.

30. "Snyder Case Sad, says Darrow," *New York Times*, May 16, 1927.

31. Hart, "An Arizona Episode," 673.

32. Confession of Ruth Snyder in People's Exhibits, Trial transcript, Volume 6, 2779, 2781.

33. Treadwell, *Machinal*, 18.

34. Statements, in order, from A Young Woman/Helen Jones [Treadwell, *Machinal*, 19]; Phyllis Nirdlinger [Cain, *Double Indemnity*, 233]; Ruth Snyder [Styron Phillips, "Dead! A Screenplay," 166; Phyllis Dietrichson [Wilder and Chandler, "*Double Indemnity*," A26]; the actual Ruth May Snyder [Confession vol. 6, Trial Transcript, 2781].

35. Confession of Ruth Snyder, Volume 6, page 2787.

36. Trial transcript, Volume 4, page 1849.

37. "Widow on Stand," *New York Times*, May 4, 1927, 1.

38. Ibid.

39. Trial transcript, Volume 5, page 2242.

40. Gray, *Doomed Ship*, 128-9.

41. Trial transcript, Volume 6, page 2762.

42. Hearn Books edition back cover.

43. Trina, "Dubious Distinctions," 58; Anderson, "Snyder & Gray"; and Dickson, "The Iron Widow," 384.

44. Knowlton and Reader, "Ruth Snyder: Still Dead," 184-5.

45. "She Goes to Death First," *New York Times*, January 13, 1928, 1. Thanks to Tom Howard and all the sensational press coverage, three weeks later, the *Times* reported, Assemblyman Jacob Nathanson proposed to restrict all reporting to a statement by the Commissioner of Correction and threatening those "publishing any other report of such execution" with a fine of up to $5,000 ["Bars Press at Executions," *New York Times*, February 6, 1928]. The measure failed. But that fine versus selling thousands more copies have been likely to inhibit the *Daily News* or any other newspaper, tabloid or otherwise?

46. Pelizzon and West, "Multiple Indemnity," 213.

47. Jones, "She Had to Die!," 1980.

48. Ramey, "The Bloody Blonde," 630, 646.

49. "Shoots Husband Over Snyder Case," *New York Times*, May 16, 1927.

50. Pelizzon and West, "Multiple Indemnity," 217.

51. Ibid, 224, quoting Birdwell's April 12, 1927 installment.

52. Pelizzon and West, 211.

53. Ibid, 212.

54. All lines quoted are from Styron and Phillips, "Dead! A Screenplay."

55. Cain, *Double Indemnity*, 232-3.

2. Human Interest [James Cain]

1. Cain, *Double Indemnity*, 219.

2. Madden, *James M. Cain*, 101.

3. Madden and Mecholsky, *James M. Cain, Hard-boiled Mythmaker.*

4. Hoopes, *The Biography of James M. Cain*, 8.

5. Cain, *Three of a Kind*, viii.

6. Cain, "James M. Cain, The Art of Fiction No. 69."

7. In fact, while it is certainly reasonable to believe that Cain did attend the trial, there is no hard evidence of that. Elizabeth Ward makes that claim in *Shadows of Suspense*, the 40-minute documentary that accompanied the 2006 DVD release of *Double Indemnity*. "He attended the murder trial in which the wife was accused of taking out insurance, accident insurance, on her husband." The cut from Elizabeth to Eddie Muller makes it seem as if he agrees, when he says, "And it really captured Cain's imagination." Of course, Snyder-Gray could have done that without him ever being in the courtroom.

8. Hoopes, *The Biography of James M. Cain*, 177.

9. Cain, *Three of a Kind*, x.

10. Ibid.

11. Hoopes, *The Biography of James M. Cain*, 247.

12. Abbott, *The Street Was Mine*, 46-7.

13. The Academy of Motion Picture Arts and Sciences (AMPAS) Margaret Herrick Library has holdings of both Paramount Pictures Production records and Billy Wilder Papers. The letter from Joseph I. Breen to Louis B. Mayer of October 10, 1935 is included in the AMPAS library PDF file SC510621080 regarding *Double Indemnity*, pages 2-3 (of 52). The letter warns specifically that:

"...The first part of the story is replete with explicit details of the planning of the murder and the effective commission of the crime, thus definitely violating the Code provisions which forbid the presentation of 'details of crime.' This part of the story is, likewise, seriously questionable, when it is not definitely offensive, because of the cold-blooded fashion in which the murderers proceed to their kill.

"The second part of the story has to do with the successful efforts of the criminals to avoid arrest and punishment, and culminates in the decision of the man to kill his accomplice. The attempt is frustrated when the woman shoots him, whereupon the wounded man, in love with the stepdaughter of his accomplice, confesses the crime to save the girl he loves, against whom a mass of circumstantial evidence has been piled up.

"This story violates the provisions of the Production Code in that:

(1) The leading characters are murderers who cheat the law and die at their own hands. They avoid successfully the consequences of their crime through a miscarriage of justice, even though, subsequently, they commit suicide. It may be argued, too, that one of these criminals is, in a sense, glorified by his confession to save the girl he loves.

(2) The story deals improperly with an illicit and adulterous sex relationship;

(3) The details of the vicious and cold-blooded murder are clearly shown. These details are definitely and specifically in violation of the Production Code.

"The general low tone and sordid flavor of this story makes it, in our judgment, thoroughly unacceptable for screen presentation before mixed audiences in the theatre. I am sure that you will agree that it is most important, in the consideration of material of this type, to avoid what the Code calls 'the hardening of audiences, especially those who are young and impressionable, to the thought and fact of crime.'"

14. Wilson, "The Boys in the Back Room," 493.

15. Shearer, "Crime Certainly Pays on the Screen," 9-12.

16. Cain memo, 1943, Wilder Collection, AMPAS Library.

17. Hoopes, *The Biography of James M. Cain*, 335.

3. The Mystery Writer [Raymond Chandler]

1. Air Cadet Chandler reflects on two articles "Women, War, and Babies" by Jane Addams and "Women in Black" by Sophie Treadwell, both in *Harper's*, July 31, 1915.

2. BBC *Light Programme* Broadcast of July 10, 1958: Chandler in discussion with novelist Ian Fleming referring to Helen Hunt Jackson's *Ramona*.

3. Cf. Stacy Perman, "Writers Still Get Typecast," *Los Angeles Times*, May 20, 2023, E1, E6. The article reflects on Chandler's disparagement of Hollywood's treatment of writers in the context of a strike by the Writers Guild of America.

4. According to Chandler because he often could not find the addresses for the assignments he got from his editor.

5. MacShane, *The Life of Raymond Chandler*, 15.

6. For a man named Horace Voules at six guineas a week (a goodly sum), but reported MacShane, Chandler's reaction was "imagine me...wearing an old school tie, with an on school band on a natty straw hat, carrying a cane and gloves, and being told by this elegant fellow to write what then appeared to be the most appalling garbage ever slung together in words. I gave him a sickly smile and left the country." [page 22]

7. Williams, *A Mysterious Something in the Light*, 51. According to Tom Williams, Chandler "wore a tailored suit, carried a silver-tipped cane, and had $40 in his pocket" Williams does not stipulate whether that was $40 American or the equivalent in pounds sterling. MacShane describes Chandler as "hair parted down the middle, wearing rounded stiff collars, a school tie, and

tweeds." How could he know these details (MacShane appears to extrapolate from Chandler's self-description above) without benefit of a snapshot is unclear. Neither proposes details of how the £500 was spent. Half of it might have gone to a second-class ticket (prices ranged from £10 to £20 for third-class/steerage to around £750 for full first-class) but perhaps Chandler had more than $40 left.

8. Letters from Chandler to publisher Hamish Hamilton (December 11, 1950) and Leroy Wright (March 31, 1957) printed in Gardiner and Walker, *Raymond Chandler Speaking*, 24-5. "Every penny of it was repaid," Chandler claimed, "with six per cent interest."

9. Ward and Silver, *Raymond Chandler's Los Angeles*, 11

10. Letter to Hamish Hamilton (November 10, 1950) in MacShane, *Selected Letters of Raymond Chandler*, 236 and *Raymond Chandler Speaking*, 25. As to having "a public school accent," who knows what he might have sounded like when he got to Los Angeles in 1913 but you can judge for yourself (the BBC Broadcast of 1958 is available several places online) whether it was long gone when Chandler spoke to Ian Fleming in 1958.

11. From 1913 at 713 South Bonnie Brae Street with the Lloyds until moving to La Jolla in 1946, they included (all in Los Angeles unless otherwise noted) 311 Loma Drive (1916); 127 South Vendome Street (1917); 224 South Catalina, Redondo Beach (1920); 3206 San Marino (after Florence's death with wife, 1921); 723 Stewart Street, Santa Monica (1923); 2863 Leeward (1924); 700 Gramercy Place (1926); 2315 West 12th Street (1927); 1024 South Highland Avenue (1928); 4616 Greenwood Place (1933); 1637 Redesdale Avenue (1934); 449 San Vicente Blvd., Santa Monica (1939); 857 Iliff St., Pacific Palisades (1941); 12216 Shetland Lane, Brentwood (1942); 6520 Drexel Avenue (1943) [compiled by Elizabeth Ward].

12. Dabney in-law John Abrams quoted by MacShane, *The Life of Raymond Chandler*, 39.

13. Hector Tobar, "Following Raymond Chandler's L.A. footsteps on his birthday," *Los Angeles Times*, July 23, 2014.

14. Macshane, *The Life of Raymond Chandler*, 40.

15. August 12, 1933 letter to William Lever quoted in Williams, *A Mysterious Something in the Light*, 359. "It took me a year to write my first story," said a later letter to William Lever, "I had to go back to the beginning and learn to

write all over again…You'll laugh when I tell you what I write. Me, with my romantic and poetical instincts. I'm writing sensational detective fiction."

16. "The Simple Art of Murder," *The Atlantic*, December, 1944, online at https:// www.theatlantic.com/magazine/archive/1944/12/the-simple-art-of-murder /656179/.

17. MacShane, *The Life of Raymond Chandler*, 22.

18. Williams, *A Mysterious Something in the Light*, 114.

19. Letter to Hamish Hamilton (November 10, 1950) quoted in Day, *The World of Raymond Chandler in His Own Words*, 21.

20. Day, *The World of Raymond Chandler in His Own Words*, 30.

21. Ibid, 32, re "The Simple Art of Murder." The Hemingway parody: "Hank drank the alcohol and water. It was warm all the way down. It was warm as hell. It was warmer than whiskey. It was warmer than that Asti Spumante they had that time in Capozzo when Hank was with the Arditi. They had been carp fishing with landing nets. It had been a good day."

22. Ibid.

23. BBC *Light Programme* Broadcast of 1958.

24. Letter to Blanche Knopf (October 22, 1942), quoted in Day, *The World of Raymond Chandler in His Own Words*, 30-1.

25. Letter to Blanche Knopf in MacShane, *Selected Letters*, 23.

26. Shaw quoted in MacShane, *The Life of Raymond Chandler*, 46.

27. Letters to William Lever cited in Williams, *A Mysterious Something in the Light*, 125, 131.

28. BBC *Light Programme* Broadcast of 1958.

29. MacShane, *The Life of Raymond Chandler*, 62-3

30. Ibid, 67.

31. Isaac Anderson, "New Mystery Stories," *New York Times*, February 2, 1939.

32. Letters of March 5, 1939 in MacShane, *Selected Letters*, 8-9. Again Chandler cannibalized earlier work. For the second novel he used "Try the Girl," "The Man Who Liked Dogs," and more of "Mandarin's Jade."

33. Letters of October 17th and December 19th, 1939 in MacShane, *Selected Letters*, 10, 13. As biographer Tom Hiney recounts: "Chandler believed that the 'smart aleck' critics had only ever accepted Hammett in a patronizing way, and that though they had been titillated by Cain's first book, they had ignored him. They were still refusing even to distinguish between good and bad writers of hard-boiled fiction. Determined to break this impasse, Chandler threw away the entire typescript of *Farewell, My Lovely* and started the book again...It was a risk he was prepared to take." [Hiney, *Raymond Chandler: A Biography*, 114.]

34. After repeated prodding from his agent Sydney Sanders, Chandler had produced a story, "I'll Be Waiting," that could be sold to the *Saturday Evening Post*. He also published a science fiction piece in *Unknown*: "The Bronze Door," about an occult device that transports a snobbish British dipsomaniac with a hyphenated last name, his carping wife and her annoying pomerian into an unknown ether. Perhaps that's where Chandler on occasion wanted to go.

35. That comment is made in Chapter 28 by Dr. Carl Moss, "a big burly Jew with a Hitler mustache, pop eyes, and the calmness of a glacier." His actual remark: "'Phil Marlowe,' he said, 'the shop-soiled Galahad.'" is on page 189 of the 1942, Knopf first edition.

36. Letter of October 22, 1942 in MacShane, *Selected Letters*, 22. Chandler would soon learn that William Irish was a pseudonym for prolific Cornell Woolrich, arguably the source of more film noir narratives that any other writer.

37. Chandler's remark is quoted by many including MacShane, *The Life of Raymond Chandler*, 105 and Al Clark, *Raymond Chandler in Hollywood*, 22. "No doubt he would have been incensed further," Clark continues, "by the discovery that the sum in question was well under half what Michael Arlen had received for his original short story, and less than Arlen was paid per film for the continued use of the Falcon character."

38. Released on Christmas Eve 1942, *Time to Kill* (directed by Herbert I. Leeds from a script by Clarence Upson Young, both B-budget specialists) was the last of several times that Lloyd Nolan would portray Mike Shayne. There were actually two literary sleuths known as the Falcon. *The Falcon Takes Over* (directed by Irving Reis, from a screenplay by Frank Fenton and Lynn Boor), released in May, 1942, featured George Sanders as Arlen's Gay Lawrence. Journeyman scripter Fenton has previously helped George Sanders take over

as the Saint. He later worked on such classic period film noirs as *Nocturne* (1946), *Out of the Past* (1947), and *His Kind of Woman* (1951). There was just about nothing hard-boiled or Marlowe-esque in the suave Sanders' multiple portrayals of the Saint (five) or the Falcon (four). Nolan on the other hand could put his feet up on an office desk and talk tough when necessary.

39. The complete list is reproduced in MacShane, *The Life of Raymond Chandler*, 79-80.

40. Letter of February 8, 1943 in MacShane, *Selected Letters*, 23-24. Chandler apparently re-read some pages and found the prose "both much better and much worse than I had expected—or that I expected. I have been so belabored by tags like tough, hard-boiled, etc. that it is almost a shock to discover signs of sensitivity in the writing. On the other hand, I sure did run the similes into the ground." Chandler does not remark on the front or back cover of the just-released "New Avon Library" version, in the series of "$2.00 Mysteries for 25¢." The earliest cover featured a fresh corpse, presumably the body of Arthur Geiger, wearing a Chinese jacket and lying on the floor beneath a couple of owl statuettes. On the back was a reprinted review from the tabloid *Los Angeles News* which proclaimed, "JAMES CAIN, JOHN O'HARA, DASHIELL HAMMETT, MOVE OVER: You've got a new pal." The Armed Services Edition, a Black Widow Thriller in monochrome with the only image being the signature arachnid. Given that General Sternwood compared himself to a new spider, that could fit quite neatly. The second Avon featured a crème-colored skull with a hint of brow line above dark eyes that from a distance were empty sockets. It had a black inverted "V" for a nose and a reasonable rendering of a cadaverous grin.

41. From "Writers in Hollywood," reprinted in Gardiner and Walker, *Raymond Chandler Speaking*, 120-21.

4. The Austrian Journalist [Billy Wilder]

1. Biographers differ as to what reference letters or "two or three things," Wilder had taken with him to Mexico. You can read his most recent version of events in Crowe, *Conversations with Wilder*, 282: "I did not have the proper paperwork with me to show that I was not a criminal...that I did not have a sexual disorder or something. The guy was walking around the desk, studying me. 'How do you expect to make a living?' And I said, 'I am a writer. A screenplay writer. With that he smiled, twisted my papers around, gave them a stamp, *dock-dock-dock-dock*, and said 'Write some good ones.'"

2. Sikov, *On Sunset Boulevard*, 8. "And you never tell the same story twice." Sikov continues. "As told by Wilder, his life was a series of themes and variations, with heavy accent on the variations and little attention paid to inconsistencies." Sikov invokes Buffalo Bill on page 5. Twenty years earlier Maurice Zolotow in *Billy Wilder in Hollywood* had held off until page 21. Even generalist Otto Friedrich in *City of Nets: A Portrait of Hollywood in the 1940s* deems to mention to it on page 44.

3. Zolotow, 21.

4. Ibid, 26 and Sikov, *On Sunset Boulevard*, 20.

5. Sikov, *On Sunset Boulevard*. According to Sikov, "after painstakingly going through volume after dusty volume on *Die Stunde* looking for articles by Billie Wilder, [Austrian biographer] Andreas Hutter found only a single signed article covering a crime. [page 21]

6. Most recently in Crowe, *Conversations with Wilder*, 140.

7. Names and colorful details can be found in Zolotow, 39-40 and Sikov, *On Sunset Boulevard*, 49-50. Both of them quote Wilder using the same words to the young lady: "Thank you, for sending me Galitzenstein [president of Maxim Films], but he is a small-time producer. Next time, please…Erich Pommer [head of UFA]." To be clear, biographer Maurice Zolotow had met Wilder while working on an earlier book on Marilyn Monroe, and over the course of months repeatedly interviewed his subject. Wilder's stories, often complete with snippets of dialogue, fill this biography. Later writers such as Friedrich and Sikov replicated much of *Billy Wilder in Hollywood*. Zolotow did interview others (as did Sikov); but in the context of that first detailed biography published a quarter century before his death, it was via Zolotow that Wilder himself is the source of the anecdotes.

8. Different sources gave Zolotow different versions. Future Hollywood agent Paul Kohner claimed it was his idea, as the project needed a breezy style. Producer Joe Pasternak disagreed, saying Wilder owed him almost $1000 from poker losses and hiring him meant the gambling debt could be repaid. One way or another it was Wilder's first screen credit.

9. Sikov tried unsuccessfully to get clarity on what Wilder actually wrote for this independent production (or how it was financed). Director Siodmak claimed "Wilder only wrote a single gag." Per producer Edgar G. Ulmer "Wilder did not write a true script." [page 59-source] Wilder claimed he sketched out the main lines of action in around 10 pages which the cast improvised.

10. Wilder did write a short script for Robert Siodmak to direct, *Der Kampf mit dem Drachen oder: Die Tragödie des Untermieters* (*The Fight with the Dragon or: the Tragedy of the Tenant*), a fantasy about a renter who kills his landlady. [Zolotow, page 43]

11. According to Zolotow Wilder was so put off by the pressure of staging scenes that "he was praying to get back to the real business of his life, which was writing. He would, of course, never direct another movie—never." [page 52]

12. Friedrich, *City of Nets*, 52.

13. In Sikov, *On Sunset Boulevard*, 98, Sikov adds "reportedly." The details are much the same as Zolotow, but Sikov's citation is Lally, *Wilder Times*, 60.

14. Sikov, *On Sunset Boulevard*, 106. Sikov adds: "Billie's life at the Chateau Marmont wasn't much fun, if for no other reason than it marked the first extended time in his life that it wasn't easy to talk [the language]. He wanted to become an American—fast."

15. The projects were *Encore* (a musical) and *Gibraltar* (spies, gambling, and romance). Zolotow, pages 59-60.

16. Zolotow, 60, and Sikov, *On Sunset Boulevard*, 112. Sikov singles out the assassination of the Austrian chancellor Engelbert Dolfuss as cementing Wilder's prescient concern long before Germany's 1938 Anschluss with Austria.

17. Perhaps he moved back into the Chateau Marmont (Zolotow) and maybe he was owed money on a spec script for sometime Paramount producer Lester Cowan who got studio story-department head Manny Wolfe [spelled this way by Brackett, Sikov and Zolotow but without the "e" in Crowe and elsewhere] to hire him. This makes sense to Zolotow [60], not so much to Sikov [Sikov, *On Sunset Boulevard*, 115], but what is certain is that Wilder became one of the 100-plus writers under contract.

18. Brackett, *It's the Pictures That Got Small*, 88. The full story from the man's diaries: "I'd gone to meet somebody with whom I was to have dinner in the Hollywood Brown Derby. While I waited, Billy came in and I asked him to join me for a drink. As we sat together, the swing door was opened on the wintry evening to admit a luminous figure. 'Look who's coming in!' I breathed. Billy gave a cursory glance over his shoulder. 'Marlene!' he snorted. 'She's old hat…Let me tell you if the waiter were to wheel over a big covered dish with her in it stark naked, I'd say, 'Not interested,' and have him wheel her away.'"

19. Zolotow has a detailed and colorful reenactment of Wilder's exchange with Manny Wolfe and official introduction to Brackett, who asks him if he plays cribbage. Of course, Zolotow gives the date as July 17, 1936. [page 62] Brackett, who was there, records it in his diary as the 17th of August. He noted: "I am to be teamed with Billy Wilder, a young Austrian I've seen about for a year or two and like very much. I accepted the job joyfully." [page 86] Wilder's retelling to Crowe: "Brackett was a very loquacious man…just hanging around Paramount and did not know what the hell to do. Manny Wolf, head of the writing department, got the two of us together. Introduced me and said, 'Now you two go and talk to Mr. Lubitsch and see whether he likes you.' About half an hour later, we had the job of *Bluebeard's Eighth Wife*. It was not a very good picture, just kind of all right." [page 40] For an independent assessment from a repeated co-worker see also Miklós Rózsa's autobiography, *Double Life*, page 118: "Wilder and his associate Charles Brackett were entirely different personalities. Brackett was a reserved New England gentleman, literate, cool, composed, and well-behaved; the volatile Wilder was all jokes and wit and couldn't sit still for a moment. They were like solid iron and quicksilver."

20. Released in the same year as *Bluebeard's Eighth Wife* (1938) was *That Certain Age* (for which they were not credited) then came 1939's *Midnight*, *What a Life*, and *Ninotchka* then *Arise, My Love* (1940), *Hold Back the Dawn* and *Ball of Fire* (both 1941). The writing work continued after Wilder started directing again in 1942: *The Major and the Minor* then *Five Graves to Cairo* (1943), *The Lost Weekend* (1945), *The Emperor Waltz* and *A Foreign Affair* (both 1948 releases), and finally *Sunset Boulevard* (1950). They also were not credited for a treatment on *French Without Tears* (1940).

21. Crowe, *Conversations with Wilder*, 40-1. As to dinner together, Brackett's diaries beg to differ, starting with meeting him and future first wife Judith Coppicus at the Brown Derby on November 25, 1936. [page 94] After Wilder got married and bought a house, Brackett records him going there for dinner on more than one occasion.

22. Brackett, 87.

23. Ibid.

24. Brackett, page 89.

25. Brackett, page 90.

26. Brackett, page 92.

27. Crowe, *Conversations with Wilder*, 40. There was no couch jumping involved but Brackett recalls a day in 1939 when "Billy arrived with a small wooden Bulgarian flute which he played all day. I took it and smashed it across my knee. Billy's face turned scarlet, he rushed from the room." [page 131] Also Brackett's diaries end in 1949 while *Sunset Boulevard* was in post-production but from that movie's release back to the initial assignment for Lubitsch is a 16 not 20-year stretch.

28. Purportedly Preston Sturges' own decision to become a director was reinforced by the cuts Mitchell Leisen made to *Remember the Night* (1940). It was during an encounter in a restaurant that Wilder and Brackett were told by Charles Boyer how their scene for *Hold Back the Dawn* had been axed: "I convinced Mr. Leisen, I'm not talking to a cockroach." [page 9] As Wilder further details it to Crowe: "I did not think I would be a director in those early days. It was only later when we were writing that last picture at Paramount…it was only after directors had fucked up things that I took any interest in staging them myself." [page 200]

29. Zolotow, 93.

30. Bogdanovich, *Who the Devil Made It*, 320.

31. Crowe, *Conversations with Wilder*, 193.

32. Ibid, 192.

33. Zolotow, 91-2

34. Brackett, 166.

35. Zolotow, 106.

36. Sikov, *On Sunset Boulevard*. Sikov adds some more details: $46,667 to Ray Milland, $10,000 for a few days work to Robert Benchley, Brackett as producer/writer, $31,500 and "working for scale" as director, only $27,033 for Wilder. [page 174]

37. Zolotow lists the attendees besides Lubitsch as E.A. Dupont, William Wyler, William Dieterle, Michael Curtiz, and Robert Koster. [page 106]

38. Miklós Rózsa, *Double Life*. As Miklós Rózsa tells it, Wilder "told me bluntly that he had actually wanted Franz Waxman (a dear friend from his Berlin days) to do the music, but he was under contract to Warners. However, he promised that, if I did a good job, I would be his first choice for the next." [page 118]

5. The Movie: A Fancy Piece of Homicide

1. Moffat, Ivan, "On the Fourth Floor at Paramount." in *The World of Raymond Chandler*, edited by Miriam Gross, New York: A & W Publishers, 1977, 47. When he quoted a variant of the line from *The High Window*, Wilder called the novel *"The Brasher Doubloon*, which was retitled," probably confounding the title of the Fox remake. In another version Wilder quoted correctly: "I was eager to work with Cain, but he was tied up working on a picture at Fox called *Western Union*. A producer-friend brought me some Chandler stories from *The Black Mask*. You could see the man had a wonderful eye. I remember two lines from those stories especially: 'Nothing is emptier than an empty swimming pool.' The other is when Marlowe goes to Pasadena in the middle of the summer and drops in on a very old man who is sitting in a greenhouse covered in three blankets. He says, 'Out of his ears grew hair long enough to catch a moth.' A great eye…but then you don't know if that will work in pictures because the details in writing have to be photographable." [Wilder, "The Art of Screenwriting, No. 1."]

2. Zolotow [page 123] says Cain was unavailable because he was polishing *Western Union* for Fritz Lang. This would not have been possible as *Western Union* was released more than two years before Paramount committed to *Double Indemnity*. Besides Zolotow, other writers claim to have heard about the Lang movie directly from Wilder, probably because Wilder said it himself to Moffat [page 44]. As noted before, Wilder tended to exaggerate and embellish and/or misremember. The likeliest is that in spring 1943, Cain was at Fox on a 22-week contract and writing propaganda for the Signal Corps. That is the sort of wartime commitment that could not be circumvented by loan-out agreements or other side deals.

3. Ibid. This comment might explain Chandler's cameo in the movie, sitting in an upstairs walkway possibly waiting to consult on some balance sheet, as Neff walks by en route from Keyes' office to his own.

4. Zolotow, 123.

5. Moffat, "On the Fourth Floor at Paramount," 46.

6. MacShane, *Life of Raymond Chandler*, 106.

7. Williams, *A Mysterious Something in the Light*, 184.

8. Paramount Pictures, "Analysis of Costs of Scenario, Supervision, Direction and Cast," June 17, 1944. 161 days x $58.33 ($350 per week ÷ 6) = $9,391.66. $750 ÷ 6 x 4 = $500. Why the kicker at the end? It might have

been indicated in Chandler's contract, which we could not find. Many staff writers at Paramount were on 26-week deals, and Chandler worked 4 days beyond that amount of time at the $350/week rate. His new agent H.N Swanson might have insisted on a renewal at that rate. Or Sistrom (or Wilder), mindful that Chandler's final weekly rate would impact his next writing salary, might have bumped it on the last 4 days of shooting to help get him better paid on the next. What is not explained is why—at a studio where, much to Wilder's consternation when writing was all that he did, writers were not allowed on sets—was Chandler physically present throughout the shooting of *Double Indemnity* and not laid off until the last day?

9. The letter of March 15, 1943 from Joseph I. Breen to Luigi Luraschi at Paramount is in the AMPAS library PDF file SC510621080, pages 10-11 (of 52). It essentially replicates the 1935 letter to MGM.

10. Zolotow, 111.

11. Sikov, *On Sunset Boulevard*, 195.

12. Brackett, 212.

13. Ibid, 213.

14. Moffat, "On the Fourth Floor at Paramount," 44.

15. Schickel, *Double Indemnity*, 34. Per Schickel Chandler returns with only 65 pages and is offered a deal at $1000 per week! That would be a whopping $17,500 per week in today's money. While the Writers Guild is currently on strike in today's film industry, an increase of 6% of last weekly scale (through May 1, 2023) for 20 out of 26 weeks as a theatrical film writer—shorter than the deal Chandler had—would be $5,527. The $350 that Chandler was paid for 26 weeks would be $6,125 today.

16. Brackett showed Wilder a screen test of silent era star Eleanor Boardman, who was 44 years old.

17. Zolotow, page 114, and Sikov, *On Sunset Boulevard*, 198.

18. Moffat, "On the Fourth Floor at Paramount," 45. Sikov embellishes: "'it's going to take ten or twelve weeks, and getting $2000 a week.' He almost fainted." [page 198] Wherever that $2000 per week number comes from, Chandler almost certainly would have fainted at a prospect of $20 to 24,000 dollars or over $400,000 in today's money.

19. Letter of November 10, 1950 to Hamish Hamilton in MacShane, *Selected Letters*, 237.

20. Williams, *A Mysterious Something in the Light*. Swanson confirmed these details of Sistrom's call in his own book initially noting, "One day I had a call from Joseph Sistrom about a situation in which he thought I could help, a contract with Raymond Chandler," from *Sprinkled with Ruby Dust* quoted in Williams. [page 184] In MacShane's version, appalled at how little Chandler wanted, "Sistrom phoned H.N. Swanson and asked him to take on Chandler and teach him how to negotiate the studios." [page 106] Of course, with Swanie protecting his interests, Chandler would no longer be doing any direct negotiating.

21. Exactly how much Warner Bros. paid for the rights, which were actually purchased by *Ball of Fire* producer/director Howard Hawks, is also unclear. The consensus is at least $5,000, up to $10,000. Some assert that Warners gave Hawks $50,000 and that he kept the rest, which would have been a neat trick to pull on H.N. Swanson, whose posh offices on Sunset Boulevard depended on him not getting flim-flammed. According to Jon Tuska (who had been known to use rhetorical embellishment): "Warners proposed to Hawks that he should make another film with Bogart and Bacall. Hawks wanted to try his hand at a hard-boiled detective story but found that virtually all of Hammett's properties had been used and reused. Talking it over with Faulkner, Hawks found that Faulkner agreed that, if you couldn't have Hammett. Raymond Chandler was the next best. Hawks purchased screen rights to Raymond Chandler's first novel, THE BIG SLEEP (1939) for $25,000. He intended to have a similar turnaround with the property as he had done for TO HAVE AND HAVE NOT." [from *Encounters with filmmakers: Eight Career Studies*, 1991, page 119] Did that turnaround ultimately involve Hawks pocketing some cash?

Screenplay

22. MacShane, *Life of Raymond Chandler*, 106-07.

23. May 24 Test Scene, File 12, Wilder collection, AMPAS Library.

24. MacShane, *Life of Raymond Chandler*, 107.

25. It is unclear whether either Wilder or Brackett reviewed Alfred Savoir's French playscript of *La Huitième Femme de Barbe-Bleue* or just used the English version by Charlton Andrews (credited for such) from the 1921-22 run on Broadway. Andrews' play with Philip Dunning "Get Me in the Movies" closed after a short run 3 months before *Machinal* in 1928.

26. MacShane, *Life of Raymond Chandler*, 107-08.

27. We are not graphologists but a comparison with other vetted examples of Wilder's handwriting on memos and autographed photographs matched the note on page 3 of the May 24 test scene.

28. Cain, *Three of a Kind*, 221. A long paragraph Huff explains to the reader how "accident insurance is sold, not bought" before concluding that "all they want is the money, and there's many a man walking around today that's worth more to his loved one dead than alive, only he don't know it yet." Sounds a lot like Albert Snyder; but at this point Cain's Huff is still more insurance salesman Leroy Ashfield than Judd Gray. To be clear, Cain has the automobile club ("Never knock the other guy's stuff," Chapter 1), the iced tea drinking (Chapter 2, second visit), the "worried sick (2), the crown block (Chapter 2, third encounter at Huff's apartment), but he doesn't even reveal her name is Phyllis until their fourth meeting (Chapter 2, next night at Huff's place).

29. Brackett, page 211.

30. Chandler's June 1 memo (and others) is in the AMPAS Library Wilder Papers, File 13.

31. Schickel, *Double Indemnity*, 44.

32. Internet opinions and algorithms vary, but as of this writing Officialdata.org reported that 90,000 1927 dollars would equal $1,578,150. 1943 dollars would equal $1,587,272.25. When Cain was writing in 1935, $2,004,365.69. Of course when the movie is set in 1938, the number would be $1,947,504.26. But did the writers know or care? And how many in the audience actually noticed when Neff dictated July 15, 1938?

33. See the details on the $97,000 in endnote 6 for Chapter 1.

34. Brackett, 225.

35. Ibid, 226.

36. "No one comes off well in this ill-advised venture. The acting is as stilted as the situation. Two characters in the play, Wilder's perky secretary [Helen Hernandez] and a frazzled producer [Joe Sistrom], seem to have blundered in from a sitcom." [Stasio, Marilyn. *Variety* review, October 20, 2014] "Any given five minutes of the classic film noir "Double Indemnity"—I am tempted to say any single frame of the classic film noir "Double Indemnity"—packs

more heat than the torpid two hours of "Billy & Ray," a play, a slumberous drama, a stolid production directed by the television veteran Garry Marshall," [Isherwood, Charles, *New York Times* review, October 20, 2014.] Apparently before the lights come up, noises suggest the tumultuous parting break-up of Wilder and Brackett. Presumably that means, ashtrays beings thrown, perhaps lamps tipping over but no jumping on sofas.

37. Brackett, 227-8.

38. Moffat, "On the Fourth Floor at paramount," 47-8.

39. Crowe, *Conversations with Wilder*, 69.

40. Ibid, 70.

41. Moffat, "On the Fourth Floor at Paramount," 46.

42. Brackett, 228-9.

43. Ibid, 230.

44. Ibid, 231.

The Hays Office

45. File 21, Wilder Collection, AMPAS Library.

46. In some accounts, "Ness" (unclear if the reference is to the novel) had to become "Neff." Likely a case of years-later confusion, as no AMPAS drafts use "Ness." The full memo is in Billy Wilder Papers (file 22) in AMPAS Library, copy of August 6, 1943 memo to Luraschi. Wilder also wrote:"We have just found out that there is actually a student at U.S.C named Sachetti. We suggest changing the name to LURASCHI and, in order to make it different from yours, to give him the first name of LUIGI. We also want to call the insurance company PARAMOUNT INSURANCE COMPANY. KEYES we can call KARP [Jack Karp, young assistant and then successor in 1959 to Y. Frank Freeman]; NORTON can be called MR. FREEMAN [the then-head of production]; PHYLLIS NIRDLINGER can be PHYLLIS BALABAN [Barney Balaban, Paramount president and part-owner since his theater chain was purchased by Famous Players-Lasky]; and WALTER HUFF can be WALTER PASTERNACKI [Joe Pasternak, then MGM producer who used Wilder's services when he was Universal's representative in Berlin, started as a busboy at Paramount's Astoria Studios in New York]. And, in order not to offend Los Angeles, we are going to change the town to BOLOGNA."

47. Schickel, *Double Indemnity*, 53.

48. As indicated the memos quoted are on letterhead from Paramount on September 21 and 28 and carbon copies of Breen replies on September 24 and 30. Luraschi and Paramount continue the strategy of doling out portions, never letting Breen make a full meal of the script. October 1, the day after Breen approves one chunk, he gets another taste. October 4, that is okayed, with the usual closing caveat: "You understand, of course, that our final judgment will be based on the finished picture." The process continues: on October 4th, 12th, twice on the 18th, 25th, 27th, and so on.

Actors

49. Moffat, "On the Fourth Floor at Paramount," 48.

50. The mouse question is Friedrich, *City of Nets*, 165, or Sikov, *On Sunset Boulevard*, 203. Alternately quoted, Schickel, *Double Indemnity*, 58, for example, as "actress or a mouse?" The longest version has Stanwyck explaining: "'I love the script and I love you, but I am a little afraid after all these years of playing heroines to go into an out-and-out killer.' Mr. Wilder looked at me and he said 'Well, are you a mouse or an actress?' I said "Well, I hope I'm an actress." He said 'Then do the part'. And I did and I'm very grateful to him." [quoted in Kevin Lally, *Wilder Times*, 126] To be clear Wilder never stipulates then the mouse bit the cheese, so the time frame ranges from early spring (Wilder's memo to the agent) to mid-summer. The ethics of Hollywood then as now permitted producers to rely on handshake deals, verbal commitments from actors or their representatives. Actual contract signing could take a while. The notes for Stanwyck's contract in the AMPAS Library production records for the studio (File 1264) are dated August 13, 1943; but all the stars were set by late July. [see Numbers]

51. Wilder to Porfirio (*Film Noir Reader 3*), 108.

52. Consensus version from Wilder (mostly Moffat, "On the Fourth Floor at Paramount," 48 blended with Zolotow 117): "I said, 'What?' He said again, "Where's the lapel?' I asked again, 'What is the lapel?' 'The lapel,' Raft said, annoyed at my stupidity, 'When the guy turns it, you see his badge, you know he's a detective or government agent, a good guy.'"

53. Wilder to Porfirio (*Film Noir Reader 3*), page 109.

54. Zolotow, page 117.

55. Wilder to Porfirio (*Film Noir Reader 3*), page 109.

56. Ibid.

57. Neff's actual comment: "It was one of those California Spanish houses every-one was nuts about ten or fifteen years ago. This one must have cost some-body about thirty thousand bucks—that is if he ever finished paying for it." Take a look at the house at 6301 Quebec Drive. The Redfin estimate is bit more than $30,000 in today's money or MacMurray's updated picture fee of $1.75 million. It's almost twice that: $3.37 million.

58. Wilder to Porfirio (*Film Noir Reader 3*), page 106.

59. First details of Robinson's contract on August 18, 1943 (the AMPAS library file) make the details of his credit no less than third position but otherwise (such as the size of lettering) of equal prominence. Note 3 of the December 16, 1943 billing recap for *Double Indemnity* is very precise:

"(a) Only the names of FRED MacMURRAY & BARBARA STANWYCK to precede the name of the Artist; the name of no other player appearing in said motion picture photoplay shall be announced in larger size type, not be more prominently displayed than the name of the Artist; co-stars shall be displayed above the title of the motion picture photoplay.

"(b) The names of the co-stars shall be announced as follows:

Fred 25%   Barbara 25%

MacMURRAY 75%   STANWYCK 75%

EDWARD G. ROBINSON 75%

"(The above percentages are in relation to the size of the title of the photoplay.)"

That's why EDWARD G's first name and middle initial in the actual titles are larger than "Fred" or "Barbara."

Numbers.

60. In 1938, after years of investigation by the Federal Trade Commission, the eight major studios (Columbia, MGM, Paramount, RKO, 20th Century-Fox, United Artists, Universal, and Warner Bros.) and some independent exhibitors were named in a civil suit over their violation of the Sherman Antitrust Act because such practices as block-booking were monopolistic restrictions of fair trade and open competition. In an initial consent decree, the defendants agreed to change practices, including using trade showings to permit theaters to bid on or pass on feature releases by 1943. When that did not happen a group representing non-studio producers sued Paramount's Detroit-theaters. The federal government took over the suit, now aimed at all the studios for non-compliance. In 1948 the Supreme Court ruled that mandated compliance including forced divestment by all the studios of their theater chains.

61. The Paramount budgets and cost reports in the AMPAS Library Files 1262-63 bear various dates. The June 17, 1944 cost report is in file 1263. The budget estimate of August 4, 1943 is in file 1262.

62. To be absolutely precise per the June, 1944 cost report, that was 49 days at the lower rate of $250/day, and 95 days at the higher. There was a Screen Writers Guild in 1943 (Charles Brackett had served a term as its president); but Wilder's rate was well above the minimum in the 1942 agreement with the MPPDA.

63. Wilder did not make, as is sometimes reported, $33,350, because $7,350 for the services of Doane Harrison, was paid via Account 4A as co-director. The 13-week minimum on features that applied to scale had not been formulated yet by the Screen Directors Guild; but oddly Wilder got paid for 13 weeks. And, in fact, the numbers on the cost report indicate not 78 but 84 days (or 14 weeks) of work. That's obviously $28,000, which means Wilder got shorted by $35,272 (in today's money). There is no record of him complaining about this.

64. Here is the full breakdown of the $2,535 ($44,708 today) total from September 25:

Bath towel, slippers: $40 ($705)

White shirtmaker dress: $275 ($4,850)

Print dress: $400 ($7,054)

Raincoat, hat, bag: $460 ($8,112)

Evening dress: $200 ($3,527)

Simple house dress: $300 ($5,290)

Camel coat, black dress: $425 ($5,290)

Gray tailored suit, bag, hat, gloves: $435 ($7,672)

Locations and Sets

65. Moffat, "On the Fourth Floor at Paramount," 48. Wilder continues: "It's very peculiar you know that the only person who caught the California atmosphere in prose was an Englishman—Chandler."

66. Paramount Files, AMPAS Library. This shot was made after studio had obtained a waiver from the Screen Extras Guild to shoot an actual "Los Angeles Railway electric welder and his assistant working on the company right of way at 5th and Olive Streets."

67. It is not specified in a memo to production manager Bertholon what the *Los Angeles Examiner* charged for its stake-bed truck and bales of newspapers—at least three of which flew off into the roadway—or if they provided items free of charge for promotional consideration.

68. At 450 Rossmore Avenue, this location, two blocks south of Melrose by the Wilshire Country Club, was somewhat restrictive in their tenant requirements. Past renters included *Machinal* actor Clark Gable, Swanson client (and co-scenarist of *The Big Sleep*) William Faulkner, and Neff prospect George Raft (whose mob associations were apparently okay with the proprietors).

69. In mid-November, while the main company was on the process stage, C.C. Coleman took a second unit back to 1825 North Kingsley Drive for an

establishing shot of the building and Phyllis dropping Walter using photo doubles and the Dodge coupe. He also got the shot of Zachette a few blocks southwest.

70. The actual Glendale Station at 400 West Cerritos Avenue now serves as Metrolink stop. The Burbank station in the movie at 201 North Front Street burned down decades ago and was never rebuilt. The Burbank Metrolink is on South Front Street across East Olive (Avenue not the Olive Street in the first shot of the movie).

71. Cain, *Three of a Kind*, 217.

72. There are two chairs. And more details: "Often times, a man will mutter his prayers while in the chair" and "Only then [after noon] is the gas let out and the body retrieved." The first cyanide gas chamber in 1924 Nevada antedates the Snyder-Gray electrocutions. But, in fact, the San Quentin gas chamber was barely open for business in July of 1938, when Neff starts his recording. Ready in June, its first customer was on December 2. 193 people (four of them women) followed, until a decade of suspension in 1967 and penal code revision a decade later. The death penalty was restored in California by Proposition 7 in 1978; and, when executions resumed, two more men died via cyanide before courts mandated a switch to lethal injection in 1996. The voters of the Golden State again voted in favor of the death penalty via Proposition 34 in 2012 and Proposition 66 in 2016. Since 2006 a de facto moratorium has been in by gubernatorial decree. Lawsuits are in process.

73. Wilder quoted in Chandler, *Nobody's Perfect*, 116.

74. Without mentioning DeSylva, Zolotow asserts the ridiculously inflated cost on page 118. The Breen memo to Luraschi is dated December 1, 1943.

75. The Bradbury Building in downtown Los Angeles—while prominently featured in scores of movies and television from the classic period *D.O.A.* (1949) or the 1951 remake of *M* through *Marlowe* (1966 adaptation of *The Little Sister*, where Chandler's investigator has his office) or *Blade Runner*—is not where *Double Indemnity*'s two-tiered, Beaux Art style insurance offices were filmed. Nor was Pereira's set modeled after it. The story of it being a copy of the Paramount Building in New York City (at 1501 Broadway) is also apocryphal.

76. Crowe, *Conversations with Wilder*, 54. When Cameron Crowe asked about the door, Wilder replied: "Yeah, that was a mistake that we made and I did not want to correct it. We'd already shot it. It worked and I did not want to reshoot it."

Design and Photography

77. Stanwyck and Head quoted in Chandler, *Nobody's Perfect*, 119.

78. Truhler, *Film Noir Style*, 138. Truhler elaborates "The wardrobe has also influenced other costume design, the most obvious example being Carl Reiner's comedy-noir *Dead Men Don't Wear Plaid* (1981). Reiner hired Edith Head to design the costumes, and…fittingly, Reiner's movie would be Head's swan song; she passed away five months after the premiere. That same year, Lawrence Kasdan's neo-noir *Body Heat* (1981) also paid tribute by taking its plot and costume cues right from *Double Indemnity*."

79. Chandler, *Nobody's Perfect*, 120.

80. Truhler, *Film Noir Style*, 133. The full details:

Ten actual costumes in film	The budgeted items
First scene at Dietrichson House: 1. Towel 2. Then simple house dress	A. Bath towel, slippers=40 ($705) B. Simple House dress=300 ($5,290)
Second scene there: 3. Floral print blouse and long black skirt with high-waisted front	C. Print dress=400 ($7,054)
At Neff's apartment: 4. Cardigan sweater, black trousers, raincoat	D. Raincoat, hat, bag=460 ($8,112)
Dietrichson Living Room again: 5. Black dress	E. Evening Dress=200 ($3,527)
First Market scene: 6. White blouse, checked vest top, knee-high skirt	Not in the budget list
Telephone call to say murder is on (at pay phone): 7. Belted Gray coat with black blouse	F. Camel coat, black dress=425 ($5,290)

In Norton's Office:
8. Gray suit, black blouse, hat with veil, and gloves
Phyllis is still wearing this outfit that night at Neff's

G. Gray tailored suit, bag, hat, gloves=435 ($7,672)

Second Market:
9. White blouse, black trousers

H. White blouse from 6, trousers from 4

Shot by Neff at end:
10. White jumper

I. White Shirt maker dress=275 ($4,850)

81. Truhler, *Film Noir Style*, 134.

82. Silver and Ursini, *Film Noir Fatal Women*, 52. The shot of Stanwyck is followed by three pages of eight other actors in similarly tight sweaters. Eventually Breen must have gotten used to film noir's outfits.

83. Truhler, *Film Noir Style*, 129.

84. Neff does pick his hat up when he walks out on Phyllis and down the steps to his Dodge. If he were not wearing his hat outside, a man in 1943 would almost certainly notice that. More importantly, when Phyllis shows up at his door and says "You forgot your hat this afternoon," her hands are in her coat pockets. She does not have any hat. It's not what the script says—"She has nothing in her hands but her bag"—but it is clear that what she really means is, "I have no excuse for coming by other than I wanted to see you again." She continues, "Do you want me to bring it in?" His reply, "Sure. Put it on the chair," really says, "I wanted to see you, too."

85. Wilder to Porfirio (*Film Noir Reader 3*), 104. Wilder frequently complained (Sikov, *On Sunset Boulevard*, 94, where Wilder says mounting cameras on trucks "was rather dangerous"; Crowe, *Conversations with Wilder*, 95) about not having money for process photography while shooting *Mauvaise Graine*. Sikov continues: "Rear projection would have look considerably worse than the vertiginous sweep of a moving camera." The high-speed return of Neff's car to his office that opens the picture did not call for camera mounts. But long before towing vehicles with insert cars (weighted trucks with railed levels of platforms for lights and cameras, that still must be used with caution) the scenes Wilder shot out of necessity with hood-mounted cameras on the streets of Paris are striking in their "documentary" style.

86. Friedrich, *City of Nets*, 165.

87. Truhler, *Film Noir Style*, 135.

88. Wilder to Porfirio *(Film Noir Reader 3)*, 116.

89. In the days before negatives could be easily duplicated, two hand-cranked cameras were placed side-by-side and operated by the first and second camera persons usually on outdoor stages lit by the sun. It is unclear who the first camera woman actually was. Candidates include Francelia Billington, Grace Davison, Margery Ordway, or someone else. [Pamela Hutchinson, "'Ever heard of a woman cameraman?': Why female cinematographers get overlooked," *Guardian*, January 25, 2018.] Brianne Murphy was the first female member of the American Society of Cinematographers. She was admitted in 1973.

90. And some "helmers" (as they were dubbed by the trade papers) barely touched the steering wheel, using "Dialogue Directors" to rehearse the cast and limiting themselves to what Wilder learned from Hawks: action, cut, print number 7.

91. Crowe, *Conversations with Wilder*, 53. Seitz shot both *The Lost Weekend* and *Sunset Blvd*. After that Wilder switched to Charles Lang, Jr.

92. Porfirio, Silver, and Ursini, *Film Noir Reader 3*, 205. 1971 interview with Seitz by James Ursini.

93. Wilder to Porfirio *(Film Noir Reader 3)*, 116.

94. Crowe, *Conversations with Wilder*, 53.

95. Ibid.

Shooting

96. The slightly banked curves of the Arroyo Seco Parkway, the first "freeway" in Los Angeles completed three years earlier were designed for that speed, as anyone who drives them incautiously today will soon realize.

97. Just to confirm that this is us, not Maurice Zolotow, channeling Wilder.

98. We've picked on Maurice Zolotow enough. This is our late colleague Richard Schickel's version: "His own car wouldn't start. He leapt out and started running back across the lot to his stage, praying the grips had not dismantled the set. Luckily, they had not. Wilder ordered retakes in which the murderers,

desperate to make a quick getaway, are momentarily, suspensefully, halted by a faulty ignition." [Schickel, *Double Indemnity*, 62] Elegantly written, Richard, as fiction often is.

99. Zolotow, page 116. MacMurray also told Maurice, "By the way, you remember that bit where I fall off the observation car platform? Where I'm pretending to be husband with the crippled leg and the crutches? I didn't do the fall right. Wilder showed me how to do the fall. That's the only time he demonstrated an action for me by doing it. Usually he just told you what he wanted and expected you to do it." Really? Of course, normally very few directors demonstrate line readings, bits of business, or anything. It's not done. Also the Production Report for Day 20 indicates that Neff's stunt double received a large adjustment (how it is done) for the jump off the train. Sometimes it's hard to remember what happened yesterday, let alone 50 years ago. Case in point: there may not have been a windshield, or dashboard, but there was steering wheel and back end to the car on the process stage, more than just a seat.

100. Sikov, *On Sunset Boulevard*, 208-9. Sikov also notes that MacMurray "took his line-reading misfires in stride. Without missing a beat, he continued, in character, speaking directly into the microphone: "Memo to Wilder— MacMurray blew his topper again."

101. Ibid. Sikov also tells of the five strikes at the bowling alley and quotes Wilder saying "I just wanted to be sure with the part before we crippled you." Then Sikov says MacMurray wasn't finished [!?]: "Principal photography on *Double Indemnity* was completed with a shot of Walter in his car at a drive-in restaurant." Did MacMurray go to a drive-in? The shot in which he drinks "the bottle of beer, the one I had wanted all along" certainly seems to be on a process stage in front of a projected drive-in façade.

102. Brackett, 232. Earlier that year Doane Harrison had edited *The Uninvited* for associate producer Brackett before reporting for work on *Double Indemnity.*

103. Rózsa, *Double Life*, 119-20. Rózsa recalled that Victor Young "became furious—one thing you don't do in Hollywood is disagree with an executive. However, Billy Wilder told him that he wasn't in the *Kaffeehaus* where he once played his violin and that he'd better stay in his office in the future and leave the composing to me."

104. Ibid.

105. Wilder to Porfirio (*Film Noir Reader 3*), page 163.

106. Rózsa, *Double Life*, 121.

107. Wilder to Porfirio (*Film Noir Reader 3*), page 164.

108. Rózsa, *Double Life*, 121-2.

109. AMPAS library in PDF file SC510621080, 38-41 (of 52). The actual reviewer for Shurlock-Lynch is listed as "L. Greenhouse." Greenhouse's synopsis is not just a recital of events, she/he does some pointed character analysis also: "Neff knows that Phyllis isn't any good for him, that he is playing with fire. But for the life of him, he can't get her out of his thoughts. The temptation is great, and though Neff fights it, he doesn't fight hard enough." There is one question the synopsis raises but does not answer. Did the print submitted for review include the last bit, the reversal on the match lighting and the "I love you, too"? Sure it did; Greenhouse just didn't get it.

110. The character description of "Sam Gorlopis"—a last name which namsor.app reports is most likely Greek (53.9%)—is detailed in the script: "a big dumb bruiser with untidy hair, broad face, and small piggish eyes"; but no ethnicity is stipulated.

111. Brackett, 237. The next day is an added note: "When I got to the studio Billy was arriving, pretending that none of his friends had liked the picture, that the cards had been bad....Most of the cards had been superb. His friends had made minor criticisms and the front office was wildly enthusiastic and the cuts suggested were minor." [page 238] Whether any "cuts suggested" became "cuts made" is uncertain.

6. The Movie: The Top Shelf

1. Comment by Richard Schickel to Alain Silver. A light snow was falling in Hillsdale. Michigan on March 5, 2007, a very cold late afternoon. Richard and Alain, two of the lecturers for that week's film noir event, were seated with coffees in plush lounge chairs in a wide-lobby at a right angle to the guest suites. Soon there would be a screening of *Out of the Past*, then the attendees dinner. That evening's topic would be "The People That Made Film Noir," for which Alain had prepared a DVD of long takes from the work of Siodmak, Aldrich, Welles, and John Farrow. The college had concerns about its DVD playback system, but Alain planned to do live commentary over the clips on the screen. Richard scoffed at the vagaries of technology and glanced through the window at a digital thermometer. It was so cold that even a Wisconsin-native

and a lifelong smoker paled at the prospect of stepping out for some nicotine. The next day's screening of *Double Indemnity* would be followed by Richard's presentation on "The Elements of Film Noir." Alain mentioned that another clip he would use that evening was a sequence shot from *Tension*, the John Berry movie, the guy who shadowed Wilder. An okay picture, Richard noted, with its odd combination of Cyd Charisse and Audrey Totter as the good and bad girls, but Totter's character hardly approached the level of Phyllis.

So what would he say about *Double Indemnity*? "It's simple," he continued, "I nit-picked a bit with the Woody Allen quote in the book; but he was right when he said it's practically anybody's best movie. But what I'll say, really…"

2. James Naremore, *More Than Night,* 81.

3. Ibid, 82.

4. Stanwyck quoted in Chandler, *Nobody's Perfect,* 119.

5. Nino Frank, "A New Kind of Police Drama," *Film Noir Reader* 2, 15.

6. Ibid, 35.

7. Charles Higham and Joel Greenberg, reprinted as "Noir Cinema" [retitled per Higham's 1996 request] in *Film Noir Compendium*, 61, 68.

8. Flinn, "Three Faces of Film Noir," 108.

9. Silver and Ursini, *Film Noir Compendium*, 88-99. From Paul Schrader's "Notes on film noir."

10. Lyons, *Death on the Cheap*, 18.

11. Silver and Ursini, *Film Noir Compendium*, 72-87: There are actually 11 but the last two, "Blacks and Reds" and "Giogol, Horror, Fantasy," delete tangential limbs of the tree. The major branches: 1. CRIME AS SOCIAL CRITICISM; 2. GANGSTERS; 3. ON THE RUN; 4. PRIVATE EYES AND ADVENTURERS; 5. MIDDLE CLASS MURDER; 6. PORTRAITS AND DOUBLES; 7. SEXUAL PATHOLOGY; 8. PSYCHOPATHS; and 9. HOSTAGES TO FORTUNE.

12. Ibid, 83.

13. *Film Noir The Encyclopedia.*

14. Silver and Ursini, *Film Noir*.

15. Silver and Ursini, *The Noir Style*, 31.

16. Ibid, 90.

17. Place and Peterson, "Some Visual Motifs of Film Noir," 110-121.

18. Silver and Ursini, *The Noir Style*, 192.

19. Silver and Ursini, *The Noir Style*, 161.

20. Silver and Ursini, *Film Noir Compendium*, 145. From the reprint of Robert Porfirio's, "No Way Out: Existential Motifs in the Film Noir."

21. Ibid, 176. From the reprint of Marc Vernet's "The Filmic Transition: On the Openings of Film Noirs."

22. Ibid, 181.

23. Marc Vernet, "Film Noir at the Edge of Doom," in *Shades of Noir: a Reader*, edited by Jan Copjec, New York: Limelight Editions, 1996, 4. Alain Silver wrote in his Introduction to the first *Film Noir Reader*, "What can one say about a viewpoint such as Vernet's. In his essay 'Film Noir at the Edge of Doom' he asserted that 'a hero cannot be both strong and vulnerable, the woman good and evil.' Of course they can, his observations were part of a simplistic, structuro-semiological rush to judgment clearly at odds with the narrative position of film noir as a whole. Where once Vernet merely puzzled over contradictory icons, in 'Edge of Doom' he indulges in pointless deconstruction. On the one hand Vernet now bemoans 'complacent repetition' about film noir. On the other hand he presents the ultimate obfuscation by calling it 'impossible to criticize.' What then is he writing about?"

24. Silver and Ursini, *Film Noir Compendium*, 91.

25. Naremore, *More Than Night*, 13.

26. Robert Porfirio, "The Noir Title Sequence, Evolution of Style" in *Film Noir Light and Shadow*, edited by Alain Silver and James Ursini, Milwaukee: Applause, 2017, 66. Originally from *The Dark Age of American Film: A Study of American Film Noir (1940-1960)*, Yale University, 1969.

27. Claire Johnston, "Double Indemnity" in *Women in Film Noir*, London: British Film Instutute, 1978, 101-2.

28. Ibid, 103.

29. Biesen, *"Double Indemnity,"* 211.

30. Hirsch, *The Dark Side of the Screen*, 3-4.

31. September 25, 1943 *Double Indemnity* script, 18.

32. Johnston, *Women in Film Noir*, 35, 45. From Janey Place.

33. Ibid, 29. From Sylvia Harvey's, "Woman's place: the absence of family in film noir."

34. Sobchack, "Lounge Time," 219.

35. Ibid, 219.

36. Imogen Sara Smith, "Rooms Like Reveries: Interiors and Interiority in Film Noir," in *Film Noir Light and Shadow*, edited by Alain Silver and James Ursini, Milwaukee: Applause, 2017, 80. Smith quotes Stanwyck from *The Edward G. Robinson Encyclopedia*, p. 109.

37. Sobchack, *"Lounge Time,"* 321.

38. Linda Brookover, "What Is This Thing Called Noir?" in *Film Noir Compendium*, edited by Alain Silver and James Ursini, Milwaukee: Applause, 2017, 355.

39. Elizabeth Ward, "The Camouflaged Femme Fatale," in *Film Noir Compendium*, edited by Alain Silver and James Ursini, Milwaukee: Applause, 2017, 431.

40. Biesen, *"Double Indemnity,"* 213.

41. Hirsch, *The Dark Side of the Screen*, 60.

42. Julie Grossman, *Rethinking the Femme Fatale in Film Noir*. London–New York: Palgrave Macmillan, 2009, 27.

43. Ibid, 121-122.

44. Bronfen, "Gender and Noir," 158.

45. Silver and Ursini, *Film Noir*, 85. From R. Barton Palmer's, "Cold War Noir."

46. Telotte, *Voices in the Dark*, 49.

47. Johnston, *Women in Film Noir*, 100-1.

48. Gerd Gemünden, *A Foreign Affair: Billy Wilder's American Films*. New York and Oxford: Berghahn Books, 2008, 30.

49. Ibid, 42. Gemünden quotes Wald in *Mildred Pierce: Script and Commentary*, edited by Albert J. LaValley, Madison: University of Wisconsin Press, 1980, 29. Yes, flashback is used in *Mildred Pierce*, and also a couple more of Wald's Joan Crawford pictures, *Humoresque* (1946) and *Possessed* (1947), but it's hardly in every one of the 40 plus movies he produced after 1944.

50. Naremore, *More Than Night*, 13, 88. The former selection regarding French invention and the latter regarding dehumanization.

51. Cf. Our book *The Zombie Film: From White Zombie to World War Z*. Minneapolis: Applause, 2014.

52. Porfirio, Silver, and Ursini, *Film Noir Reader 3*, 94. Preminger took issue in 1975 in his interview with Robert Porfirio. Porfirio recapped the following exchange regarding influences from German expression and its stage sets:

    Preminger: This is nonsense. What are you talking about? Where did Reinhardt bring Expressionism?

    Porfirio: During World War I, when the sets couldn't be grandiose, so he began to throw certain lights onto the stage so that actors would walk in and out.

    Preminger: Who told you all this nonsense?

    Porfirio: It's in most books on German theater.

    Preminger: Well, that's nonsense. That has nothing to do with the sets.

53. Wilder to Porfirio (*Film Noir Reader 3*), 109.

54. Naremore, *More Than Night*, 89.

55. Ibid, 90.

56. Robertson, *The Big Lebowski*, 97. In a "A Short History of Bowling Noir" sidebar, Robertson continues: "And just as quickly, the moment [of grace] is gone. Fred goes back to Babs. The inexorable darkness closes in. Put another way: bowl or die. This is Fred MacMurray's lesson in *Double Indemnity*."

57. Scenes E-5 and E-8 on page 136 of the September 25, 1943 script.

58. Schlotterbeck, "The Dynamism of Violent Death," 314.

59. Moffat, "On the Fourth Floor at Paramount," 49. The exact date of the Moffat interviewer is not stipulated in *The World of Raymond Chandler* that was published in 1977. What he told Bob Porfirio was much the same, it was likely a bit earlier: "We were delighted with [the gas chamber scene] at first… But then I realized, this thing is already over. I have one tag outside that office, when Neff collapses on the way to the elevator, where he can't even light the match. And from the distance, you hear the sirens, be it an ambulance or be it the police, you know it is over. No need for the gas chamber." Porfirio, Silver, and Ursini, *Film Noir Reader 3*, 107.

60. Schlotterbeck, "The Dynamism of Violent Death," 309.

61. Dickos, *Street with No Name*, 159.

62. Allyn, *Double Indemnity: A Policy That Paid Off*, 122.

63. September 25, 1943 script, Scene B-46 on page 70.

64. Allyn, *Double Indemnity: A Policy That Paid Off*, 117.

65. Porfirio, Silver, and Ursini, *Film Noir Reader 3*, 108. From the interview with Wilder.

66. Ibid, 101-2. The Preminger comment is from the transcript and was cut from the book.

67. Ibid, 102.

68. This list originated in *Film Noir The Encyclopedia*, has been refined repeatedly since then—its most recent iteration is in *Film Noir Light and Shadow*, page 9—and is revised again here.

69. Zolotow, page 118.

70. Leroy riffed on the title of "Impression Sunrise" by Monet to say: "*Impression*, I knew it. I was telling myself, it made an impression on me, so there has to be some impressionism in there. What freedom, what sense of ease emanates from its manufacture," and concludes with just a touch of Gallic sarcasm, "The first inkling of a wallpaper pattern is more finished than this

seascape." Branding the work as unfinished and unworthy in 1874 simultaneously dismissed the entire content of the alt-salon by the Anonymous Society of Painters, Sculptors, Printmaker as just about worthless. Monet, Edgar Degas, and Camille Pisarro, and Renoir never called themselves "les SACDAPS (acromym for 'Société anonyme des artistes peintres, sculpteurs et graveurs" which leaves out the "g"). But they liked the term "Impressionists." And from that point on it stuck. But all those earlier canvasses? How could they be examples of impressionism before the fact? [the original in *Le Charivari*, le 25 avril 1874: *"Impression*: j'en étais sûr. Je me disais aussi, puisque je suis impressionné, il doit y avoir de l'impression là-dedans...Et quelle liberté, quelle aisance dans la facture! Le papier peint à l'état embryonnaire est encore plus fait que cette marine-là"]

71. Porfirio, Silver, and Ursini, *Film Noir Reader 3,* page 101. From the interview with Wilder.

72. Crowther, *"Double Indemnity*: A Tough Melodrama."

73. With music by Victor Schertzinger, lyrics by Johnny Mercer, "Tangerine" became a hit for Jimmy Dorsey after it debuted in Paramount's *The Fleet's In* (1942, directed by Schertzinger). Of course that would be after the evening of July 16, 1938 when Neff gets shot for closing the window on it. Bob Eberly croons a first verse than after the bridge Helen O'Connell's uptempo riposte agrees that her lips are bright as flame but "she's only fooling one girl. She's only fooling Tangerine!"

74. Maxfield, *The Fatal Woman*, 34.

75. Silver and Ursini, *Film Noir*, 48. From Janet Bergstrom's "German Expressionism and American Film Noir."

76. Bronfen, "Gender and Noir," 159.

77. Hoopes, *The Biography of James M. Cain*, 334.

78. Elizabeth Ward in the documentary *Shadows of Suspense* (Minute 16).

79. Peter William Evans, *"Double Indemnity* (or Bringing Up Baby)," in *The Book of Film Noir*, New York: Continuum, 1993, 166.

80. Perkins, *Film as Film*, 142.

81. Dennon, *The Emergence of the Feminist Fatale in American Film Noir*, 33.

82. What was cut from the film or never shot begins with a dissolve from the drive away into the car with them in mid-conversation:

> DIETRICHSON: Aw, stop squawkin', can't you, Phyllis? No man takes his wife along to a class reuninon. That's what class reunions are for.
>
> PHYLLIS: Mrs. Tucker went along with her husband last year, didn't she?
>
> DIETRICHSON: Yeah, and what happened to her? She stayed in the hotel lobby for four days straight. Never saw the guy until we poured him back on the train.
>
> CLOSEUP ON NEFF'S FACE LOW DOWN IN THE CORNER BEHIND DIETRICHSON
>
> He looks up at Dietrichson and Phyllis in the front seat.
>
> PHYLLIS' VOICE: All right, honey. Just so long as you have a good time.
>
> DIETRICHSON'S VOICE: I won't do much dancing, I can tell you that.
>
> [Next there are three lines of dialogue in the movie, ending with his "…Monday at the latest."]
>
> PHYLLIS: Don't forget we're having the Hobeys for dinner on Monday.
>
> DIETRICHSON: The Hobeys? We had them last. They owe us a dinner, don't they?
>
> PHYLLIS: Maybe they do but I've already asked them for Monday.
>
> DIETRICHSON: Well, I don't want to feed the Hobeys. And I don't want to eat at their house either. The food you get there, and that rope he hands out for cigars. Call if off, can't you?

It could be argued this would be interesting to see, Stanwyck as Phyllis engaged in chit-chat knowing what is about to happen and relishing the irony of her husband's request to "call it off." Talk about cold-blooded. How about, talk about an overbearing husband, redolent of Mr. Snyder of Snyder-Gray infamy.

83. Krutnik, *In a Lonely Place: Film Noir, Genre, Masculinity*, ix.

84. Phillip Sipiora, "Phenomenological Masking," 104.

85. Conversation in Wilder's office in early 1979 about his place in the history of the noir movement. Between Wilder and Elizabeth Ward (co-editor of *Film Noir, an Encyclopedic Reference*).

86. Porfirio, Silver, and Ursini, *Film Noir Reader 3*, 168. From Porfirio's conversation with Rózsa.

87. Arnold, *The Essentials*, 91.

88. Sipiora, "Phenomenological Masking," 102

89. Silver and Ursini, *Film Noir Compendium*, 376. From Philip Gaines' "Noir 101."

7. Aftermath and Movement: The Rise of Film Noir

1. Schickel, *"Double Indemnity,"* 65.

2. Moffat, "On the Fourth Floor at Paramount," 47.

3. James M. Cain, *"Double Indemnity,"* New York Daily News, August 14, 1944.

4. MacShane, *Selected Letters*, 298. From a letter to Dale Warren (November 7, 1951).

5. *Variety,* April 26, 1944.

6. *The Hollywood Reporter*, April 24, 1944.

7. *Film Daily*, April 24, 1944, 14.

8. *Motion Picture Herald*, April 29, 1944.

9. Donald Kirkley, *The Baltimore Sun*, July 3, 1944, 6.

10. Marjory Adams, *Boston Globe*, August 15, 1944, 8.

11. Harold V. Cohen, *Pitts Post-Gazette*, July 15, 1944, 12.

12. Mildred Martin, *Philadephia Inquirer*, July 15, 1944, 12.

13. Albert Goldberg, *Chicago Tribune*, November 3, 1944, 22.

14. Ida Belle Hicks, *Fort Worth Star-Telegram*, August 11, 1944, 20.

15. Bob Fredericks, *The Miami Herald*, July 8, 1944, 2B.

16. Kate Cameron, *New York Daily News*, September 7, 1944, 35.

17. "*Double Indemnity*," *Times,* July 10, 1944.

18. Crowther, "*Double Indemnity: A Tough Melodrama*."

19. James Agee, "*Double Indemnity.*"

20. "*Double Indemnity*," *The Tidings*, August 14, 1944.

21. Scheuer, "Film History Made."

22. *Sydney Morning Herald*, December 4, 1944, 7.

23. Crozier, "*Double Indemnity*," 3.

24. Dilys Powell, 1944 review reprinted in *The Golden Screen: Fifty Years of Films*, London: Pavillion, 1989, 44.

25. Sikov, *On Sunset Boulevard*, 212.

26. Brackett, 244-5. Brackett says no more but one can imagine him smirking with Wilder while writing the copy that Sikov details for the Oblath joke: "Dear Mr. Billy Wilder, I certainly do appreciate the opportunity to see your picture *Double Indemnity*. It held my attention, it held my wife's attention, it held my sister-in-law's attention. It certainly was a good picture, one of the best pictures we have seen in several days. Sincerely, George Oblath." [212-13]

27. Sikov, *On Sunset Boulevard*, 212.

28. Ibid, 211.

29. Ibid.

30. Jerry Wald to Billy Wilder, Memo, July 9, 1944, Billy Wilder Collection, AMPAS Library.

31. Schickel, "*Double Indemnity*," 67. While the consensus is that *Going My Way* was number one in domestic earnings for 1944, the reported numbers vary considerably. On its second page, the contemporary source, *Box Office Digest Annual for 1945*, has "The BIG TEN: Top Ten Pictures of 1944 Gross $62,000,000," which is headed by *Going My Way* at $8.5 million (followed by *Wilson* and *Since You Went Away*, both at $6.5 million; *Song of Bernadette* and *Lady in the Dark*, both at $5 million; and *Meet Me in St. Louis*, $4.5

million, etc.). The current online site The Numbers lists *Going My Way* at $16.3 million (which would be $291 million today) and *Meet Me in St. Louis* number two at $12.8. Wikipedia reports earnings for *Going My Way* at $6.5 million, *Meet Me in St. Louis* at $5 million, and *Since You Went Away* at $4.9 million, which are essentially the same as the IMDB Pro numbers. The Wikipedia page for *Double Indemnity* (which is riddled with errors) lists an unsourced "Box Office" of $5 million. That is clearly wrong and would make it Number 3 on Wikipedia's own 1944 list. The Ultimate Movie Rankings site just throws up its hands: "Finding box office information for movies made in the 1930s and 1940s is extremely difficult. For somebody looking for box office information on 1944 it is very, very frustrating."

32. The key numbers used to record returns in 1944 were ticket sales; but the cost of tickets varied considerably. A key number for the industry, as reported in *Box Office Digest*, was the percentage of release costs, that is the net revenue from theaters divided by the total costs of both production and distribution (prints and advertising). Again *Going My Way* was the leader atop column A of all movies with earnings above $500,000 at 258% [page 6, "All Features Released in 1944"]. The next five of the "Big Ten" from *Wilson* through *Meet Me in St, Louis* are 240%, 238, 237, 221, and 207% respectively. *Double Indemnity* is 51st position at 147%. Even though, like most studios (especially during the war), Paramount limited its print costs by cycling a limited number prints through the country on a region-by-region basis. 147% was a decent, if not "huge" profit. Per *Box Office Digest* in 1994 102 releases were profitable in covering their costs. A final consideration is that all the studios would add overhead to their budgets. Extrapolating from that any studio that covered their release costs, which Paramount did in 1944, would cover its overhead. So what did *DI* gross. The costs of prints and advertising were likely between $500,000 and $750,000. Using the BO Digest percentage would yield gross returns of $2.2 to 2.6 million. IMDbPro indicates $2.5 million.

33. Shearer, "Crime Certainly Pays on the Screen," 13.

34. Ibid.

35. Ibid.

36. The entire article is reprinted in both Gross, *The World of Raymond Chandler* and the published screenplay of Bruccoli, *The Blue Dahlia* listed in the Bibliography. Further details on all the other events in Chandler's life post-*Double Indemnity* are chronicled by biographers MacShane, Hiney, and Williams.

37. Idem, pages 214-215.

38. Barbara Stanwyck to James M. Cain, Letter, Manuscript Division, James M. Cain Collection, Library of Congress, Feb. 23, 1950.

39. Hoopes, *The Biography of James M. Cain*, 417-418.

40. Peter B. Flint, "Fred MacMurray Is Dead at 83," *New York Times*, November 6, 1991.

41. James M. Cain to Fred MacMurray, Letter, Manuscript Division, James M. Cain Collection, Library of Congress, February 4, 1944.

42. Fred MacMurray to James M. Cain, Letter, Manuscript Division, James M. Cain Collection, Library of Congress, February 9, 1944.

43. Staggs, *Close-Up on Sunset Boulevard*, 146.

44. Bogdanovich, *Who the Devil Made It, Conversations with Legendary Film Directors*, 67. From the interview with Edgar G. Ulmer.

45. Billy Wilder, *Double Indemnity*, Internet Movie Database, *Trivia*.

46. "Mercedes McCambridge, 87, Actress Known for Strong Roles," *The New York Times*, March 18, 2004.

47. Cf. "What is Thing Called Noir" and "Mad Love is Strange: More Neo-noir Fugitives" by Linda Brookover and Alain Silver, in *Film Noir Compendium*, pages 247-269 and *Film Noir Reader 2*, pages 188-195.

48. Cf. The interview with Robert Wise about his noir films in *Film Noir Reader 3*, pages 120-135, which also has an interview with *Murder, My Sweet*'s femme fatale Claire Trevor, pages 215-227.

49. Roger Ebert, "*Out of the Past,*" *Chicago Sun-Times*, July 18, 2004.

50. Cf. The complete, contentious interview with Preminger in *Film Noir Reader 2*, pages 86-99.

51. Cf. The interview with Fritz Lang, in *Film Noir Reader 2*, pages 50-66.

52. Cf. The extensive analysis of those scenes in the sidebar on the movie's entry in *Film Noir The Encyclopedia*, pages 322-327.

53. Cf. Our study of Farrow in *Film Noir: The Directors*, pages 70-87.

54. Raymond Borde and Étienne Chaumeton, *Panorama du Film Noir Américain*, Paris: Les Éditions de Minuit, 1983, 277, translated by Alain Silver in
"Kiss Me Deadly: Evidence of Style, *Film Noir Compendium*, 304-25.

55. Cf. Our auteur study *What Ever Happened to Robert Aldrich?*, New York:
Limelight Editions, 1995.

56. Charlotte Chandler, *Nobody's Perfect*, 114.

Proto-noir

1. James M. Cain to Billy Wilder, Memo, 1943, AMPAS Library.

2. Nino Frank, "A New Kind of Police Drama," 33-5.

3. Kael, "Raising Kane."

4. Cf. The extensive visual comparison in the most recent iteration of "The
Gangster and Film Noir" in *Film Noir Light and Shadow*, pages 26-63.

5. Cf. Our survey and comparative analysis in the Introduction of *Film Noir
Graphics Where Danger Lives*, Santa Monica: Pendragon Books, 2012.

ACKNOWLEDGMENTS

As we have so often in the past, we must thank first our frequent collaborators the late Robert Porfirio, Linda Brookover, and Elizabeth Ward (as regards both film noir and Raymond Chandler), some of whose writing underlies many of our new comments. Particularly valuable were the interviews Bob conducted in conjunction with his dissertation in the 1970s and the collection of Chandler studies initially assembled by Elizabeth.

For this volume, our research of the Paramount and Wilder collections was assisted by Louise Hilton and many other staff members at the Margaret Herrick Library maintained by the Academy of Motion Pictures Arts and Sciences. Stills from *Double Indemnity* and other motion pictures are courtesy of Turner Classic Movies. The photo of the house on Quebec Drive (page 119) is by India Brookover. Several writers, including Megan Abbott, Penelope Pelizzon, Nancy M. West, and Phillip Sipiora, kindly provided us with copies of recent work. Others, including the late Ian Cameron (long ago), Sheri Chinen Biesen, Julie Grossman, Robert Miklitsch, James Naremore, R. Barton Palmer, and William Park, had previously sent us copies of their book-length anthologies and studies of film noir. Besides several persons already mentioned, we are also grateful to all those who contributed essays reflecting on *Double Indemnity* and the noir movement to the various volumes of our *Film Noir Reader* series.

Lastly thanks for help on illustrations from Eileen Flanagan at TCM and, of course, our editors at Running Press, Cindy Sipala, ably supported by Joe Davidson. In collusion with our agent Lee Sobel, Cindy had the vision for this book, that originated as an hour-long lecture in March of 2018 with 150 PowerPoint slides for a theater full of festival attendees who had just seen *Double Indemnity*. We can only hope that we have done justice to the movie they and so many before and since have watched.

On the set of *Arise My Love*: Wilder pointedly peers down at a prop letter being typed by Claudette Colbert while Charles Brackett feigns interest a bit more subtly.

INDEX

Page numbers in italics indicate illustrations.

film noir *(continued)*
  end of period, 243
  feminist perspective of *Double Indemnity*,
    157–65
  flashback trend and, 169
  German expressionism and, 256–57
  Hays Code and, 87, 175
  horror series of Universal, 260–61
  lighting for, 212, 257–58
  MacMurray in, 212
  mood and femme fatale in, 258
  motifs of, 263–64
  as movement, 153–55
  neo-noir films, 222, 225, 237, 256
  origins of, 147–49, 156, 255–56
  Robinson in, 210–11
  set designs and visual motifs, 258–59
  Stanwyck in, 210
  Wilder on, 180, 187
  WWII influence in, 49
Film Noir The Encyclopedia (Silver &
    Ursini), 149–50, 155, 233
Film Noir Reader (Silver), 312n23
Fischer, Dorothy, *63*
Fisher, Steve, 90, 207
Five Graves to Cairo (1943), 81–82, 141
flashback technique, 166, 169
The Fleet's In (1942), 316n73
Fleischer, Richard, 21
Fleming, Ian, 60
Flinn, Tom, 147
Ford Theater (anthology radio series),
    228–30
Frank, Leo, 17, 21
Frank, Nino, 146–47, 255–56
Frankenstein (1932), 260–61
Freeman, Mona, 111, 113, 135–36, 247–48

Freeman, Y. Frank, 109, 111, 204
Freund, Karl, 260–61
Friedrich, Otto, 130

G
Gable, Clark, 8, *8*
Gage, Jack, 113, 134
gangster films, 261–63
Gardner, Erle Stanley, 59, 60, 61
Garrett, H. P., 76
Geller, James, 43
Gemünden, Gerd, 167–69
German expressionism, 256–57
"Get Me in the Movies" (play), 298n25
Giannini, A. P., 45
The Girl on the Red Velvet Swing (1955), 20
The Glass Key (1942), 87
Going My Way (1944), 204, 319–22nn31–32
Goodis, David, 239
"A Good Man Gone Wrong" (Menchen),
    279n14
Granada Television, 217
Granger, Bert, 124
Gray, Henry Judd, 3, 9–12. *See also* Trial of
    Snyder-Gray murder case
Greene, Graham, 173
Greene, Ward, 21
Greenhouse, L., 157, 184, 310n109
Greer, Jane, *239*
Griffith, D. W., 14
Grossman, Julie, 164
Gun Crazy (1950), 174
The Gunsaulus Mystery (1921), 21

H
Hall, Porter, 222
Halliday, Lizzie, 280n17